32-Bit Microprocessors

32-Bit
Microprocessors

Second Edition

Editor: H. J. Mitchell

CRC PRESS

BOCA RATON · ANN ARBOR · BOSTON

This edition published by CRC Press, Inc.
2000 Corporate Blvd., N.W., Boca Raton, Florida, 33431

First printed in Great Britain by
Blackwell Scientific Publications 1991

Library of Congress
Cataloging-in-Publication Data

32-bit microprocessors / edited by Hugh Mitchell. – 2nd ed.
    p.   cm.
  Includes index.
  ISBN (invalid) 0-8493-7713-7
  1. Microprocessors. I. Mitchell, H. J. II. Title: Thirty-two
bit microprocessors.
QA76.5.A135 1991
005.26—dc20   90-21059
                                            CIP

International Standard Book Number 0-8493-7713-7

Contents

Preface

Today there are many 32-bit microprocessors on the market. Some are based on CISC architecture techniques, others on RISC technology. Some are sold freely, others are sold on a restricted basis or embedded as the central processor of a manufacturer's computer system.

The purpose of this book is to give an insight into, mainly, the CISC architectures that are around today. The book provides detailed, technical, information on the architectures, the base technology and the necessary support devices and tools. The majority of the book deals with CISC devices, however one chapter is included on the Inmos Transputer. While the Transputer is most certainly a RISC device, the novel system architectures that can be created by its use deserve a specific mention.

The chapters on the Intel 80386/486 and the Inmos Transputer have been written by independent users, while the remaining chapters have been produced by application specialists from the device manufacturers.

Today a microprocessor cannot be considered as an isolated device. It needs support devices as well as extensive hardware and software tools to ensure that any development is manageable, controllable and successful. While competent systems engineering skills are essesntial, at the managerial level, coverage of these aspects are beyond the scope of this book.

In a book, such as this, one is governed by the willingness of individuals and organisations to make the time to provide the appropriate chapters. To attempt to cover a wide variety of devices would have produced a book of unmanageable size. The overall aim has been to produce a book that provides a balanced view of today's 32-bit microprocessors.

H. J. Mitchell

List of Trademarks

The following trademarks have been used within the text:

Ada	registered trademark of the US Department of Defense.
HP-UX	registered trademark of Hewlett-Packard Inc.
Inmos	trademark of the INMOS Group of Companies. INMOS is a member of the SGS-THOMSON Microelectronics Group.
Macintosh	registered trademark of Apple Computer Inc.
Occam	trademark of INMOS Group of Companies.
Unix	registered trademark of AT&T.
VAX, VMS, VAXELN, ULTRIX, MicroVAX	registered trademarks of Digital Equipment Corporation.
WE	registered trademark of AT&T.

CHAPTER 1
Introduction

H. J. MITCHELL
Digital Equipment Corporation, UK

1.1   Evolution

Some years ago I remember listening to a marketing manager who told his audience to estimate how many electric motors they thought they had in their homes. He went on to predict that within a few years most people would have as many microprocessors in their homes as electric motors. At the time I did not believe him; however, a quick check today shows that in my own home I probably have half as many microprocessors, embedded in domestic equipment, as there are electric motors. Whether these devices are 4, 8, 16 or 32 bits is irrelevant. What is illustrated is not only the incredible growth in microprocessor technology but what to me is somewhat worrying, is how one's life has now become partially dependent on the quality of someone else's software.

For those of us who have worked with microprocessors and microcomputers since their inception, the progression from the first 4- and 8-bit devices to the 32-bit devices of today has been a steady evolution. We are now at the stage when the second generation, 32-bit, devices are starting to appear. In the early 1970s every semiconductor manufacturer seemed to produce his own microprocessor. How many organisations have been caught out by a bad choice of device and/or manufacturer? Today the microprocessor manufacturers have segmented in much the same way as the computer industry. We have the giants, the second and third division players and the niche vendors. To add some confusion to the scene, we also have some of the large computer vendors either selling directly or licensing to others their proprietary architectures.

1.2   Compatibility

Throughout this book, phrases such as object code and upwards/downwards compatibility are used. The latter is generally used to describe the code compatibility between earlier or modified versions of a standard product. When a new product or an update to an existing system is being planned, it is usually necessary to consider the cost impact of redeveloping existing software for a new architecture. Today, with many projects involving hundreds of man years of software development effort, protection of investment is a key business decision. This criterion has been understood for many years in the computer industry; however, it is only fairly recently that microprocessor users have started to understand this need.

1.3 CISC v. RISC

During the past few years we have seen the desktop market dominated by the Intel-based IBM pc, the technical workstation market by Motorola-based systems, the minicomputer market by Digital and the mainframe market by IBM. All these different architectures have one common element, i.e. they are based on Complex Instruction Set Computers (CISCs).

Recently we have seen the emergence of the Reduced Instruction Set Computer (RISC)-based technical workstations. Most manufacturers have now adopted RISC-based architectures for their high performance, top end systems. Today we have, for example, Digital, Hewlett Packard and Sun Microsystems selling both CISC- and RISC-based products.

This has led to many software vendors having to port their products to new architectures and new versions of operating systems. Most organisations are finding that this porting activity is not easy and they are now having to support their products on more platforms than they would probably wish.

While the new RISC products are providing exceptional Central Processing Unit (CPU) performance, the 'high tech' compilers, necessary to support the quirks and optimisation requirements of these devices, are causing users numerous problems. It is probable that it will take several years for the quality problems of the RISC compilers to stabilise.

1.4 Unix ™

Without any doubt, the most commonly mentioned operating system in this book is Unix™ and its many derivatives. Unix is now probably available on most manufacturers' machines. Implementations range from desktop pcs through to mainframes. Whether one loves or hates it, Unix and its derivatives will be around for many years to come.

Recognising that Unix is important for its hardware strategy, most microprocessor vendors are providing features within their architectures to support C and Unix. National Semiconductor and as one might expect, AT&T, have designed their devices for efficient support of C and other high level languages. They have also included primitives to improve Unit performance.

1.5 Real time operating systems

While Unix provides a portable environment in a general purpose time-sharing environment, there is no real standard for real time. While there are real time extensions from some vendors, Unix implementations and even some claims for real time Unix-like operating systems, there are no products that yet compare to the performance of a dedicated product.

The best known dedicated operating systems are RMX from Intel and VAXELN from Digital. As the need for real time operating systems increases, we are likely to see more of the portable products, such as VRTX and VXworks, appear.

1.6 Multiprocessor support

Once the domain of dedicated real time applications and very large mainframe computers, multiprocessor applications are now appearing in all levels of computer systems. Virtually all microprocessor vendors provide on-chip support for multiprocessor applications.

Probably the most novel of the on-chip multiprocessor support still comes on the Inmos transputer, with its high-speed serial links to other transputers.

With all 32-bit microprocessors there is a need to provide on-chip support for dedicated co-processors. The most common types of co-processors are probably the dedicated floating point processors and memory management units.

1.7 Memory systems

With users demanding higher performance from every new product release, and memory sizes forever on the increase, memory system design and control is a complex area of system design. While memory management support is essential for 32-bit microprocessors, the system designer now has to consider whether he needs to increase complexity and cost by utilising cache memory. To allow systems to operate at anywhere near their true potential, it is necessary to implement memory systems with expensive static memory or to front-end and slower dynamic memory with some form of caching. With small cache memory appearing within most chips it is probable that, to achieve acceptable system performance, designers will need to implement some form of high-speed cache memory within their products.

1.8   Software tools

It is probably safe to assume that most 32-bit microprocessors will be used in medium and large, technically complex projects. These projects will need careful planning, resourcing and support to achieve their aims. Any medium-to-large scale project will need extensive integrated support tools. Such tools need to include those for design and analysis, publishing, project management and code and configuration management. While these tools are becoming commonly available, care must be taken to ensure that the chosen products can be integrated together to provide the desired environment.

Closely allied to the need for good software tools is the need for improved software reliability. With microprocessors starting to appear in mission and safety critical systems, draft standards are now emerging. When such standards are accepted by industry, system suppliers will find that their contracts will include contractual targets for software reliability.

1.9   The future

While RISC products are available, it is probably safe to say that it will be many years before this architecture dominates the market. With today's CISC products, users and suppliers have made major investments in products and tools for their chosen architectures. The investment necessary and, initially, lower levels of productivity are unlikely to make RISC technology appear in anything other than applications that need the high, raw performance available.

Where the industry moves to in the future is currently in the hands of the users, semiconductors' houses and the direction of their future markets. Whether these moves are towards RISC, increased functionality, parallelism or greater word lengths, only time will tell.

CHAPTER 2
AT&T's WE™ 32-Bit Microprocessors and Peripherals

PRISCILLA M. LU and VICTOR K. HUANG
AT&T, USA

2.1 Introduction

The WE™32100 and 32200 microprocessors (CPUs) are AT&T's second and third generation microprocessors, respectively. They are complemented by six peripheral chips consisting of memory management support (WE32101 and 32201 Memory Management Units (MMUs)), floating point arithmetic acceleration (WE32106 and 32206 Maths Acceleration Units (MAUs)), Direct Memory Access Control (WE32104 DMAC controller); and Dynamic Random Access Memory Control (WE32103 DRAM controller). Photographs of the 32100 family devices are shown in Figs. 2.1–2.5.

Fig. 2.1   WE32100 microprocessor chip.

Fig. 2.2 WE32101 memory management unit chip.

The chip sets form the basic building blocks for a high performance 32-bit system. The architecture supports efficient implementation of the Unix operating system and provides high level language support. the I/O architecture[1] is designed to simplify system design and maximise system level performance.

2.2 AT&T WE32100 and 32200 microprocessor architectures

Sections 2.2.1 and 2.2.2 describe the architectures of the WE32100 and WE32200 microprocessors, respectively.

2.2.1 WE32100 MICROPROCESSOR ARCHITECTURE

The WE32100 microprocessor is implemented in 1.5 μm, CMOS

Fig. 2.3   WE32106 maths acceleration unit chip.

technology. The first generation WE32000^2 CPU was implemented in 1981, in 1.75 μm, CMOS technology. The WE32100 CPU, upwardly compatible with its predecessor, is enhanced with a 64-word instruction cache (I-cache) and a general purpose co-processor interface. The I-cache has a hit rate of about 65–75% for most Unix system programs, and provides about 20–25% improvement in performance of programs. The WE32100 CPU operates at 18 MHz, with an overall performance of 2–3 MIPS.

The microprocessor has a 32-bit bi-directional bus with status decoding, bus arbitration for external access, DMA control, interrupt handling, trace enable and pin out visibility to facilitate testing and debugging.

The WE32100 processor supports four data types: bytes (8-bit), halfwords (16-bit), words (32-bit), and bit field (1 to 32 bits in length). Bytes, halfwords and words can be interpreted as either signed or unsigned in arithmetic or logical operations. Strings are supported by special block instructions (STRING COPY, STRING LENGTH). The string format conforms to the C language and is terminated by a 'null' or zero byte.

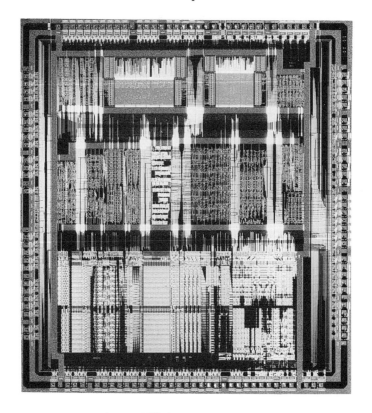

Fig. 2.4   WE32104 DMA controller chip.

Fig. 2.5   WE32103 DRAM controller chip.

Instructions are byte addressable and defined by a one- or two-byte opcode followed by zero or more operand descriptors. All byte or halfword operands are sign or zero extended to 32 bits when they are fetched.

The operand descriptor identifies the location of the operand. There are several addressing modes: literal, byte/halfword/word immediate, register, register deferred, short offset (for frame and argument pointers), byte/halfword/word displacement, byte/halfword/word displacement deferred, and expanded operand type. These are covered in more detail in the following sections.

There is a special program counter register and 15 other registers in the processor that can be referenced in any of the addressing modes. Three of the 15 registers are privileged, i.e. they can be written only when the processor is in kernal execution level. These three registers are used to support operations in the operating system. They are used as interrupt stack pointer, process control block pointer and processor status word. Another three registers are used by special instructions as a stack pointer, a frame pointer and an argument pointer.

2.2.2   WE32200 MICROPROCESSOR ARCHITECTURE

The WE32200 microprocessor, successor to the WE32100 CPU, is implemented in 1 μm, CMOS technology. It is protocol and object code upward compatible with the WE32100 CPU. Object code for the WE32100 microprocessor runs without modification on the WE32200 CPU. The WE32200 CPU performs all the system address generation, control memory access and processing functions required in a 32-bit microcomputer system. The system memory space is addressed over the 32-bit address bus using either physical or virtual addresses. Data is read or written over the 32-bit bi-directional data bus in byte (8-bit), halfword (16-bit), word (32-bit) or bit field (1 to 32 bits in length) widths, using arbitrary byte alignment for data and instructions. In addition, dynamic bus sizing allows the WE32200 microprocessor to communicate with both 16-bit and 32-bit memories in the same system. Twenty-five addressing modes result in a symmetric, versatile and powerful instruction set. The WE32200 CPU operates at 24 MHz. A block diagram of the CPU is shown in Fig. 2.6. Sections 2.2.2.1 to 2.2.2.4 describe the enhancements incorporated into the WE32200 CPU.

2.2.2.1   *WE32200 CPU registers.*   In addition to the WE32100 CPUs 16 registers, the WE32200 CPU contains an additional 16 32-bit registers (r16 – r31). Registers 16 through 23, like Registers 0 through

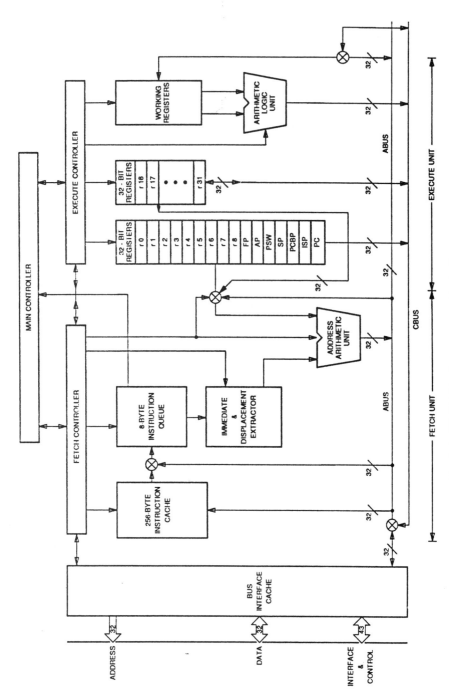

Fig. 2.6 WE32200 microprocessor block diagram.

8, may be used for accumulation, addressing or temporary data storage. They may be used in any of the 25 addressing modes by any privileged or non-privileged program. Similarly, Registers 24 through 31 may be used for accumulation, addressing or temporary data storage but, in addition, they are kernel level privileged. This means that they may be read in any addressing mode, but may only be written by kernel level instructions (privileged programs).

2.2.2.2 *WE32200 CPU addressing modes.*   The addressing modes incorporated in the WE32100 microprocessor are labelled Format 1 modes when discussing the WE32200 microprocessor. In addition to these modes, which are fully supported by the WE32200 CPU, there are eight more addressing modes labelled Format 2 which are not supported by the WE32100 CPU.

The auto pre-post increment/decrement modes are convenient when performing arithmetic or sort operations on contiguously addressed blocks of memory. When using the auto pre-increment/decrement modes, the specified register is first incremented or decremented; then, the value of that register is used as a pointer to the address of the operand. With post-increment/decrement modes, the value of the specified register is used as a pointer to the address of the operand which is then incremented or decremented.

The indexed register modes are useful for the efficient manipulation of arrays. The indexed register modes with byte or halfword displacement add the sum of the two specified registers to the byte or halfword offset. This total is then used as a pointer to the address of the operand.

Using indexed register mode with scaling, the contents of the first register (r0 – r15) is multiplied by 1, 2 or 4 (for byte, halfword or word) depending on the size of the operand mode descriptor. Then, the contents of the second register (r16 – r31) are added to that product. The result is used as a pointer to the address of the desired operand.

The Format 2 addressing modes also contain the modes specified in Format 1. As the WE32100 CPU had only 16 registers, the Format 1 addressing modes apply only to Registers 0 through 15. These Format 2 addressing modes are basically the same as those in Format 1 modes, but may be used with Registers 16 through 31.

2.2.2.3 *Dynamic bus sizing.*   The dynamic bus sizing feature allows communication with both 16-bit and 32-bit memories and peripherals. When a 16-bit port is accessed, the CPU generates additional memory accesses if the data size is word, 3 bytes or a halfword located in the middle of a word boundary. A very useful application of dynamic bus sizing is in boot ROMs. A 32-bit ROM can be substituted by a 16-bit boot ROM, therefore reducing board space requirements.

2.2.2.4 *Arbitrary byte alignment.* The arbitrary byte alignment feature enables the microprocessor to efficiently handle non-aligned memory accesses for both reads and writes. The microprocessor automatically generates multiple accesses when non-aligned data types cross word boundaries.

2.3   Programming language support

In designing the WE 32-bit microprocessors, a major goal was to provide support for the C programming language. The resulting architecture, however, supports the needs of high level programming languages in general, as well as C. Language support features include useful instructions for implementing arithmetic and logical operations, special instructions for manipulating strings and bit fields, and both simple and high level subroutine linkage operations. Several features of the WE 32-bit microprocessors simplify the interface to an operating system, including the machine's 'process oriented' design as needed for tasking, and a special 'controlled transfer' mechanism which implements both user defined and system exception control.

2.3.1   ARITHMETIC AND LOGICAL INSTRUCTIONS

Instructions, addressing and, to some extent data types, are fully orthogonal on the WE 32-bit microprocessors. The operation code defines the function to be performed, and the operand descriptor (or addressing mode) specifies the data type. The operand descriptor can be any one of the possible addressing modes. There are no register or data type restrictions on operands with any operation. Machine instructions associate a 'default' data type with the operands if their data type is not otherwise specified.

The WE 32-bit microprocessors offer a complete set of the 'usual' arithmetic and logical operations. Briefly the functions provided are:

logical: clear (i.e. zero data) one's complement, inclusive or, and exclusive or

arithmetic: negate, add, subtract, multiply, divide, modulus, increment and decrement (by one).

The unary operator's negate and complement are formulated as a move instruction; consequently, the result can either replace the existing datum or be placed in a new destination. All binary operators have both dyadic and triadic forms of instructions. All operations are internally performed as 32-bit functions; however, an overflow occurs if the computation result size exceeds that of the output operand's size.

Having all operations occur in all the same forms is convenient for compilers. For example, using dyadic and triadic forms for evaluating an expression is sometimes ignored in compiler optimisation because of operand restrictions. Coding the C expression

a = b + c*(d+e)

can be done easily with three instructions (assume all variables were integer words):

```
addw3    d,e,%r0    R0 = d + e
mulw2    c,%r0      R0 = c*(d+e)
addw3    b,%r0,a    a = b + c*(d+e)
```

where the variable names represent some operand descriptor to access the variable data. The same sequence could be used with different (binary) operators in the C expression with the corresponding opcode replacements; also, the variables need not be integer words.

One addressing mode of particular interest is the *short literal* mode that can represent a small integer (between –16 and 63) using only a single byte for data and descriptor. Using this mode provided an average space reduction of 5% and, as a consequence of this reduction, improved execution time by about 1.8%. The WE 32-bit microprocessors also have *immediate* modes for the different data types, where the data follows the mode descriptor. As with many machines, short literals and immediates need not be the same data type as the other instruction operands and these modes cannot be used as an operation destination.

An instruction associates a predefined data type with its operands, such as 'add word' and 'add byte'. However, this default data type is essentially a convenience that provides abbreviated addressing descriptions. The WE 32-bit microprocessors have an *expanded type* operand mode that explicitly specifies the data type of the operand along with its addressing form. The WE 32-bit microprocessors execute arithmetic and logical operations internally in words; the CPU performs any data type conversion while fetching and storing operands.

As an example of expanded type operands, consider adding a byte integr 'a' to a word integer 'b' and storing the result in a halfword integer 'c'. Typically, this computation requires several steps of instructions. The sequence of operations for most machines would look like:

```
movbw    a, temp    convert a to word
addw2    b, temp    compute the sum in a temporary
movwh    temp, c    convert result to a halfword.
```

Using the expanded type operands on the WE 32-bit microprocessors, this operation needs only one instruction:

addb3   a, {word} b. {halfword} c

where the desired operand data type is specified in brackets. In this example 'add byte' was used as the instruction to specify the data type of the first operand. If the first operand also used an expanded type mode, then any of the add instructions would produce identical computations.

As seen in the above example, the expanded type mode is convenience when the operand data types happen to be inconsistent since its use eliminates temporaries that can compete for registers. Expanded type also provides some operations that are not directly available with the instructions. For example, there is no unsigned multiplication operation but this operation can be achieved with a multiplication instruction using unsigned expanded type'd operands.

2.3.2   OTHER DATA TYPE OPERATIONS

Other data operations in the WE 32-bit microprocessors include functions to manipulate strings and bit fields. The string operations are destined specifically for a C string representation, where a *string* is a sequence of bytes ending in a null character (zero).

There are two string primitives:

string copy: copy one string into another
string end: locate the terminating (null) character in a string.

The addresses of the operands for these operations are specified in predefined registers. The *string end* operation can be used to compute the string length or in combination with *string copy* to produce a string append function. No length specification is given in either of these operations (string copy assumes target memory space is adequate and string end assumes the string is properly represented). These instructions are suitable for C but not necessarily for other languages. The WE 32-bit microprocessors also provide an instruction for moving a block of storage similar to the string copy, except the length is specified.

A *field* on the WE 32-bit microprocessors is a variable length sequence of bits occurring entirely within a word. Instructions are provided to extract a field from storage and to insert a field, with the operations specifying the number of bits and bit offset of the bit field as well as the target and source addresses. Fields can be manipulated in terms of types, halfwords or words. Using these operations, most of the necessary bit manipulation functions for high level languages can be easily implemented.

The WE 32-bit microprocessors support floating point and decimal arithmetic co-processor instructions. These instructions are supported by a co-processor interface that allows the CPU to initiate instruction and operand fetch from memory. The co-processor is activated by a co-processor command from the CPU. The co-processor proceeds to monitor the data bus for latching the operands for that operation. Data is fetched from memory by the CPU and this is latched by the co-processors on the data bus.

The CPU is blocked during the co-processor's execution of that instruction. Upon completion, the co-processor would assert the 'done' signal. Status conditions are sent back to the CPU, the result is placed on the data bus by the co-processor and is written out to memory by the CPU.

2.3.3   PROCEDURE LINKAGE

The WE 32-bit microprocessors offer high level procedure linkage operations as well as a set of primitive instructions for subroutine jump and return. The high level operations are useful for many programming languages, including C.

The high level procedure linkage operations manipulate the stack frame, save registers and transfer control between procedures. They are implemented to be efficient and include procedure call/return, and register save/restore. The push operation can be used to push arguments onto the stack. The procedure linkage process manipulates the stack and execution. Four registers are modified:

pc: The program counter is changed to start executing in the subroutine and to return to the calling program.

sp: The stack pointer is adjusted properly to point to the top of the stack.

fp: The frame pointer points to the position in the stack just above the register save area (usually the start of local variable space for a procedure).

ap: The argument pointer points to a list of arguments used by the procedure. This list precedes the other linkage data on the stack.

In addition to these registers, other registers have presumed semantics. Specifically, Registers r0 through r2 are viewed as 'temporaries' whose values are not saved in the WE32100 CPU between procedure calls. Registers r3 through r8 (in addition, r16 through r23 for the WE32200 CPU) can be saved across procedures calls.

A typical stack frame, such as used in C, contains the arguments, return information, saved registers and local variable. This stack frame is displayed in Fig. 2.7.

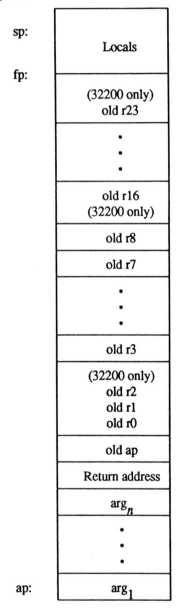

sp:

Locals

fp:

(32200 only)
old r23

•
•
•

old r16
(32200 only)

old r8

old r7

•
•
•

old r3

(32200 only)
old r2
old r1
old r0

old ap

Return address

arg_n

•
•
•

ap:

arg_1

Fig. 2.7 Sample stack frame.

Stack frames using the WE 32-bit microprocessors' high level linkage operations can differ from the above in the number of registers saved.

There are four instructions used in procedure linkage. The calling procedure uses the Call instruction to save the ap and return address on the stack. The first instruction of each procedure is the Save instruction that saves the old fp and a specified sequence of registers from r8 through r3 (in addition, r16 through r23 for the WE32200 CPU). Conceptually, only the registers to be used are saved. As noted earlier, Registers r0 through r2 are not saved and consequently can be used to store the result. When the procedure completes, it executes a 'Restore' instruction to restore any needed values in r3 through r8 and r16 through r23, and then a 'Return' instruction that resets the stack frame to that of the calling procedure, and then resumes its execution. Arguments are typically placed on the stack with the 'Push' or 'Push-Address' instructions. The 'Return' instruction automatically pops them off. Using these instructions proved to give a 20% speed-up in execution time over direct coding of these four functions.

Coupled with the above procedure linkage scheme are two addressing modes called ap-offset and fp-offset. These modes provide a one-byte descriptor that can reference data whose address is an offset to the ap or fp registers in a range of 0 to 14. Since procedures typically have few arguments and often only a few local variables, most arguments and locals can be referenced with a one-byte descriptor. For an example of where these modes can be used, consider the variables in the C program:

```
foo(a,b,c)
int a,b,c;
{   int d,e,f;
    . . .

}
```

All the given variables (a to f) could be addressed with a one-byte descriptor. Our analysis showed that each of these addressing modes gave an average space reduction of 5% and an average execution speed improvement of 1.8% over not using these modes.

If it is inconvenient to use the above procedure linkage scheme, 'Jump to Subroutine' and 'Return from Subroutine' instructions are also provided. The 'Jump to Subroutine' instructions act as in many machines by pushing the return address on the stack and transferring control to the subroutine. This operation comes in both jump (that gives the address) and branch (which gives a pc offset) formats. The

Return from Subroutine unwinds this operation but is interesting in that it comes in a conditional form, i.e. the execution of the return can depend on the condition codes, where all available codes can be tested.

2.3.4   ENVIRONMENTAL CONTROL: TASKS AND EXCEPTIONS

Providing 'operating system' functions in a programming language, such as tasking and exception control, have typically been difficult to implement. Many articles on compilers have cried for assistance in machine architecture. The WE 32-bit microprocessors provide some assistance to these problems, particularly with exceptions.

The process oriented architecture of the WE 32-bit microprocessors eases this requirement by establishing the process design with the machine architecture. A compiler can represent a task as a WE 32-bit microprocessor process with the appropriate memory mappings that can be constructed by either the language run time system or operating system. Also, this approach simplifies the mutual exclusion aspect of task rendezvous, since it is provided by the hardware. The other rendezvous issues, synchronisation and data exchange, are not directly assisted by the hardware and need some assistance by the system scheduler. Section 2.4 on operating system support discusses this process structure for the WE 32-bit microprocessors.

The WE 32-bit microprocessors have a table-driven *interrupt* mechanism that is used to manage system exceptions (and other system calls) and can be employed to implement user exceptions as well. When a system level exception occurs, the WE 32-bit microprocessors effectively execute a *controlled transfer* call instruction using a predefined set of operand vlues. This transfer operation is best viewed as a form of Jump to Subroutine where tables select the appropriate subroutine address. If the operating system provides an interface for modifying the controlled transfer tables, a user-written exception handler can be called automatically by inserting its address into the appropriate table entry. The user defined exceptions can be managed with this operation by adding exception handler address for each user exception and having the user execute a controlled transfer call instruction when the exception occurs. The controlled transfer can transfer to a normal user routine. To resume processing at the point of the exception (user or system), the code for the handler simply executes a controlled transfer return instruction.

2.3.4.1   *Common libraries and packages.*   One approach to implementing common libraries and packages (abstract data types) is to use

the controlled transfer mechanism discussed above. Conceptually, the call to a package entry can be viewed as a user exception.

One (or more) of the transfer tables could be allocated to package control. Each entry in this table would correspond to a function entry in some package. To invoke a package procedure, a controlled transfer call instruction would be used and each package procedure would return via a controlled transfer return. A major advantage of this approach is that code for package procedures could be shared across processes and generating code for package calls would be simplified.

2.4 WE 32-bit microprocessors' operating system support

The WE 32-bit microprocessors were designed to provide an efficient environment for a sophisticated operating system. An operating system is not built into the processor, nor is the processor optimised for any particular operating system. Instead, the processor provides two mechanisms that can be used to manipulate processes, control transfers to the operating system, and respond to interrupts and also the handling of exceptions.

2.4.1 PROCESSES

The WE 32-bit microprocessors support a 'process oriented' operating system; a particular model of a process is implicit in the machine architecture. This model has several characteristics:

- There are four levels of privileged execution to allow flexibility in constructing multi-level operating systems. The hierarchy among the four levels is enforced only by the controlled transfer mechanism.
- There is only one execution stack per process. This stack is used by the procedure call mechanism as well as the controlled transfer mechanism, and it is used independent of execution level.
- A process is defined to the processor by a *Processor Control Block* (PCB), which stores copies of the processor's resources used by the process (e.g. the on-chip registers).
- It is intended that at least the kernel of the operating system reside in the address space of every process.

With four execution levels, a system that required a separate stack for each execution level would have to maintain at least four growable segments for stacks. With a single stack, the operating system need maintain only one, and a single stack overflow mechanism is sufficient to grow the stack. The stack fault mechanism, which handles overflow conditions as well as other violations, is described in Section 2.4.6.2. In addition, at least four registers would be required to point to these four stacks, and the management of such special registers is expensive in a VLSI design. The execution stack can also be used to pass arguments from user code to system functions; the regular parameter passing mechanism can be used without elaborate copying operations.

If the kernel of the operating system is in the address space of every process, copying of data from user buffers to system buffers is not required since the system can access user buffers, and vice versa. A common address space for user and operating system code is necessary

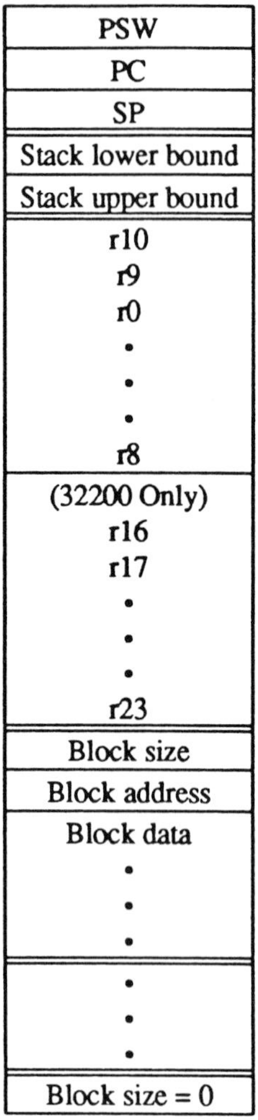

PSW
PC
SP
Stack lower bound
Stack upper bound
r10
r9
r0
•
•
•
r8
(32200 Only)
r16
r17
•
•
•
r23
Block size
Block address
Block data
•
•
•
•
•
•
Block size = 0

Fig. 2.8 Process control block layout.

if the single execution stack mechanism is to work because changing the address space would lose the stack and the procedure chain it contains. The exception mechanism of the WE 32-bit microprocessors expects the kernel to be in the address space of every process, so the processor does not change memory management to access an exception handler.

Two data structures are associated with processes on the WE 32-bit microprocessors, the PCB and the interrupt stack. The PCB (see Fig. 2.8) has space for the 14 registers (22 for the WE32200 CPU) used by a process. These are the 11 user registers (19 for the WE32200 CPU) plus three control registers, the *Stack Pointer* (SP), the *Program Counter* (PC) and the *Processor Status Word* (PSW). Two words in the PCB are used to store the upper address limit and the lower address limit of the execution stack; these bounds are checked in the controlled transfer mechanism. The rest of the PCB is unbounded in length and is intended to be used by (but is not restricted to) memory management. The interrupt stack is not associated with any one process, and contains pointers to PCBs. One of the two on-chip registers not associated with any one process, the PCB Pointer (PCBP), points to the PCB of the process running on the processor. The second of these registers, the *Interrupt Stack Pointer* (ISP), points to the top of the interrupt stack. Both the PCBP and the ISP are privileged in that they can only be written when the processor is in the kernel execution level.

2.4.2   PROCESS SWITCH

The first of the two mechanisms used to support operating systems on the WE 32-bit microprocessors is the *process switch* mechanism, which is used in process switching, interrupt handling and exception handling. The process switch mechanism has four parts that are used by the microsequences in various combinations:

(1) Store the control registers in the PCB pointed to by the PCBP (the 'old' PCB). Store the user registers in the 'old' PCB (optional).
(2) Update the PCBP to point to the 'new' PCB. Load the control registers from the 'new' PCB. Move PCBP past the initial context of the 'new' PCB (optional).
(3) Perform a series of block moves (optional).
(4) Load user registers from 'new' PCB (optional).

The data in the block move section of the PCB is intended to be a memory map specification. Since all I/O on the WE 32-bit microprocessors is memory mapped, the starting address in the block move section would be the base of translation registers in an MMU. With this mechanism, the process switch would automatically establish the virtual address domain of the new process without any further intervention by the operating system. Of course, if the WE 32-bit microprocessors' mechanism is undesirable for some application, it can be disabled by setting the block move count to zero in all PCBs.

2.4.3   CALL PROCESS/RETURN TO PROCESS

Explicit instructions are provided in the WE 32-bit microprocessors for switching processes by the operating system. They are not used for scheduling processes which, in the WE 32-bit microprocessors, are still the responsibility of operating system software. Instead, they provide a means of dispatching processes and co-ordinating process switches determined by the operating system with those that arise unexpectedly from interrupts. The two instructions, Call Process and Return to Process, are analogous to the pair Jump to Subroutine and Return from Subroutine. In the subroutine transfer instructions, the starting address defines the subroutine. The jump pushes a return address on the execution stack and the return pops the return address off that stack. In the process transfer instructions, the address of the PCB defines the process. The call pushes the address of the current PCB on the interrupt stack and the return pops the address of a PCB off the interrupt stack. Like the subroutine transfer instructions, the process transfer instructions only transfer flow of control and do not explicitly pass arguments.

The Call Process instruction has the address of a PCB as its argument. It saves the context of the old process in the old PCB, with the saved PC pointing to the next instruction to be executed, and gets a new context from the new PCB. The Return to Process instruction just loads a new context from the new PCB.

2.4.4   INTERRUPTS

The interrupt mechanism of the WE 32-bit microprocessors is intended to be efficient, reliable and consistent with the process model of the processors. Since interrupts are asynchronous, they are not likely to be associated with the process running on the processor. Ideally, an interrupt should be handled by a new process, which is exactly what the WE 32-bit microprocessors do. This concept has a number of advantages. An interrupt process has an entirely new context and is unlikely to interfere with any other process. If the interrupting device is not a critical resource, the interrupt handler need not run in kernel mode, but can be dispatched directly in user mode. A special execution stack used by interrupts is not necessary, since each interrupt process gets a new execution stack that does not need any special treatment.

2.4.4.1 *Interrupt mechanism.*

An interrupt in the WE 32-bit microprocessors is handled as an unexpected Call Process instruction. An interrupting device presents the processor with an 8-bit interrupt id. This id selects one of 256 PCB pointers in a table starting at a fixed virtual address. Each PCB pointer corresponds to an interrupt handler process. The microsequence is then exactly the same as in the Call Process instruction. The interrupt process will then run unless it is interrupted by a higher priority interrupt. When the interrupt handler process is completed, a Return to Process instruction should be issued which will restart the process that was suspended when the interrupt occurred.

The interrupt stack keeps track of the nesting of interrupts. Unless the interrupt stack is explicitly manipulated by the operating system, the PCBP at the bottom of the stack points to the PCBs of interrupt handler processes of increasing priority, with the PCBP pointing to the PCB of the highest priority interrupt currently in a state of execution.

2.4.5 CONTROLLED TRANSFER

The controlled transfer mechanism in the WE 32-bit microprocessors provides a means for controlled entry into a procedure or handler along with a new PSW. It can be used as the system call mechanism. The controlled transfer consists of a 'controlled call' and a 'controlled return'. The controlled call operates like the Jump to Subroutine instruction except that the PC/PSW pair is stacked and replaced. This instruction has two operands that operate as a double table index to determine the new PSW and the appropriate address to branch to. The PC/PSW pair is popped off the stack on a controlled return.

At a predefined location in memory there is a 'first level' table of pointers, each of which can point to a 'second level' table of PC/PSW pairs. The first index operand selects the appropriate 'second level' table. The second index operand determines the appropriate address to branch to (see Fig. 2.9). The 'first level' allows for 32 entries and each 'second level' table can have up to 4095 entries. The 'second level' table can be located anywhere in memory. In particular, they may be shared by some (or all) of the users or be unique to a process.

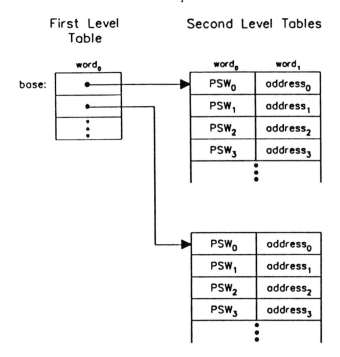

Fig. 2.9 Process index tables.

2.4.5.1 *Use of controlled transfer.*   In more conventional architectures, a single Supervisor Call instruction exists which loads a new
PCC and PSW from a predetermined location. It is up to the operating
system software to determine which procedure to invoke.

In the WE 32-bit microprocessors, this software procedure is
assisted by their internal architecture. The controlled transfer mechanism is the only way a processor can change its execution level. There
is no notion of execution level in the microsequence implementing the
call, because the new PSW will determine the execution level of the
process. The controlled return instruction is the only place in the WE
32-bit microprocessors that explicitly identifies privilege; it will not
allow a procedure to return to a more privileged one.

Since there is only one execution stack per process, it is especially
important to maintain integrity of this stack. The controlled transfer
mechanism is where the sanity of the stack is preserved. There are two
entries in the PCB. These correspond to the upper and lower bounds
of the execution stack. The controlled call instruction checks to make
sure that the stack pointer lies between these boundaries before
executing the transfer. The operating system on the processor has to
maintain the stack bounds in the PCB.

2.4.6   EXCEPTIONS

Exceptions are events that indicate something is wrong with the current execution. They can be detected internally by the processor or generated externally. The WE 32-bit microprocessors can handle all exceptional conditions without halting and they use the two basic mechanisms provided for the operating system, i.e. the controlled transfer mechanism and the process switch mechanism. Four levels of exceptions are invoked by the WE 32-bit microprocessors, depending on the severity of the error and the resources available at the time. These levels are normal exception, stack exception, process exception and reset exception.

2.4.6.1   *Normal exception.*   Most exceptions are normal exceptions. These include such internal exceptions as illegal instruction, integer overflow, and privileged register access, as well as externally generated memory faults. The processors record an index of the exceptions in a 4-bit field of the PSW called the *Internal State Code* (ISC). The action the processors take is exactly the same as the controlled transfer call. The first level index is always zero, and the second level index is the ISC. Therefore, when any normal exception occurs, the controlled transfer mechanism automatically transfers control to a routine that can handle the exception. The exception handler need not be privileged or even part of the operating system. If the user provides a handler for an exception, it is sufficient to change the table entry of that exception to point to that code.

2.4.6.2   *Stack exception.*   The execution stack on the WE 32-bit microprocessors is a critical resource and hence must be maintained carefully. If the execution stack is bad, a normal exception sequence cannot be invoked, since the first thing a normal exception sequence does is push a PC/PSW pair onto the stack. Therefore, a special type of process switch is provided to handle stack exceptions. Stack exceptions are detected in the controlled transfer mechanism, either when the stack bounds check fails, or when a read from the stack or write to the stack fails. When a stack exception is detected, the processors fetch a pointer to a new PCB from a fixed virtual location. They then push the current PCBP onto the interrupt stack, save the old control registers and load a new set, obtaining a new stack. They do not execute the block moves, so the memory managements are not forced to change. The new process can repair the stack, adjust the stack bounds, kill the process or whatever else it likes.

2.4.6.3 *Process exception.* A process exception occurs when a read from, or a write to, the PCB during a microsequence causes a memory fault. Since the PCB is bad, the process is effectively dead; there is no way registers can be saved or the process restarted. All that the processors can do is to start a new process. When a process exception occurs, the processors fetch a pointer to a new PCB from a fixed virtual location, push the current PCBP onto the interrupt stack and load a new set of control registers. Because the process exception handler should do its job quickly, it is more efficient to include one in the domain of every process and avoid executing the block moves of the process switch.

2.4.6.4 *Reset exception.* A reset exception is invoked when all else fails or when the processors reset externally. It occurs during a microsequence, when a memory fault occurs when reading from, or writing to, the interrupt stack, when a memory fault occurs in reading an address vector or when there is a memory fault in processing a process exception. When a reset exception occurs, the processors disable virtual addressing, fetch a pointer to a new PCB for a fixed physical location, and then load a new set of control registers. If a memory fault occurs in processing a reset exception, another reset exception is generated and the processors try again. The microprocessors are fully restartable on any fault.

2.4.7   UNIX SYSTEM USE OF THE HARDWARE PROCESS SWITCH
        AND THE MMU

The process switching features of the CPU and the virtual memory features of the MMU combine neatly to support operations typical in modern operating systems. Use of these features to implement a user-process to user-process switch is explained in this section.

The MMU provides the concept of 'sections' of virtual address space, where each section consists of one quarter of the 32-bit address space and is mapped through one segment descriptor table. The MMU can automatically flush its internal descriptor caches on a per-section basis, in response to a single write from the CPU. That is, in one operation, the operating system can change the mapping of one quarter of the virtual address space, and the MMU will guarantee that the appropriate portions of its internal caches are flushed.

A natural way to partition the virtual address space is to dedicate one or more sections to the operating system, and the remaining sections to the currently active user process. That is, all user processes will reside at the same virtual addresses (of course, only one user process can reside there at any one time). By rewriting the MMU registers that contain the addresses of the segment descriptor tables for those sections, the operating system can switch one user process out of the virtual address space, and another one into the virtual address space, in a few operations.

In fact, the complete operating system code for a user-process to user-process switch in such a system would be as follows:

{Currently running in user process A}

```
/* process switch to switcher process in operating system,*/
MOVAW switcher, %r0
CALLPS
```

{Now running in switcher process in operating system}

```
/* rewrite MMU registers for two sections*/
MOVW newpointer1,mmureg1
MOVW newpointer2,mmureg2
```

```
/*process switch "back" to new user process B*/
RETPS
```

{Now running in user process B}

This code has accomplished a complete user-process to user-process switch. The CALLPS (Call Process) instruction saved the register contents of the current process (user process A) and obtained the register contents of an operating system process designated as the 'switcher' process. The 'switcher' process, after determining which user process to switch to (not shown), wrote the addresses of user process B's segment descriptor tables into the MMU registers, thus making user process A 'disappear' from the virtual address space and making user process B 'appear' in it. Finally, the 'switch' process executed a RETPS (Return to Process) instruction, which obtained the register contents of user process B from where they were saved when process B last executed a CALLPS instruction to get to the 'switcher' process.

The advantage of providing support for the operating system are that the primitives are guaranteed to be correct, i.e. protected from alteration or corruption, and the accessing of internal CPU facilities for disabling interrupts, initiating fault sequences, etc.

2.5 Usage of common peripheral chips with the WE 32-bit microprocessors

The WE 32-bit microprocessor chip-sets provide a pseudo-synchronous interface to the system designer. The interface protocol is compatible with common industry peripherals such as UARTs, interrupt controllers, etc. The WE 32-bit microprocessor chip-sets allow easy memory interface to dynamic RAMs, static RAMs, and cache memory designs.

The basic memory transaction is a 3–7 clock cycle transaction (zero wait states) with an additional cycle used by the MMU to provide a virtual memory environment when the designer uses an MMU. This additional cycle may be eliminated with the use of the on-chip data cache of the WE 32201 MMU.

Some unique features of the hardware interface provided by the WE 32-bit microprocessor chip-sets are:

(1) A dynamically selectable block fetch feature which improves CPU performance by eliminating trivial virtual address translation.
(2) Delayed bus exceptions allowing a designer longer time to detect faults.
(3) Two-wire bus arbitration.

2.5.1 CO-PROCESSOR INTERFACE

The co-processor interface supported by the WE 32-bit microprocessor chip-sets provide a high speed interface between the CPU and MAU, along with the flexibility for easy expansion of additional co-processors. A total of ten CPU opcodes have been reserved for co-processor instructions, providing a flexible assortment of zero, one and two operand instructions with each operand being either one, two or three words in length. Communication between the CPU and a co-processor takes the form of a minimum length bus transaction, with optional wait states. Data fetched from, or written to, memory is performed concurrently by the CPU and co-processor in a single bus transaction, rather than routing data through the CPU as two separate bus transactions. This approach provides the highest possible speed for operand transfers.

A co-processor operation is initiated with a 'co-processor broadcast' transaction, in which an 8-bit co-processor ID field allows the CPU to address up to 256 different types of co-processors on the bus. The remaining 24 bits of the transaction word can be interpreted by the co-processor in any fashion it desires, usually as opcode and operand information. All operands are then fetched, and taken in directly by the co-processor. At this point, the co-processor executes the requested operation, and indicates completion of the CPU with a DONE signal. The CPU then latches status from the co-processor into its PSW, and provides the address for any memory writes which may be required for the result of the co-processor operation. Any exceptions which may have been detected by the co-processor during execution can be signalled to the CPU during the status transfer bus cycle.

2.6 WE32101 and 32201 memory management units architecture

The WE32201 MMU is the third generation MMU while the WE32101 MMU is the second generation.[3] The first generation was implemented in 2.5 μm CMOS technology and runs at 7.2 MHz. The WE32101 MMU is implemented in 1.5 μm CMOS technology and has a clock-rate of 18 MHz. The WE32201 MMU is implemented in 1 μm, CMOS technology and has a clock rate of 24 MHz. The MMUs provide address translation for contiguous (WE32101 MMU only) and paged segments simultaneously. The memory management architecture has the following attributes:

- Facilitates systematic memory organisation for operating systems by partitioning virtual address space into manageable units of sections, segments and pages.
- Access protection checking for continuous and paged segments.
- Support of demand paging and segmentation algorithms by automatic update of 'referenced' and 'modified' bits.
- Automatic miss-processing for on-chip segment and page descriptor cache entries.
- Support of variable size segments from 8 bytes to 128K for the WE32101 MMU and 2K to 128K, in 2K increments, for the WE32201 MMU.
- Support of shared segments through the use of indirect segment descriptors.
- Descriptor cache flushing facilities.
- Detailed fault detection and resolution.

To minimise memory translation time, the MMU has descriptor caches on-chip. There is a directly mapped, 32-entry segment descriptor cache and a two-way set associate, 64-entry page descriptor cache.

To translate an address, the MMU searches its descriptor caches for relevant descriptors. If the descriptors are present, the MMU checks for length violation and access permission violation.

For contiguous segments, translation is done by adding the segment base address from the cached segment descriptor to an offset, from the virtual address, to form the physical address.

For paged segments, the MMU concatenates a page base address, from the cached page descriptor, to the page offset, from the virtual address, to form the physical address.

If there is a miss in the cache, the MMU will perform 'miss-processing'. The MMU will access the descriptor tables in memory and fetch the descriptor into the on-chip caches.

2.6.1 ADDRESS SPACE PARTITIONING

The MMU supports up to 2^{32} bytes of virtual or physical memory. Virtual address translation can be selected dynamically by a virtual/physical signal from the CPU.

Virtual address space is divided into sections, and sections into segments. Segments are paged (or contiguous, non-aged, for the WE32101 MMU).

The virtual address space of a process is divided into four sections. An important purpose of sections is to optimise the flushing of cache entries of shared virtual address space. The cached descriptors for a section can be flushed independently of the other sections during a process switch. Therefore, sections of the virtual address space (such as libraries of system calls or kernel routines) that are common among multiple processes can be maintained in the descriptor caches of the MMU between process switches.

Each section may consist of up to 8K segments. Section identifiers stored in the MMU designate the segment descriptor tables associated with the sections. Rewriting a section identifier in the MMU automatically flushes the corresponding entries in the descriptor caches for that section.

Segments can be contiguous or paged. Both types are supported simultaneously by the WE32101 MMU. A paged segment is divided into 2K byte pages for the WE32101 MMU or 2K, 4K or 8K byte pages for the WE32201 MMU.

2.6.2 FEATURES

2.6.2.1 *Virtual address fields.* The subdivisions of virtual address space require the division of virtual addresses into three fields for contiguous segments and four fields for paged segments.

A virtual address that references a contiguous segment (WE32101

31   30   29   17   16   0

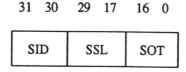

Fig. 2.10   Virtual address fields for a contiguous segment.

31 30   29   17   16 13/12/11*   12/11/10† 0

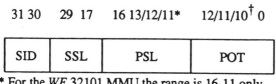

* For the *WE* 32101 MMU the range is 16-11 only.
† For the *WE* 32101 MMU the range is 10-0 only.

Fig. 2.11   Virtual address fields for a paged segment.

MMU only) is divided into *Section ID* (SID) field (which section of virtual address space), a *Segment Select* (SSL) field (which segment within the section) and a *Segment Offset* (SOT) field (which byte within the segment). See Fig. 2.10.

For paged segments, the SOT field is subdivided into a *Page Select* (PSL) field (which page within the segment) and a *Page Offset* (POT) field (which byte within the page). See Fig. 2.11.

2.6.2.2   *Map tables and descriptors.*   Segment Descriptor Tables (SDTs) and Page Descriptor Tables (PDTs) specify mappings between virtual and physical address space in terms of segments and pages. The tables must always reside in physical memory whenever the MMU is using them. A contiguous segment is represented by only a single SDT entry, while a paged segment is represented by both an SDT entry and an entire PDT. In the latter case, the SDT entry contains the physical base address of the PDT.

The MMU chip stores pointers to the table in memory and also contains the length of each table. This information is used during miss-processing.

2.6.2.3   *Segment descriptors and tables.*   The mapping from virtual address space to physical address space for a section is defined by the SDT associated with that section. An SDT contains one 8-byte entry, a Segment Descriptor (SD) for each segment in the section. Each segment may consist of up to 128K. The SSL field of the virtual address is used as an index into the SDT. (See Figs. 2.12 and 2.13.)

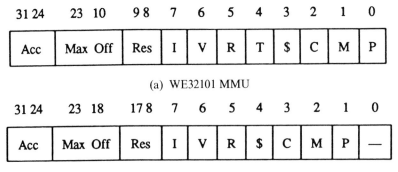

(a) WE32101 MMU

(b) WE32201 MMU

Fig. 2.12 Format of first word of an SD.

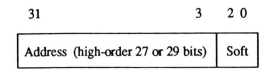

Fig. 2.13 Format of second word of an SD.

V (Valid).   V==1 indicates a valid segment descriptor. If V==0 an access causes a fault.

C (Contiguous).   C==0 means the segment is paged and C==1 means that it is contiguous. If C==0 then the MMU uses the second word of the SD as the physical base address of a PDT. If C==1 the MMU uses the second word of the SD as the physical base address of a contiguous segment.

P (Present).   P==1 means the segment or PDT is present in memory. If the MMU attempts to use the SD during miss-processing and P==0, a fault occurs.

I (Indirect).   I==1 indicates an indirect segment descriptor (one that points to another segment descriptor). During miss-processing, if I==1, the second word of the SD is used as the physical address of another SD and the second SD is fetched. In addition, if I==1 in the second SD, another SD is fetched using the second word of the second SD. Up to six fetches may occur but if the sixth SD has I==1, a fault occurs. Indirect segment descriptors may be used to implement shared segments that may be easily swapped out. The only segment descriptor that has to be modified by the operating system when the shared segment is swapped or moved is the last one (the one with I==0).

R (Referenced).   If the MMU is configured to do so and a segment descriptor (in a segment descriptor table) is referenced via miss-processing and the reference is not faulted, then the R bit in the segment descriptor is set to 1.

M (Modified).   If the MMU is configured to do so, it sets the M bit to 1, if the MMU successfully translates an address using this SD for a write access.

$ (Cachable).   Whenever the SD is used for a translation, the MMU sets its cachable pin to reflect the value of this bit. Cachable bits may be used by the system to prevent or allow the caching of instructions and data on a per-segment basis.

T (Object Trap, WE32101 MMU only).   If there is a valid translation using the segment descriptor (maximum offset and access permissions are not violated), the segment is contiguous (C==1) and the T bit is set, an object-trap fault occurs. The T bit is ignored on paged segments.

Res (Reserved).   These bits are reserved for future MMU use.

Soft (Software Reserved).   These bits are reserved for use by software and are guaranteed not to be changed by the MMU.

Max Off (Maximum Offset).   This field is used to calculate the maximum offset from the beginning of the segment that a virtual address may specify. If a virtual address specifies a byte outside this limit, a fault is signalled to the CPU.

This value is equal to the number of double-words (8-byte) in the segment, minus one. Thus it is impossible to specify a segment containing 0 bytes via this mechanism.

Whenever a segment descriptor is used to perform a translation, the MMU checks the access permissions field of the SD, the type of access being requested by the CPU, and the execution level at which the access is being requested. If the MMU determines that access is not allowed under the given condition, a fault occurs.

The MMU uses the execution level (kernel, executive, supervisor, user) at which the access is being requested and the contents of the access permissions field to determine whether the given execution level is allowed Read/Write (RW), Read/Execute (RE), Read-only (RO) or No-access (NA) permissions to the segment. It then checks the type of access requested by the CPU to determine which permissions are needed to allow the access. If the permissions needed for that type of access are not satisfied, a fault occurs; otherwise, the access is allowed.

The access permissions field is 8 bits wide and is structured as four 2-bit fields, one for each execution level. The type of access allowed to a given execution level is encoded in its 2-bit field.

The address field of the second word of a segment descriptor in an SDT may be used by the MMU in one of the following ways:

(1) As the physical base address of a contiguous segment. This is the address in physical memory where the contents of the segment start.
(2) As a PDT address for a paged segment. This is the address in physical memory where the page descriptor table starts.
(3) As the physical address of another SD, in the case of an indirect SD.

2.6.2.4 *Page descriptors and tables.* For a paged segment, the second word of the segment descriptor is used by the MMU as the address of a page descriptor table. A PDT contains one 4-byte page descriptor for each page in the segment. A PDT may consist of a maximum of 64 page descriptors, but may contain fewer. (See Fig. 2.14.)

P (Present). P==1 if the page is present, P==0 if it is not. If the MMU attempts to fetch a PD during miss-processing and P==0, the remainder of the PD information is ignored and a fault occurs.

R (Referenced). The MMU sets R to 1 when it successfully translates an address for any type of address.

M (Modified). The MMU sets M to 1, if not already 1, when it

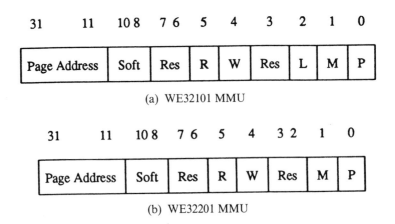

(a) WE32101 MMU

(b) WE32201 MMU

Fig. 2.14 Page descriptor format.

successfully translates an address for a write access to any byte of the page.

L (Last, WE32101 MMU only). During translation, if L==1 the MMU will access the maximum offset field of the corresponding SD and perform a length check. If L==0, the translation proceeds without this action occurring.

It is intended that L==1 if the page descriptor corresponds to the last page in the segment whose length is not an integral multiple of 2K. If L==0, the page length is 2K.

W (Fault-On-Write). If access permissions and length are not violated and the access type is a write and W==1, a fault occurs. This bit can be used to minimise copying of pages when duplicating a process. Instead of copying every page, each may be shared and have W==1. An attempt to write to a shared page by either process then causes a fault and only then does that page have to be duplicated.

Page Address. The page address * 2K (or 4K or 8K when using the WE32201 MMU) is the address of the first byte of the page in physical memory.

2.6.3 INTERNAL STRUCTURE

The following entities in the MMU may be accessed in the memory mapped peripheral mode:

(1) The segment descriptor cache (32 descriptors; directly mapped; total of 64 words).

(2) The two-way set associative page descriptor cache (64 descriptors; two-way set associative; total of 128 words).

(3) Section RAM A. SRAMA contains the addresses of the SDTs, and can be used to flush sections from the descriptor caches.

(4) Section RAM B. SRAMB contains the number of entries of each SDT.

(5) The Fault Code Register (FLTCR). This is used to record information about faults that the MMU detects.

(6) The Fault Address Register (FLTAR). This contains the virtual address that was being processed when a fault occurred.

(7) The Configuration Register (CR). This contains bits that specify configurable aspects of the MMU behaviour.

(8) The Virtual Address Register (VAR). This contains the virtual address to be translated by the MMU, and can be used to flush single entries from the descriptor caches.

Additional entities accessible for the WE32201 MMU are:

(9) Flush data cache register (write only). When all zeros are
    written to the FDCR by the operating system, the data cache (see
    Section 2.6.5) is flushed.
(10) ID number cache (read only). The IDNC is used by the MMU
    to transparently assign ID numbers to each section of the MMU.
    It is organised as a 16-entry, fully associative configuration
    containing the segment table tag and ID number.
(11) Current ID number registers (read only). CIDNRs contain the
    four current ID numbers.
(12) Flush ID number register (write only). Writing the address of a
    SDT to the FIDNR causes all page descriptor cache entries
    associated with the flushed ID to be flushed from the PDC and all
    entries to be flushed from the SDC.

2.6.3.1 *Descriptor caches.* The SDC consists of 32 descriptors, each
of which is 64 bits wide. These descriptors have a format that differs
from the format of the SDs in SDTs that were described earlier.
Cached SDs contain a tag field and do not contain V, I, P and R bits,
among other differences.

The SDC is a directly mapped cache divided into four parts that
correspond to the four sections. It requires a 5-bit index to select an
entry and a 10-bit tag for unique identification of the descriptor.

The page descriptor cache consists of 64 64-bit descriptors organised
in a two-way set associative fashion. The format of cached PDs is
different from the format of PDs in PDTs in memory. Cached PDs
contain a tag field and an access permissions field (copied from the SD)
and do not contain P and soft bits, among other differences.

The PDC is divided into four parts that correspond to the four
sections. As in the SDC, the index is 5 bits. The tag, however, is 16 bits.

2.6.3.2 *Other objects.* Section RAM A consists of four 32-bit
words. Each word is used as the physical base address of an SDT
during miss-processing.

Section RAM B contains the number of segments in each section,
minus one. This is used for segment descriptor table bounds checking
during miss-processing. SRAMB consists of four 32-bit words.

The virtual address register contains the virtual address to be
translated by the MMU.

The fault code register keeps a log of faults and operational states in
the MMU chip. Its contents are overwritten every time a fault occurs.

The FLTAR contains the virtual address that was being processed when the last fault occurred. The FLTAR contents are changed when the CPU writes to it in peripheral mode, and when faults occur.

The configuration register is a 32-bit register containing three one-bit items called $, Ref and Mod. The Ref and Mod bits enable or disable setting of segment R and M bits in memory. During miss-processing and R and M update, the $-bit determines the state of an output pin. This may be tied to an external cache to prevent or allow caching of descriptors in the external cache.

2.6.4 OPERATIONS

This section describes several operations that the MMU performs in response to actions by the CPU. Most of the operations are quite complex, yet they all occur with no CPU intervention.

2.6.4.1. *Translation, miss-processing and R and M update.* Translation is the operation during which the caches are assessed to determine whether or not there are hits (whether the necessary descriptors are in the caches). If necessary descriptors are missing, miss-processing is invoked. If the descriptors are present, or after miss-processing is completed, access permissions and segment length are checked and the physical address is calculated (simultaneously). If there are no faults, R and M updating is invoked. When it completes, the physical address is output.

When a segment or page descriptor needed to translate a virtual address into a physical address is not present in the descriptor caches, the MMU must access descriptor tables in memory to fetch the appropriate descriptors into the descriptor caches. This activity is called miss-processing. Miss-processing to fetch a segment descriptor, a page descriptor or both may be necessary. Faults may occur during this activity. Invalid (V==0) or not present (P==0) descriptors are never put into the caches.

The R and M bits of page descriptors are always kept up to date both in the descriptor cache and in memory. The process of checking and setting R and M bits in the caches and in memory is called R and M updating. It may involve miss-processing to fetch a segment descriptor (because the segment descriptor contains the address of the page descriptor in memory).

2.6.4.2 *Faults.* If the address translation process cannot be completed for some reason, a fault will be triggered. All faults cause the

MMU to set the Fault Code Register (FLTCR) fields appropriately, copy the contents of VAR into FLTAR, and signal a fault to the CPU. The FLTCR and FLTAR contents will not be altered in the course of successful (non-faulted) translations and miss-processing. Only another fault or a peripheral mode write can change their contents.

The FLTCR contains three fields: access requested, access Xlevel and fault type. The access requested field contains a code that specifies the type of access (instruction fetch, data fetch, etc.) attempted by the CPU when the fault occurred. The access Xlevel field contains a code that specifies the execution level at which the faulted access was attempted.

The fault type field of the FLTCR may contain many values corresponding to different fault types. They fall into several categories, from the operating system point of view. User mistakes may cause the segment offset, access, access-&-seg-offset, SDT length, PDT length or invalid SD faults. A need for swapping may be signalled by the seg not present, PDT not present or page not present faults. Serious operating system problems cause the double-page hit, miss proc mem, R-M-update mem or too many directions faults. The other fault types are object trap, page write and no fault.

2.6.4.3 *Memory mapped peripheral mode and flushing.* The MMU can be used as a memory mapped peripheral. In this mode, many of the internal registers of the MMU and its descriptor caches can be addressed as memory locations. Each of these locations can be read or written.

A peripheral mode access to the MMU occurs when external logic asserts the MMU chip select pin. Various bits of the address sent to the MMU are used to select an object within the MMU and (for some objects) a word within the object.

All objects described in Section 2.6.3 may be accessed in peripheral mode.

Writes to the FLTCR cause the fault type field to be sent to no-fault.

When the CPU writes an address into SRAMA, the MMU will flush all SDC and PDC descriptors that are in the section corresponding to the newly written SRAMA entry. When the CPU writes an address into the MMU VAR, the MMU will flush any segment and page descriptor cache entries corresponding to that virtual address.

2.6.5 ADDITIONAL FEATURES OF THE WE32201 MEMORY
       MANAGEMENT UNIT

The WE32201 MMU is protocol upward-compatible with the

WE32101 MMU. All signals that are defined in the WE32101 MMU are in the same location on the WE32201 MMU.

A fully associative, CAM-based, 64-entry PDC has been incorporated in the WE32201 MMU to improve the hit rate. The PDC on the WE32101 MMU can map only two out of 64 PDC entries. The WE32201 MMU can map all 64 entries, greatly increasing the hit rate.

In addition, a 4K on-chip data cache has been built into the WE32201 MMU. This cache is enabled by a bit in the Configuration Register, and its use is automatic. Its purpose is to increase the system performance by reducing the average system access time. This is accomplished by storing instructions and data on chip instead of accessing system memory.

2.7 Operating system considerations

It is the responsibility of the operating system to initialise the MMU and the overall system by setting up the SDTs and PDTs in physical memory and writing values into MMU registers that provide necessary information, such as table addresses.

The operating system is also responsible for changing SRAM values when process switches occur. This will cause the MMU to flush and fill its caches.

The transfer of descriptors between the MMU caches and physical memory (miss-processing) is handled by the MMU without any operating system intervention.

Operating system action is required when the MMU signals to the CPU that a fault has occurred. There are a number of fault types that relate to errors that the MMU detects in critical data, such as memory faults when the MMU tries to read the SDTs or PDTs. These faults require unusual and perhaps drastic action by the operating system.

Two other types of faults are the page not present fault (for a paged segment) and the segment not present fault (for a contiguous segment). In either case, the MMU is telling the CPU that a required page or segment is not present in physical memory, and must be brought into physical memory. The operating system is responsible for these activities, and must do any I/O that is necessary and adjust the appropriate SDT and/or PDT entries.

The MMU provides hardware support for operating system page or segment replacement algorithms by setting the R (referenced) and M (modified) bits in the segment and page descriptors whenever a segment or page is referenced or modified. If the operating system periodically clears all of the R bits, for example, it can use the R bits to implement a variation of the LRU replacement algorithm. It could choose to replace segments or pages that still have their R bits clear when swapping is called for, reasoning that those segments or pages have been referenced less recently than the ones with the R bit sets.

The operating system will occasionally alter the contents of the descriptor tables in memory. For example, it must do this to set and clear P (present) bits whenever pages or segments are swapped in and out of physical memory. Any alteration to the table contents must be followed by some type of flushing of the MMU caches, to prevent the chaos that would result from tables and caches that contain conflicting information.

2.8   WE32106 and WE32206 maths acceleration units architecture

The WE32106 and WE32206 Maths Accelerator Units (MAUs)[4] provide the WE 32-bit microprocessors with complete IEEE standard floating point support as a co-processor. Figure 2.15 shows the block diagram of the MAUs. The MAUs support both co-processor and peripheral mode operations. Floating point data types of single (32-bit), doublt (64-bit), and double extended (80-bit) precision are supported. In addition, the 32-bit integer data type and an 18-digit decimal data type are supported for conversions. All four IEEE standard rounding modes are supported (round to nearest, round to zero, round to plus infinity, and round to minus infinity), as well as all five maskable exception types (invalid operation, overflow, underflow, divided by zero, and inexact). In addition, a maskable integer overflow

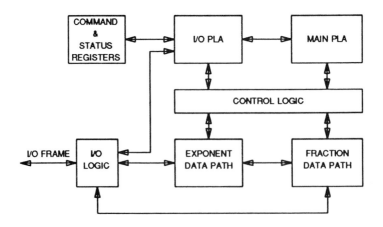

Fig. 2.15   WE32106 and WE32206 MAUs block diagram.

exception is supported for integer and decimal conversions. The MAUs support the following instruction operations:

(1) *Arithmetic.*   Add, subtract, multiply, divide, remainder, square root, negate, absolute value, compare (four versions), move.
(2) *Conversions.*   Float to integer, integer to float, float to decimal, decimal to float.
(3) *Control and status.*   Read status register, write status register, extract result on fault, load data register, no operation.
(4) *Transcendental functions* (WE32206 MAU only).   Sine, cosine, arc tangent, pi.

The control and status instructions allow the MAU context to be saved and restored on process switches, and also provide valuable debugging information when an operation generates an exception.

The MAUs support all required data types, including positive and negative zeros, positive and negative infinites, and trapping and non-trapping NANs (Not a Number). Gradual underflow is also supported, in the form of de-normal numbers in single and double precision, and un-normal numbers in extended precision. Sign, zero and overflow status flags are automatically returned to the CPU, and use of the MAUs instructions with the CPU is totally transparent to the user in co-processor mode. In addition, the MAUs are compatible with all microprocessor chip-set features including DMA, interrupts and restartability.

The MAUs contain many hardware optimisations to achieve a high floating point performance. The data path interconnections have been carefully optimised to obtain a high level of performance on the high-runner Add and Subtract operations. The addition of a full barrel switch (BSW) is especially helpful for these operations. The Multiply operation is implemented with a highly encoded form of Booth's algorithm which processes three bits of the result per iteration of a heavily pipelined loop. The Divide operation uses a highly pipelined implementation of the non-restoring divide algorithm. In addition to these internal optimisations, the co-processor interface to the MAU allows exceptionally high speed transfers of data to/from CPU and memory on a 32-bit data bus. The combined effect of these optimisations is a total execution rate for the familiar Whetstone benchmark in single precision IEEE standard floating point of 1.0 Whetstones (this number is for the WE32100 CPU and WE32106 MAU running together in co-processor mode with zero wait-state memory access at 14 MHz). Double precision execution rates are slightly lower.

2.8.1   SUPPORT FOR THE IEEE FLOATING POINT STANDARD IN THE MAUs

The IEEE standard for binary floating point arithmetic facilitates:

- Generation of high quality numerical software
- Software portability between complying implementations
- Careful and deterministic handling for the exception conditions and anomalies.

The standard does not impose any restrictions on complying implementations. That is, an implementation can be realised entirely in software, entirely in hardware or in any combination of software and hardware. The MAUs are a hardware implementation of the standard.

2.8.1.1   *Data formats.*   A floating point number consists of three parts: a biased exponent, a significant (or mantissa) and a single bit in the leftmost position of the number that indicates the sign of the significant. The significant consists of an implicit or explicit leading bit to the left of the implied binary point and fraction to the right. The standard categories data formats into basic and extended, with each having two widths, single and double. The conforming implementation must support the single format. The support of the extended format corresponding to the widest supported basic format is also strongly recommended.

The MAUs support single, double and double extended formats of the IEEE standard.

2.8.1.2   *Data types.*   The MAUs support all the required data types. What follows is a brief discussion of these data types.

(1) Normalised floating point numbers. This is the working data type that the user will interact with. This data type is identified by the exponent value not being at format's minimum or maximum.
(2) Denormalised floating point numbers. These numbers have non-zero mantissa with the exponent corresponding to the format's minimum exponent value. The most significant implicit bit of the mantissa (to the left of the binary point) has a value of zero. A denormalised number is generated when a masked underflow exception occurs. Denormalised numbers provide gradual underflow to zero.
(3) Zeros. This is a number with the exponent at format's minimum and a zero significant. Zeros are signed.
(4) Infinites. This is a number with a zero significant and format's

maximum exponent is infinity. Again both positive and negative infinities are encoded.

(5) Not a Number (NaN). These are symbolic entities that are intended for diagnostic purposes and to allow enhancements that are outside the scope of the standard. They are numbers that have format's maximum exponent with a non-zero fraction. NaNs are further classified into two categories, *signalling* and *quiet*. A quiet NaN can be used to detect an error which had propagated through a sequence of operations. It can also be used to indicate usage of uninitiated variables. A quiet NaN propagates through operations without causing any exception. When a signalling NaN is encountered, an exception is taken. If the exception condition is masked, an operation with a signalling NaN as an operand completes normally and produces a quiet NaN as a result.

2.8.1.3 *Operations.* The conforming implementations must provide operations to add, subtract, multiply, divide, square root, remainder, round to integral value, conversions between various floating point integer and decimal formats and compare. The MAUs directly support all of these operations in hardware.

2.8.1.4 *Rounding.* Rounding takes an infinitely precise number and modifies it to fit in the destination format. The standard requires all floating point operations to produce an intermediate result that is correct to infinite precision with unbounded range, then round it according to the mode of rounding selected. The standard proposes four different rounding modes:

- Round to nearest. In this mode, the representable value closest to the infinitely precise result is delivered. This is the default rounding mode.
- Round towards positive infinity.
- Round towards negative infinity.
- Round towards zero.

The MAUs directly implement all four rounding modes.

2.8.1.5 *Exceptions.* The IEEE standard specifies five different types of exceptions: invalid operation, underflow, overflow, divide by zero and inexact. The standard requires individual trap enable/disable control for each exception. The default response is to proceed without the trap. Also, individual status flags are required for each exception. The status flags can be 'sticky' in nature, i.e. once set to indicate exception condition, an explicit operation to reset the flag is necessary. The stick nature of the flags allows the exception status information to propagate through a sequence of operations when the corresponding trap is disabled. The exception handling in the MAUs conforms to the standard as described above.

2.8.2   ADDITIONAL FEATURES OF THE WE32206 MATHS ACCELERATION UNIT

The WE32206 MAU is protocol upward-compatible with the WE32106 MAU. All signals that are defined in the WE32106 MAU are in the same location on the WE32206 MAU. The WE32206 MAU provides significant performance improvements over the WE32106 including greater speed and fewer memory accesses. The maximum operating speed for the WE32206 MAU is 24 MHz.

A faster square root algorithm improves performance by a factor of 4 for single-precision numbers and by a factor of 2 for double-precision numbers. Multiplication and division speed has been improved by a factor of 2 for single-precision numbers.

Four functions have been added to the WE32206 MAU to provide high-performance support for trigonometric calculations. These functions include sine, cosine, arctan and pi.

Other features incorporated on the WE32206 include four additional user registers, improved rounding control, improved write-fault handling, a better compare operation, four data register bits – Least, Guard, Round and Sticky (for conformance to strict IEEE requirements), MAU version detection bits (for OS detection of either MAU), arbitrary byte alignment access handling, additional peripheral mode control, modified data ready sensing, and additional power and ground pins (to improve noise margins).

2.8.3   SUMMARY OF IEEE STANDARD

The IEEE standard for binary floating point arithmetic differs from generic floating point arithmetic processors in many ways. Some of the features of the standard that increase the hardware complexity are:

(1) The standard recommends three data types: single, double and extended. The number of bits in the exponent is different in each format. This makes conversion from one format to another more complex than other floating point implementations, in which single and double precision formats have identical exponent fields.

(2) The special data types (e.g. NaN, infinity, denormalised numbers and unnormalised numbers require special hardware to recognise and process.

(3) The standard defines five exceptions with individual enable/disable control for each exception and corresponding status flags. The standard is also very specific about the default response to the exception when it is masked and about the information supplied to the exception handler when it is enabled.

(4) The definition of the remainder operation requires it to be broken down into several steps in order to avoid locking out interrupts.

2.9   WE32104 DMA controller architecture

The WE32104 DMA Controller (DMAC) is a 4-channel direct memory access controller designed specifically for 32-bit applications. A unique 2-bus architecture allows for simple, efficient interconnection of byte oriented peripheral devices, such as UARTs, disk controllers and network interfaces, with a 32-bit processor memory system bus. Isolating the slower peripheral traffic on a separate bus not only simplifies interconnection logic, but greatly reduces contention for the system bus, thereby increasing overall system throughput.

To support its dual bus architecture, the DMAC provides a 32-byte data buffer for each channel. Data read from the byte-wide peripheral bus is packed into larger operands (up to 16-byte quad-word) before being written to memory. In addition to byte, halfword, and word transfers, the DMAC supports double-word and quad-word transfers on the system bus for improved memory handwith, and reduced bus arbitration overhead. A block diagram of the DMAC is shown in Fig. 2.16.

Each of the four channels is independently controlled and can be programmed for burst or cycle-steal transfer mode. In burst mode, the DMAC will hold the system bus as long as needed, while in cycle-steal mode the system bus is relinquished after every bus transfer. Four transfer types are provided: memory-to-peripheral, peripheral-to-memory, memory-to-memory and memory fill. Other programmable options include selection of peripheral device transfer characteristics, enabling interrupts on channel completion, and enabling a channel for chained transfer mode. In chained mode, a linked list of request blocks containing source/destination and transfer count information is loaded in memory by the processor. The DMAC can then execute this list, fetching transfer parameters directly from memory, without further intervention by the host processor.

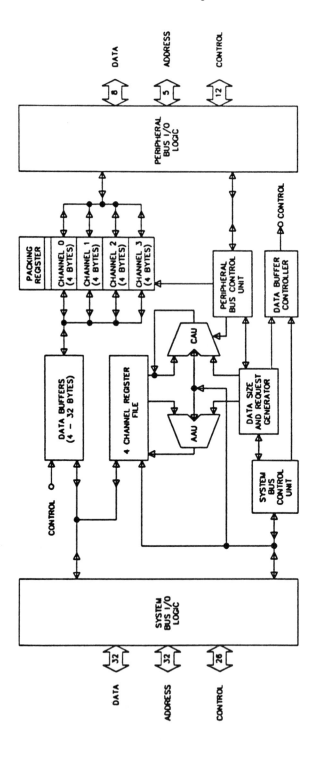

Fig. 2.16   WE32104 DMAC block diagram.

In burst mode, a 14 MHz DMAC can perform memory-to-memory copies at 11.2 Mbyte/s, and memory-fill operations at 20.3 Mbyte/s. Given that these rates are as much as five times greater than can be achieved with equivalent CPU instructions, many system level functions can be coded for higher performance by making use of the DMAC.

For transfers to and from the peripheral bus, the maximum data transfer rate obtainable is 6 Mbyte/s, when the peripheral bus burst feature is employed, and 3.7 Mbyte/s, when a single byte is transferred for each peripheral bus request. Equally important, however, the DMAC only requests the system bus once a quad-word has been packed into its data buffer, performing in one bus cycle what would otherwise require 16 bus cycles. Including the overhead incurred during bus arbitration, bus utilisation is reduced by a factor of ten.

2.9.1 DMAC MEMORY-TO-MEMORY COPY IMPROVES UNIX SYSTEM PERFORMANCE

The DMAC's memory-to-memory copy and memory fill operations are up to five times faster than equivalent operations executed by the CPU. Unix system routines, such as fork, exec, and logical I/O between system and user buffer areas, rely on fast buffer copy and block clear routines which can be optimised by making use of a DMA channel. Unix system profiling demonstrates that the CPU spends approximately 10% of its time performing these routines. Making use of the DMAC's fast memory copy cabilities would thereby improve overall system throughput by 8%.

2.9.2 ADVANTAGES OF 8-BIT PERIPHERAL BUS ON DMAC

The 8-bit peripheral bus on the WE32104 DMAC is ideally suited to 8-bit peripherals such as disk controllers and local area network interfaces. Separating the peripheral bus from the 32-bit system bus reduces contention for the system bus. This allows the CPU to execute more efficiently while the DMAC is servicing peripherals. In one model, the CPU has ten times the system bus allocation compared to a model without the peripheral bus, when a 10 Mbit/s peripheral was being serviced by the DMAC.

2.10 WE32103 DRAM controller architecture

This controller provides address multiplexing, access and cycle time management, and refresh control for Dynamic Random Access Memory (DRAM). The DRAM controller's extreme flexibility allows a wide selection of DRAM components to be used, in varying memory system configurations.

Among the features supported by the WE32103 DRAM controller are: several different modes for refresh (distributed/burst, internally/ externally timed), programmable time constants to meet diverse DRAM component requirements, and support for many DRAM sizes, e.g. 256K by 1, 64K by 4, and 1M by 1 DRAMs. The DRAM controller is capable of addressing up to 16 Mbyte of DRAM using 1 Mbyte chips. Page and nibble mode operation may be selected for fast double and quad-word memory access. In addition, a unique pre-translation mode is provided to improve access time for systems incorporating paged virtual memory. For applications requiring highly reliable operation, a full set of handshake signals is provided for (optional) error detection and correction hardware.

The WE32103 DRAM controller has an asynchronous mode which permits it to operate with other commercial microprocessors. However, enhanced performance can be achieved using synchronous mode when configured with the WE32100 chip-set. Synchronous operation will, in general, save a wait-state for processor reads and writes. Pre-translation mode further reduces access time by overlapping the row portion of a memory access with the WE32101 MMU's address translation. Finally, fast double and quad-word memory cycles, utilising page and nibble mode DRAMs are supported to enhance both CPU and DMAC performance.

2.10.1   WE32103 DRAM CONTROLLER PRE-TRANSLATION MODE USING 256K DRAMS

The DRAM controller has the capability to begin a memory access before the MMU has translated the virtual address. This early start is advantageous in systems utilising a paged virtual memory scheme. In such a system, the low order address bits are the page offset, and thus equivalent in virtual and physical address spaces.

If programmed for early RAS, the DRAM controller will drive the page offset contained within the virtual address as the row address, and assert the ROW Address Strobe (RAS0) in parallel with the MMU's address translation. Utilising the pre-translation feature, one cycle can be saved from the memory access. A block diagram of the DRAM controller is shown in Fig. 2.17.

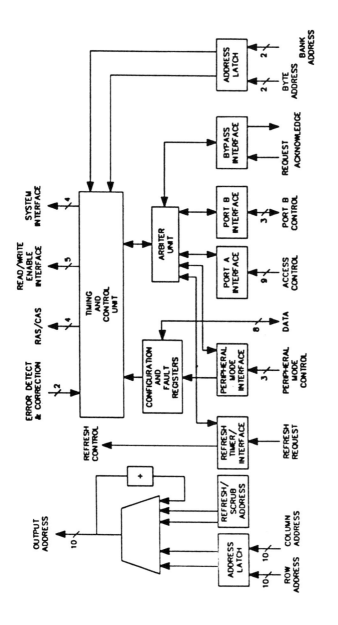

Fig. 2.17   WE32103 DRAM controller block diagram.

2.11 Summary

The WE32100 and WE32200 microprocessor chip-sets and their first generation predecessor (WE32000) are operational in a number of AT&T systems, spanning time sharing, real time and transaction oriented applications. The microprocessor chip-sets are used in the 3B2 and 3B5 systems. The CPU is also used as an intelligent peripheral controller for the 3B5 system. Other applications include the Teletype DMD 5620 terminal, where the CPU is used to execute graphics primitives as well as resident programs. Network interfaces using the CPUs are available to handle flow control and higher level protocols in the 3B systems. VME-bus based boards have been built to take advantage of the chip-set capabilities, and can be used as basic building blocks for single-board computers or multiple processor systems. Several multiprocessor systems have also been built.

The chip-set is supported by a completed set of Unix system based development support tools that provides easy access to internal signals and status for hardware debugging and development, and symbolic debugging for software development.[5]

Acknowledgments

This chapter was written jointly by many people who worked on the architecture and the design of the chips. Some of the sections were extracted from previous papers.[2,3] We would like to acknowledge the written contributions of the following: A. D. Berenbaum, M. W. Condry, W. A. Dietrich, J. A. Fields, M. L. Fuccio, A. K. Goksel, L. N. Goyal, U. V. Gumaste, M. E. Thierbach and P. A Voldstad.

References

1. 'Hardware Configuration and I/O Protocol of the WE32100 Microprocessor Chip Set'. Fuccio, M. L. and Goyal, L. N., WESCON 1985.
2. 'The Operating System and Language Support Features of the BELLMAC-32 Microprocessor'. Berenbaum, A. D., Condry, M. and Lu, P. M. *Symp. Arch. Support for Prog. Lang. and Op. Sys.* Palo Alto, Cal., 30–38, 1–3 March 1982.
3. 'Architecture of a VLSI Map for BELLMAC-32 Microprocessor'. Lu, P. M., Dietrich, Jr, W. A., Fuccio, M. L. Goyal, L. N., Chen, C. J., Blahut, D. E., Fields, J. A., Goksel, A. K. and LaRocca, R. D. *Spring Compcon 1983*, San Francisco, CA., 213–17, 28 February to 3 March 1983.
4. 'An IEEE Standard Floating Point Chip'. Goksel, A. K., Diodato, Phil W., Fields, John A., Gumaste, Ulhas V., Kung, Chew K., Lin, Kingyao, Lega, Mario E., Maurer, Peter M., Ng, Thomas K., Oh, Yaw T. and Thierbach, Mark E. *ISSCC 1985*, 18 and 19 February 1985.
5. 'Hardware/Software Development System for the WE32100 CPU and MMU'. Clark, M. H., Rango, R. A., Rusnock, K. J. and Stubblebine, W. A. *WESCON 1984*.

CHAPTER 3
The Inmos Transputer

J. R. NEWPORT
Keywood Computer Services Ltd, UK

3.1 Introduction

Transputers, manufactured in Britain by Inmos, are high performance single-chip computers with integral processor-to-processor serial links and optional on-chip memory. However, such a simple description vastly underrates the potential of this relatively new range of devices.

The name 'Transputer' is derived from two words: *transistor* and *computer*. The intention is that just as transistors have been the building blocks of computers, so transputers will be the building blocks of a whole new range of machines from compact array processors to vast supercomputers.

Attempts to build multiprocessor systems from conventional microprocessors have always been fraught with problems, not least of which have been those concerned with inter-processor communication. Bandwidth problems are usually encountered when more than about four processors are linked via a shared bus. This effect can be clearly seen if total system performance is plotted against the number of constituent processors (see Fig. 3.1(a)). Plots will vary slightly, depending on the types of bus and processor being used, but a point will be reached at which adding further processors will tie up the bus and then actually reduce total system performance. This limit is usually reached when between six and eight processors share a common bus.

Transputers have their own built-in serial links, each capable of concurrently inputting and outputting at up to 20 Mbit/s. A typical transputer has four such links, giving it a communications capacity of 80 Mbit/s into the device and 80 Mbit/s out. As these links are an integral part of each individual transputer, the greater the number of transputers in a network, the greater the total bandwidth of the system. Because communication bandwidth is far less of a problem, it is now found that plotting system performance against the number of constituent processors for a transputer network gives a near linear graph (see Fig. 3.1(b)).

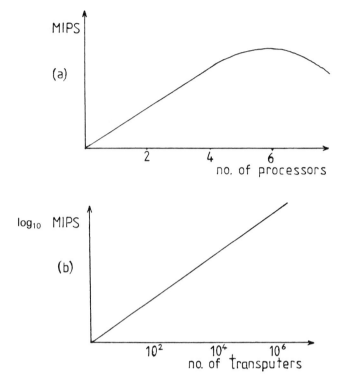

Fig. 3.1 (a) Plot of performance against number of processors for a conventional multiprocessor system; (b) the same plot for a multi-transputer system but using a logarithmic scale to show that the linear relationship continues ad infinitum.

The size at which closely coupled networks of transputers, connected by their serial links, becomes impractical has yet to be determined. In theory there is no reason why supercomputers containing thousands or even hundreds of thousands of transputers should not be constructed.

One area where very high performance figures are required is in Artificial Intelligence (AI). The performance rating of AI machines is measured in Logical Inferences Per Second (LIPS), with one logical inference being roughly equivalent to one hundred machine instructions. The target set by the Japanese team developing fifth generation architectures was for a prototype machine capable of one billion (or giga) logical inferences per second by 1991. It is believed that such a machine would, for example, be capable of translating from Japanese to English (and *vice versa*) in real time, using either text or voice input. The capability to build a machine of the required performance using transputers (about 10 000 of them) has existed since 1986. This is five years ahead of what was considered by many to be a highly ambitious goal.

As Inmos has realised that simply providing hardware with a high performance potential does not necessarily produce a high performance system, a new programming language, Occam, has been developed hand-in-hand with the transputer. A number of more well-established languages such as Pascal, FORTRAN and C are now available for use on transputers, but it is Occam which will enable the full performance potential of transputer-based systems to be fully realised. Occam provides direct software support for both concurrency and for the 20 Mbit/s inter-processor serial links.

The transputer architecture combines several features developed for other processors over the years to achieve sustained performance rating of 15 Million Instructions Per Second (15 MIPS). However, the key elements which allow high performance systems to be contructed from transputer devices are parallel processing, inter-processor communication and the support provided for both these features by the Occam language.

3.2 The transputer generic architecture

As can be seen in Fig. 3.2, the transputer architecture does not define a single device but rather a whole family of transputers. The T425 32-bit transputer, with four serial links and 4K of on-chip static RAM, is the standard general purpose transputer, but various combinations of on-chip facilities are possible. Transputers always include a processor, system services and one or more serial links, but they may have 4K of on-chip RAM, 2K or no on-chip memory at all.

The first 32-bit transputer to become freely available was the T414, released by Inmos in October 1985. The T414 has four serial links but only 2K of on-chip RAM. A 16-bit family of transputers is also being developed, the first of these being the T212. Released at the same time as the T414, the T212 also has 2K of on-chip memory. The T222 is now the standard 16-bit transputer. Like its 32-bit cousin, the T425, the T222 has 4K of on-chip RAM and 4 × 20 Mbit/s serial links.

The second digit in a transputer's product name indicates the amount of on-chip RAM in units of 2K. A 4 following the T indicates a 32-bit processor, and a 2 in the same position, a 16-bit processor. However, Inmos has been less logical with the last digit which, it says, provides 'product uniqueness' rather than indicating the number of available links on the chip (the T212 has 4 links, not 2, as might be expected). The speed of a particular device in MHz may also be

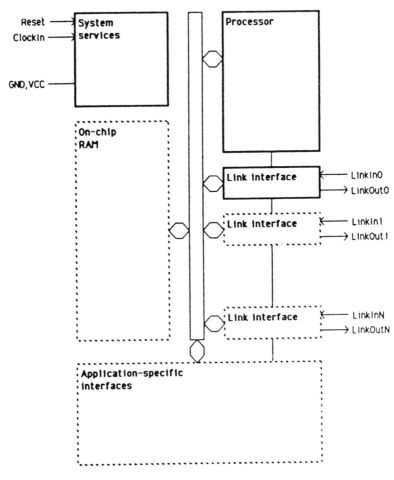

Fig. 3.2 Transputer generic architecture. (Courtesy of INMOS. INMOS is a member of the SGS-Thomson Microelectronics Group.)

included in the name, following a hyphen, e.g. a T425-30 would run at 30 MHz, and a T425-17 would run at 17.5 MHz (transputer speeds go up in 2.5 MHz steps from 17 to 30 MHz).

All transputers have a timer which runs off a 5 MHz external clock. Both the processor clock frequency and the link clock (which controls the transfer rate of the serial links) are derived from the external clock frequency by internal scaling. Future transputers will be capable of operating their links at much higher speeds but all transputers will support the 10 Mbit/s standard. Link speed selection pins on each device allow one or more links to be set to the standard speed, thus allowing communication between any two transputers. A tolerance of $\pm0.02\%$ is allowable on the external clock signal for correct operation of the serial links. This means that two communicating transputers do not have to use the same external clock. Further, the tolerance is such that relatively cheap crystal oscillators can be used to provide the signals. Links are intended for use only between transputers on the same board or between those on adjacent boards on the same backplane. Over long distances (>400 mm) links will require some form of buffering. RS422 driver/receivers can be used to extend the link communication distance.

The link protocol, like the link speed, is standard across the whole range of transputers. Data is transmitted one byte at a time in packets, with each packet being acknowledged by the receiving transputer. The acknowledgement packet is sent as soon as the data packet is identified and, since each link is bi-directional, data packets and acknowledgement packets can be communicated in parallel. Acknowledgement packets consist of just two bits, a 1 and a 0. The second bit identifies the packet type. Data packets consist of two 1s followed by a byte of data and terminated with a 0 (see Fig. 3.3).

The characteristics of transputer products in the future will be governed more and more by the specialist needs of the customer. As experience is gained in running development systems, and in many cases by developing actual products incorporating T414 and T425 processors, these specialist needs will become more apparent. Some applications may benefit from having more on-chip RAM while others may require more links. As links and on-chip memory are both contending for space on the same chip, there will always be a trade-off between the two, with the ideal balance depending on the application. In a single processor system, for example, it may be more useful to have only one or two links for input and output and to have more on-chip

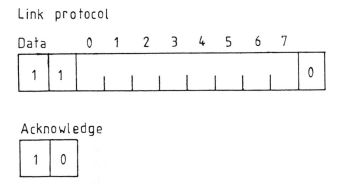

Fig. 3.3 Link protocol. (Courtesy of INMOS. INMOS is a member of the SGS-Thomson Microelectronics Group.)

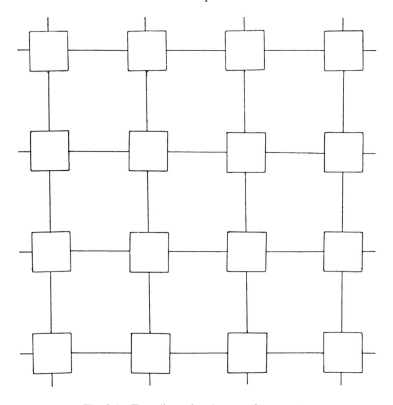

Fig. 3.4   Two-dimensional array of transputers.

RAM, which can be accessed more quickly than off-chip RAM. This would in turn improve the overall processing performance.

Many of the planned applications of the T425 have processors arranged in large two-dimensional arrays, with each T425 connected to its four nearest neighbours via its serial links (see Fig. 3.4). As system designers become more familiar with building transputer networks, they will start to think, 'Why just connect the nearest four neighbours, why not eight?' More adventurous designers are already planning three-dimensional networks, requiring at least six links and even n-dimensional networks requiring at least $2n$ links on each transputer. The problem of building three-dimensional transputer networks can be solved in the short term by pairing transputers. Connecting two T425s, using one link each, leaves six links available for connecting to the six nearest neighbours in three dimensions. The need for hypercubes, super-clusters and other novel architectures will be considered in more detail in Section 3.10.

The characteristics of future transputers will depend on demand, investment and technological advancements. It would be unrealistic to expect an 8-link transputer with 16K of on-chip RAM to be released immediately after the T425. But if the demand exists, a 6-link chip with 4 to 16K may be entirely practical.

In addition to serial links and on-chip memory, the generic transputer architecture also provides for the inclusion of application specific interfaces on-chip. Special purpose transputers for such purposes as drive control have already been developed. The M212 peripheral processor is an intelligent peripheral controller which can be programmed like a normal transputer. These specialised transputers provide a convenient means of communicating directly with peripheral devices. Although these are not actually transputers in their own right, it is worth mentioning the Inmos link adaptors in this section. The C series of devices, C011, C012, etc., are specialised devices which can be attached to a transputer's serial link to adapt it to an 8-bit parallel link. A third method of interfacing peripherals is to memory map them on to the transputer's memory bus. A peripheral can be memory mapped anywhere in the off-chip address space and can then be controlled using instructions written in Occam.

A processor which has caused a mini-revolution in the construction of high performance, numeric processing machines, is the hardware floating point transputer, the T800. The T800 is not an add-on co-processor for the T425, as has been the standard practice for conventional microprocessors such as the Intel 8086/8087 combination, it is a complete transputer in its own right. It retains all the functionality of the T425 in addition to having floating point arithmetic facilities, conforming to the ANSI–IEEE 754-1985, implemented on-chip. Operations on both single precision (sign bit, 8-bit exponent and 23-bit fraction) and double precision (sign bit, 11-bit exponent and 52-bit fraction) floating point numbers will be supported. The speed of the T800 transputer is pin selectable from 17.5 MHz up to the maximum allowed for that part. A T800-30 running at its maximum speed of 30 MHz can perform floating point operations at a sustained rate of 2.25 MFLOPS.

Many applications, such as aircraft simulation, signal processing and the analysis of seismic data, require large numbers of floating point operations to be performed in as short a time as possible. Just as fifth generation computer designers have a target of 1000 LIPS, so those involved with the development of array processors and mainframes with floating point accelerators have set a target of 1000 MFLOPS, or 1 G FLOPS. A machine with this performance can now be constructed from 500 T800-30 (30 MHz) transputers.

3.3　The T425 transputer

Having considered the generic features of the transputer family, a specific member of the family, the T425, will now be considered (see Fig. 3.5). The T425 has 4K of on-chip static RAM with an access time of 50 ns, four 20 Mbit/s bi-directional serial links, a 32-bit wide 40 Mbyte/s external memory interface and, of course, a processor and system services. This represents approximately 250,000 devices fabricated using a 1.5 μm CMOS process.

Like most 32-bit processors, the T425 is able directly to address 4 Gbytes (2 to the power of 32) of memory. Memory addresses are signed, which means that they can be handled just like any other 32-bit integers. Figure 3.6 shows the memory map of the T425's address space. ROM-based code is by convention located at the top (most positive) end of the address space and, when configured to bootstrap from ROM, the processor will commence execution from address Hex 7FFF FFFE. The on-chip RAM is organised as 1 kword of 32 bits each, situated at the most negative end of memory, i.e. at addresses

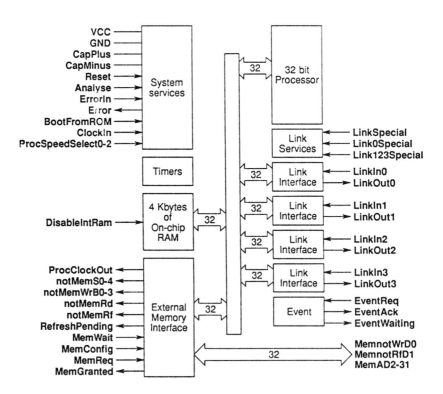

Fig. 3.5　IMS T425 block diagram. (Courtesy of INMOS. INMOS is a member of the SGS-Thomson Microelectronics Group.)

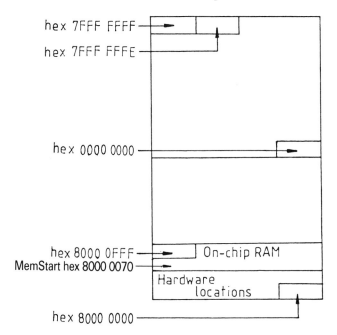

hex 7FFF FFFF

hex 7FFF FFFE

hex 0000 0000

hex 8000 0FFF — On-chip RAM
MemStart hex 8000 0070

Hardware
locations

hex 8000 0000

Fig. 3.6 T425 memory map. (Courtesy of INMOS. INMOS is a member of the SGS-Thomson Microelectronics Group.)

Hex 8000 0FFF to Hex 8000 0000. Twenty-eight words (112 bytes) of on-chip memory, from Hex 8000 006F to Hex 8000 0000, are used for system purposes, the last eight words in this range being associated with the four links (one input word and one output word for each link).

The remainder of the on-chip RAM (Hex 8000 0FFF to Hex 8000 0070 is available for applications code and data. The start address for user memory, Hex 8000 0070, is given the name MemStart. Since on-chip memory can be accessed in 33.3 ns (30 MHz device), which is typically half the access time of off-chip RAM, small programs requiring high performance should ideally be located exclusively in on-chip RAM. Where arrays of transputers interconnected by their serial links are being used, it may be possible to subdivide larger programs and locate them just in on-chip RAM. If this is not possible, the most time critical processes need to be identified so that they can be located within the on-chip memory. The Occam language provides facilities for placing code at specific locations within the transputer's address space. These facilities will be explained further in Section 3.6.

Some microprocessors make use of high speed cache memories which may be on or off-chip. As the processor executes the instructions within a program, dedicated microcode prefetches a block of code including and immediately following the current instruction pointer and places this code in the cache. When the instruction pointer reaches the end of the cache or when a Jump instruction points to an instruction outside the code contained in the cache, the microcode will automatically fetch a new block of code and place it into cache. One advantage of cache memory is that the user does not have to be aware that it exists. On the other hand, transputer on-chip RAM is treated by the processor in just the same way as off-chip RAM – it simply takes less time to access. This means that the onus is placed on the user to make the best use of the fast RAM. Whether this is considered to be an advantage or a disadvantage will depend on the needs and preferences of the user.

It is useful to remember that a transputer instruction is only one byte long, but memory is always accessed as words. Therefore, one access to external memory will fetch either four instructions or just one 32-bit data item. Inmos has conducted an experiment to demonstrate the effect of locating either code or data on-chip. The times given in the following table are relative to the case where all the program and all the data are located on-chip, this being taken as 1.

	Data intensive	Computation intensive
All program and data in on-chip RAM	1	1
Program off-chip, data on-chip	1.3	1.1
Program on-chip, data off-chip	1.5	1.2
All off-chip	1.8	1.3

These are very important findings, particularly for applications which have large amounts of code but only small amounts of data (less than 4K). The T425 processor also incorporates an instruction prefetcher which holds eight instructions (two words). This has been found to be the ideal compromise between reducing code access time and fetching instructions which may not be executed.

The general trend with microprocessors has been to include more and more registers, but the T425 uses just six to execute a sequential program. These consist of an operand register, an instruction pointer, a workspace pointer and three registers which make up an evaluation stack. In addition to these six, there are no further registers which are used by the chip's priority scheduler to time share between parallel processes located on the same transputer. Although Occam allows any number of priority levels, only two are supported on the T425 and T414, these being priority 0 and priority 1, with 0 being the higher. If one or more priority 0 process has been placed on one transputer, one will be selected to proceed by the scheduler and will then run until completion or until it has to wait for communication or for a timer input. High priority processes should therefore be kept relatively short, otherwise they will tend to monopolise the processor. Priority 1 processes will only be scheduled when no priority 0 processes can proceed. Priority 1 processes are time sliced so that no one process is kept waiting too long. Time slice periods on early versions of the transputer lasted 4096 cycles of the 5 MHz input clock. In later devices, however, this has been extended to 5120 cycles of the input clock, which corresponds to a time of just over 1 ms.

3.4 The T425 instruction set

Transputers are a form of RISCs. The characteristics and advantages of using a RISC are well documented. In brief, it has been found that programs running on CISCs use only a small percentage of these instructions on a regular basis. Some of the remaining instructions are used only in rare situations. RISC machine designers concentrate their efforts in supporting the more frequently used instructions, with less frequently used functions being implemented either by using combinations of instructions or by adding modifiers or extenders. Some of these functions may well require more machine cycles to execute on a RISC than on a CISC. However, on the whole, RISCs achieve high performance and efficiency by requiring less effort to decode instructions and requiring fewer registers.

Generally speaking, designing a compiler for a RISC is a relatively straightforward task. The compiler is presented with a relatively simple and predictable task and the resulting object code tends to be compact and efficient. Although a relatively simple task for a machine, generating code for a RISC tends to be both tedious and error prone when performed by a human programmer. This could well be a contributory factor in Inmos' decision not to release details such as instruction code values or even the complete range of instructions offered on particular transputers. Occam is intended to be the lowest level language used on any transputer and Inmost does not support the use of machine code by the user. There are, in fact, more sound reasons behind this apparently strict policy decision than being worried about error prone hand-coded programs. VLSI technology is advancing rapidly and techniques are being developed whereby new features can be quickly incorporated into a chip's hardware design. By supporting Occam as the standard language for all the members in the transputer family, a new device can be developed with a totally new instruction set and with, for example, a significant increase in performance. All the user would have to do would be to buy the new compiler for the device and he could run all his old Occam programs. Minor changes to a program may well be required to optimise the performance when porting between transputers. This would be particularly true if the new device incorporated more on-chip RAM or had more serial links. Having a separate compiler for each device is far less trouble than maintaining separate versions of the same programs in what would effectively be different languages. The following information is therefore included purely as a matter of interest as the reader is unlikely to need to program in transputer machine code. No values are given for the various functions and instructions since these may vary, even between different versions of the same device.

All instructions on the transputer are just one byte long and are split into two fields. The four most significant bits contain the function and the four least significant bits the data (see Fig. 3.7). Four bit fields allow up to 16 local data items to be manipulated by up to 16 instructions. Thirteen of these values are used to represent the most frequently used functions. These are known as the direct functions. These functions are:

Byte	Abbreviation	Function
#0x	j	jump
#1x	ldlp	load local pointer
#2x	pfx	prefix
#3x	ldnl	load non local
#4x	ldc	load constant
#5x	ldnlp	load non-local pointer
#6x	nfix	negative prefix
#7x	ldl	load local
#8x	adc	add constant
#9x	call	call
#Ax	cj	conditional jump
#Bx	ajw	adjust workspace
#Cx	eqc	equals constant
#Dx	stl	store local
#Ex	stnl	store non-local
#Fx	opr	operate

Two of the functions, Prefix and Negative Prefix, can be used to extend the operand of any function to any length. All instructions start by loading the four data bits from the instruction's data field into the least significant four bits in the operand register as shown in Fig. 3.7. All functions except Prefix and Negative Prefix end by clearing the operand register ready for the next instruction. The Prefix function

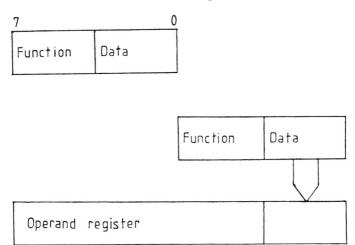

Fig. 3.7 T425 instruction format. (Courtesy of INMOS. INMOS is a member of the SGS-Thomson Microelectronics Group.)

loads its four data bits into the operand register and then shifts them four places to the left (i.e. four places more significant). The Negative Prefix function is similar except that it complements the operand register before shifting it up. Using a single prefixing function, any operand from −256 to 255 can be represented. By using several prefixing instructions, any operand in the full 32-bit range can be represented.

The other type of instructions are the zero address instructions. These use the operand to define operations on values already in the evaluation stack. Refer to the Transputer Instruction Set[1] for more detailed information.

3.5 The history and philosophy of the Occam language

Occam was named after William of Occam, a 14th century English philosopher who studied at Oxford. William was credited a Latin quotation known as Occam's Razor:

Entia non sunt multiplicanda praeter necessitatem

which states that entities are not to be multiplied beyond necessity. At the second meeting of the Occam Users' Group, held appropriately in William of Occam's home town of Oxford, one speaker made the point that he had extreme doubts about a philosopher who contrived such a complex way of saying:

KEEP THINGS SIMPLE

This less formal translation of Occam's Razor presents a much clearer view of the philosophy behind the language. The simplicity of Occam is a reflection of the simplicity of the underlying instruction set. The Occam language and the transputer have been developed hand-in-hand to produce a language which combines the performance benefits of an assembly language with the readability, programmer productivity and maintainability aspects of a higher level language.

In terms of complexity, Occam can be seen as being at the other end of the spectrum to Ada, the US DoD's new standard language for embedded systems. The designers of Ada were set an extremely difficult task in that they were given an extensive list of essential features which the new standard language was to support. Not only did the Ada language have to support programming features such as structured constructs and strong typing, it was also required to support the principles of software engineering, such as abstraction information hiding and modularity. It is arguable whether these higher level software management aspects should be addressed by the features of the language itself. Some suggestions as to how large Occam systems might be developed and managed will be given in a later section.

One indication of the complexity of a programming language is to measure the size of the language's definition. As a benchmark by which to judge the other two languages, Algol 60 can be defined in 43 pages of text, with 50 lines of text to one page, and Pascal can be defined in 38 pages. Occam can be defined in just 18 pages. When its far reaching brief is taken into consideration, it will come as no surprise to discover that Ada requires a definition of 275 pages. Although this is by no means an absolute measure of language complexity, it provides a useful comparison. If nothing else it gives an idea of the size of the problem facing the Ada compiler writer.

Ada and Occam have one important feature in common: both languages support concurrent processing. Not only do they both support concurrent processing but in each language the model of concurrency was based on the work carried out by Professor Hoare at Oxford University, on communicating sequential processes. Professor Hoare was closely involved in the definition stage of the Occam language, which was developed at Inmos by David May.

Concurrency has been recognised as the key feature in freeing the system designer from the physical limitations of the available hardware. The performance of sequentially executed software is limited to the speed of the single processor on which it runs. Only by subdividing that software into tasks which can execute independently, and in parallel on separate processors, can the performance of the total system be increased. Running totally independent software in parallel has never presented a problem. A company with an expanding workforce divided equally between two factories which finds its computer can no longer run payroll program in the required time simply buys a second computer. Real time systems in critical applications present much greater problems. Let us suppose that a particular processor has been chosen on which to run an air traffic control system. The system is required to track up to one hundred aircraft at a time. Because of extra functions, however, and safety checks specified in the requirement, performance calculations indicate that one of the chosen processors can only track one aircraft at a time. Should one aircraft be plotted on each processor and their outputs combined in some way? Obviously not. The software processes modelling each aircraft need to be able to examine the states of processes modelling other aircraft. This may be performed either directly, or via control processes which plan the aircraft's future movements and predict when aircraft may approach each other too closely. The essential features which should be supported by a real time language should therefore be concurrency and communication.

Ada provides objects known as *tasks* to support concurrency, but these are just one of many object types from which Ada programs can be constructed. In Occam, the object which supports concurrency is the *process*, which is in fact the only object type within the Occam language. Occam programs are constructed exclusively of hierarchical levels of processes. At the lowest level, the language is built up from just three primitive process types: *assignment*, *input* and *output*. Input and output primitives directly support communication between named processes via channels.

At the start of this section, it was stated that the philosophy behind the Occam language was to keep things simple. It can now be seen that this is achieved by recognising that a real time language needs to support just two essential features:

concurrency and *communication*

3.6 The Occam language

Occam programs are constructed of hierarchical levels of processes. At the lowest level, the language is built up from just three primitive process types: *assignment*, *input* and *output*. The symbol used for assignment is := as in several other high level languages. In Occam, however, no symbol is required to terminate a primitive process, but only one primitive may appear on each line. For example:

        x := 1

assigns the value of the expression to the right of the := symbol to the
previously declared variable on the left, in this case assigning the literal
value 1 to the variable x.

The symbol ? is used to indicate input, e.g.:

        c ? x

inputs a value from a previously declared channel, c, and assigns this
value to the variable x.

The symbol ! is used to indicate an output. For example:

        c ! y

outputs the value contained in y to channel c.

Primitive processes may be built up into higher level processes by the
use of constructs. The sequential construct, SEQ, indicates that the
processes which follow it are to be executed sequentially. Component
processes are indented by two characters with respect to the construct:

    SEQ
      cl ? x
      x := x + 1
      c2 ! x

In the above example there is no alternative other than to execute the
three processes sequentially. The value must be input from c1 and
assigned to x before it is incremented, before it is output to c2.
However, if two values are input from different channels into different
variables, then the two inputs could conceptually execute in parallel.
This condition is catered for in the Occam language and is implemented by the parallel construct, PAR.

    PAR
      cl ? x
      c2 ? y

If x and y were to be summed and the result assigned to x then
obviously this could not be evaluated until after both inputs had
occurred. Similarly, if expressions containing the new value of x were
to be output, they would have to follow the summing process. The
program below consists of three sequential processes, the first
consisting of two parallel input processes, the second being a primitive
process (an assignment) and the third consisting of two parallel output
processes.

```
SEQ
  PAR
    c1 ? x
    c2 ? x
  x := x + y
  PAR
    c3 ! x + 1
    c4 ! x - 1
```

The positions of the three constituent processes of the sequential construct can be seen to be aligned with each other and indented two places with respect to the SEQ. In this way, more and more complex processes can be constructed. However, in order to increase the readability and maintainability of a program, it is good practice to have named processes, or PROCs, each of which has only a few levels of constituent processes. The above process could be named as follows:

```
PROC P1 (CHAN c1, c2, c3, c4) =
  VAR x :
  VAR y :
  SEQ
    PAR
      c1 ? x
      c2 ? y
    x := x + y
    PAR
      c3 ! x + 1
      c4 ! x - 1
  SKIP :
```

SKIP simply terminates with no effect. (Note that the end of a named PROC must also be indicated by a : symbol.) Named processes communicate by means of channels which connect two processes together. When the processes at either end of a particular channel are on the same transputer, communication occurs by means of a memory-to-memory data transfer. If the processes are located on different transputers, communication occurs via a standard Inmos link. In either case the processes will be concurrent and the communication will be synchronised, with the transfer occurring when both the inputting and outputting processes are ready.

The locating of processes onto specified transputers is controlled by placement commands. Both separately compiled processes and components of a PAR construct can be individually located in this way.

PLACE is also used to associate named channels connecting processes on separate transputers with actual serial links.

PRI PAR applies a priority to the component processes of a PAR construct. This only applies to the outermost PAR. The first of the parallel processes is given the highest priority, priority 0, the second is given priority 1 and so on. The number of priority levels depends on the implementation of the priority scheduler on a particular transputer. The T414 and T425 support two priority levels, 0 and 1.

Replication can be used with both SEQ constructs to create conventional loops and with PARs to construct arrays of concurrent processes.

```
SEQ  i = 0  FOR  n
   P

PAR  i = 0  FOR  n
   Pi
```

The first example will loop n times, the second will create n parallel processes, P0 to Pn−1.

The IF construct allows one of a number of processes to execute depending on the condition which precedes it:

```
IF
   x > 0
      x := x − 1
   x > 0
      x := x + 1
   x = 0
      SKIP
```

The ALT construct can be particularly useful where signals might appear on one of a number of alternative channels:

```
ALT
   c1 ? ANY
      count1 := count1 + 1
   c2 ? ANY
      count2 := count2 + 1
   c3 ? ANY
      count3 := count3 + 1
```

The use of ANY indicates that the actual value of the signals is not important, only the presence of a signal on that particular channel is of interest.

Repetition is implemented by the use of WHILE:

```
WHILE (x - 1) > 0
    x := x - 1
```

The WHILE TRUE condition allows processes to run continuously once started:

```
PROC square (CHAN Xin, SquareOut) =
    WHILE TRUE
        VAR x:
        SEQ
            Xin ? x
            SquareOut ! x*x :
```

(This example also shows the syntax for declaring channel parameters, Xin and Square Out.) All implementations of Occam support a number of basic types:

CHAN, TIMER, BOOL, BYTE and INT

Other implementations may also support the signed integers INT16, INT32 and INT64, and the IEEE Standard P754 draft 10.0 floating point number types REAL32 and REAL64.

Expressions may be constructed using the following operators:

Arithmetic operator:	$+,-,*,/,\backslash$
	($\backslash$ is a remainder)
Modulo arithmetics:	PLUS, MINUS, TIMES, DIVIDE
Relational:	$=,<>,>,<,>=,<=$
Boolean operators:	AND, OR, NOT
Bit operators:	BITAND, BITOR, $><$, BITNOT
	($><$ is exclusive OR)
Shift operators:	$<<,>>$

All transputers incorporate a timer which can be read into a variable of type integer:

tim ? t

Delayed inputs are also supported and are of the form:

tim ? AFTER t0

3.7 Transputer system development

In an ideal world, the user provides the system designer with a requirement and a performance specification but he does not specify a particular hardware configuration. It should be left to the designer to specify what hardware is required to implement his design and to deliver the required performance. Terminology varies from application to application and from company to company, but software development is usually broken down into three phases:

- Requirements specification
- Design
- Implementation.

As no one is so naive as to expect an implemented system to work first time and to continue to work for years to come, two further phases need to be considered:

- Testing and debugging
- Maintenance.

The initial phase, requirements specification, is simply the process of taking the user's requirements and presenting them in a form which is unambiguous and understood by both the user and the developer. In the not too distant future, machines exhibiting some degree of artificial intelligence will be capable of executing the requirements specification directly, but until that time is reached a design phase is still necessary in order to generate code which can be compiled and run.

Experience with developing many large software systems has shown that in order to produce code which has any chance of being both correct and maintainable, the use of a rigorous development method is essential. The most promising design methods applicable to the design of concurrent Occam software are those based on dataflow diagrams and software modelling. Dataflow diagrams represent software designs as networks of processes connected by data streams (see Fig. 3.8). This representation maps directly onto Occam's model of

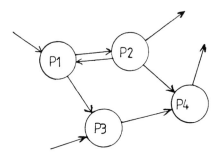

Fig. 3.8   Occam processes shown as dataflow diagram.

processes connected by channels. Some design methods, notably Jackson System Development (JSD), use software processes to model processes in the real world. JSD goes on to consider a network of these processes, each of which is considered to execute conceptually on its own individual processor. If there are more processes than processors on the target hardware then the processes are 'inverted', which is a means of transforming a process so that it can be called like a procedure. The transputer's hardware scheduler can run Occam processes directly. This removes the need for the inversion phase in JSD.

Whichever design method is adopted, a high degree of automation will be required, particularly if large software designs are to be implemented on transputer networks. Some software tools already exist, but as yet they are basic and stand alone. It was mentioned earlier that it is arguable whether a language itself should provide facilities to check the correctness of code, to handle run time errors and configuration control. When a fully integrated software toolset incorporating all the necessary facilities has been developed, there will be no need to duplicate these in the programming language. The fact that Occam provides only a limited number of facilities for software management and error checking will not therefore be a problem.

The area in which Occam offers several positive advantages over other languages is in its flexibility at the implementation phase. When a design for a system has been developed it can be implemented in Occam on any host computer for which a compiler has been produced. Once tested, this same Occam code can be recompiled and run on a single transputer or on an array of interconnected transputers. By using the PLACED operator, processes can be located on specified transputers. A performance estimator is available from Inmos which runs on the host machine (Digital VAX series, running under VMS, are currently supported as host machines) and allows the performance on the target hardware to be predicted. Therefore, the number of transputers necessary to meet the performance specification can be determined before the software is run on the target hardware. If the performance requirement is increased by the user, it is a relatively simple task to retarget the software onto a larger array of transputers.

The transputer and Occam would seem to offer an extremely attractive combination of hardware and software for developing concurrent systems. However, there are still several problems to be solved. For real time software development, generating syntactically correct code is not the end of the story. One of the features of real time software is that code tested on the host can still deadlock when it is run on the target hardware. The only way in which deadlocks can be avoided is to provide mechanisms to guard against them in all possible situations in which they could occur. It is Occam's interprocess channels which present the greatest potential for deadlocks occurring. If for any reason a process is unable to output to a channel, the process at the other end of the channel will hang, which could cause a chain reaction and hang a complete system. Occam provides no assistance in avoiding or recovering from such a deadlock. At the third meeting of the Occam Users' Group meeting (23–24 September 1985), channel associated deadlocks were highlighted as being the problem requiring most urgent attention. This should not present a major problem to the development of transputer based systems, but it is an area which requires some fairly urgent research effort.

Let us now look ahead, hopefully months rather than years, to when a toolset capable of handling the design of a moderately large system implemented in Occam has been developed. An Occam program has been tested on the host, is located on a single transputer and runs a particular application in three seconds. The performance specification, however, states a requirement for it to run in one second. Seeing that the top level of process hierarchy consists of three processes in a parallel construct, the developer changes the PAR to a PLACED PAR, and locates the three processes on three separate transputers coupled by their serial links. The same application is run and to the dismay of the developer it takes two seconds to run!

The answer to this problem is quite simple: one of the three parallel processes in the program takes twice as long to execute as the other two processes added together. This process therefore represents the critical path and needs to be decomposed into smaller processes. This trivial example highlights the need to consider what might be called the first law of processing:

Share the workload evenly between the available processors.

The next section will consider some of the other problems which need to be addressed when designing and implementing concurrent Occam software on transputer networks.

3.8   Sharing the load

The secret of realising the full performance potential of any multi-processor system lies in the even distribution of the workload. Parallelism is the most obvious and the most attractive means of sharing the workload between processors, but frequently a parallel solution to a problem is simply not possible. Consider the Occam program:

```
SEQ
  P1
  P2
  P3
```

The processes P1, P2 and P3 contain totally dissimilar sequences of primitive processes. P3 uses the end results of P2 and P2 uses the end results of P1; therefore the above construct is the only possible way of implementing the program. How can the workload of such a sequential program be shared between multiprocessors? The answer is to pipeline the program's processes. Pipelining involves locating sequential processes on a linear arrangement of processors.

In Fig. 3.9 each of the software processes, P1, P2 and P3, is located on its own processor. P1 starts, inputs a data item D1, processes this data and outputs an interim result to P2 and then terminates. P2 starts, processes the interim result from P1, outputs its own interim result to P3 and terminates. P3 starts, runs and outputs the overall program's final result R, and terminates.

Fig. 3.9 Transputer arranged as a pipeline.

It will immediately be apparent that only one of these processes is executing at any one time. In fact, if all three processes could be located within the on-chip memory of a single transputer, they would execute just as quickly on that one processor as they would on three. The areas in which pipelines are useful are where continuous streams of data need to be processed. Consider a stream of data items D1, D2, D3, D4, . . . Dn, being input into the above pipeline. This time, when P1 has processed D1 it outputs the interim result to P2, but does not terminate. Instead it repeats the sequence with data item D2. In the second time period, P2 is processing the derivative of D1 while P1 is processing D2. Therefore both P1 and P2 are operating in parallel. If the workload has been equally divided between the processes then each set of data will remain in each processor an equal length of time, T. After time, $3T$, D1 will have been processed to produce a result R1 at the end of the pipeline and all the processors will continue to execute as long as new data items can be input into P1.

It can now be seen that two techniques exist to share the workload: pipelining and parallelism. Let us now consider how the two techniques can be combined. Returning to the earlier problem of how to distribute three unequal processes which are capable of operating in parallel, how can the workload be evenly distributed between three processors if P1 runs in four time units and P2 and P3 each run in one time unit?

> PAR
>   P1
>   P2
>   P3

Running these processes on a single transputer takes six time units. We would therefore expect to run the same software on three

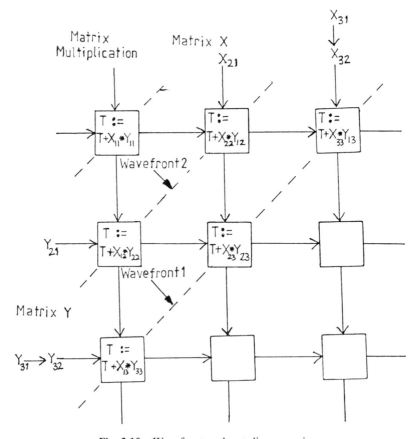

Fig. 3.10   Wavefront and systolic processing.

transputers in two units. As P1 takes four time units to execute, it has to be subdivided. If P1 consists of a set of sequential processes, which may be primitive or complex, it can be split into two processes, P1a and P1b, which take roughly the same length of time to execute. These two processes can now be pipelined together and located on two of the available processors. The Occam processes P2 and P3 will then be located on the third processor where they can execute conceptually in parallel and be scheduled by the transputer's hardware scheduler. Of course, as this is now a pipelined solution, it will only execute efficiently if streams of data items are being processed.

A technique has been developed in recent years which implements pipelines in two dimensions; this is known as *systolic processing*. Systolic processing is ideal for implementing on two-dimensional arrays of transputers, where each transputer is connected to its four nearest neighbours via their serial links. Figure 3.10 shows an array of transputers with pipelines running from top to bottom and from left to right. Processes in each transputer input the data from the left channel and the top channel, process the data and pass data or interim results to the right and bottom channels. Such an array could be used for matrix multiplication where the two inputs are multiplied together and added to a running total:

```
SEQ
  PAR
    top ? x
    left ? y
  PAR
    total := total + (x * y)
    bottom ! x
    right ! y
```

In the above Occam code, x, y and 'total' have been declared as variables with 'total' initialised to zero. Top, bottom, left and right have been declared as channels. It will be seen that x and y are output in parallel with the evaluation of the expression assigned to 'total'. In this way, neighbouring processors below and to the right are not kept waiting unnecessarily. It has been stated earlier that the components of a parallel construct, implemented on a single processor, will only execute 'conceptually' in parallel. However, in this particular case the two output processes are handled by link interfaces which are able to operate independently of the main processor. As soon as the processor has initiated the two outputs, the communication with the neighbouring transputers proceeds in parallel with the evaluation of the expression. Parallel communication processes will actually have a slight effect on the overall processor performance. Inmos claims that the performance of the processes not directly involved with communication will only be reduced by 8%, even when the links are operating at their peak rates.

Figure 3.10 shows how data injected into pipelines in two dimensions creates diagonal wavefronts of data items. In this example, the wavefronts pass across the processor array from top left to bottom right. Because of this analogy, matrix manipulations implemented in this way are referred to as *wavefront processing*. The name 'systolic' is derived from the analogy between the pulsing of data through the array and the systolic beat of the heart. Although systolic processing is not usually appropriate to software problems in general, for particular mathematical applications it can be highly efficient.

3.9   Design of concurrent systems

Any application which at present runs on a conventional array processor can usually be implemented on an array of transputers. Some excellent work has been carried out in the area of wavefront and systolic processing (particularly by S. Y. Kung who originally adopted the word 'systolic') and these techniques are particularly well suited for implementation on two-dimensional arrays of transputers. However, transputer system development should not be thought of as the means of transforming every application into a systolic process on a two-dimensional array of processes.

System design with the transputer presents a totally different level of problem than most designers will have been used to. In the past, devising mechanisms for interprocessor communication, task scheduling and process synchronisation has taken up a large proportion of the system designer's time, effort and creative skills. On the transputer, the majority of these problems are handled by the Occam language and the transputer itself. Freed from the need to consider these more mundane problems, the system designer can address himself to the particular problems associated with concurrency and the architecture of large systems.

The design of concurrent systems will be a totally new experience to most designers, simply because concurrent machines have been a rarity until quite recently. The design of a sequential program, running on a conventional von Neumann type machine, can be compared to the task of a design engineer who has to consider a single factory production line. He must ensure that all the necessary specialist workers, machines and resources are available to process items on that one production line. Taking a similar analogy, the design of a concurrent computer system is like the design of a complete factory. Here the designer must not only provide all the specialist workers, machines and resources required by all the factory's production lines, he must provide them all in the right numbers. If particular machines, resources or skills are to be shared between production lines, then the designer must ensure that bottlenecks are not created. More importantly, he must avoid critical shared resources being monopolised in such a way that the whole factory grinds to a standstill. The complexity of such a task is such that the designer may not be able to solve all the problems on the drawing board. Some problems may only become apparent after the factory is in operation. In just the same way, concurrent computer systems will always require some degree of debugging before they are fully operational.

Besides considering the special problems of concurrency, many transputer system designers will also have to address the problems of designing extremely large arrays of processors. Some of these problems will be considered in the following section.

3.10   System architecture

To the conventional designer, some of the more esoteric architectures being put forward for the transputer may seem unnecessarily complex. In fact, the reaction of many to such ideas as multi-dimensional hypercubes is to classify them in the field of science fiction rather than in the area of practical system design. There are, however, sound reasons for actually using these novel architectures in real systems.

Transputers provide a means of distributing software across a number of processors, but it should still be remembered that a communication overhead will always exist, particularly when the communication needs to pass across more than one transputer. As a general policy the designer should aim to minimise inter-processor communication wherever possible. If at all possible, certain groups of closely coupled software processes should reside on the same processor. These groups are identified by analysing dataflow representations of the software design. Processes connected by frequent or high volume data flows are said to be *closely coupled*. This group of processes might typically form a subsystem of an embedded computer system, such as an aircraft's autopilot or a section of a signal processing algorithm, taking in relatively small amounts of data and returning results. If performance studies indicate that a group of tightly coupled processes

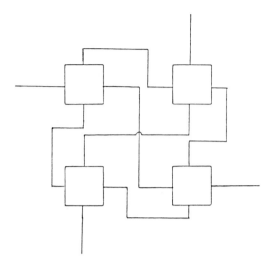

Fig. 3.11   Four interconnected transputers.

will have to run on more than one processor, then in order to minimise communication overheads, every processor supporting this subsystem should be connected directly to all the other processors supporting that same task. This configuration will be familiar to any network analyst. If *n* processors are required to provide the necessary performance for the subsystem then, if possible, each processor should have $n - 1$ links to connect directly to all the other processors and one link to connect to other subsystems or to the outside world. This makes a total of $(n - 1) + 1 = n$ links required for each processor in the subsystem. Therefore the number of processors which can be networked to form a cluster is equal to the number of links which each has available. T425 transputers should therefore be linked in clusters of four (see Fig. 3.11).

Students of chemistry, or anyone who has used a molecular modelling kit, will know that connecting objects to their nearest neighbours by four regularly distributed links forms a three-dimensional tetrahedral structure (see Fig. 3. 12). It is this structure which gives the diamond crystal its strength. It is also the ideal way of connecting a large network of four linked transputers to minimise communication overheads. The problem with such a network is that it does not lend itself to being tracked onto a two-dimensional printed circuit board. Figure 3.13 is a three-dimensional representation of Fig. 3.11. It can be seen that this is different to the diamond structure in Fig. 3.12 in that it is not totally regular but is built up from clusters of four processors each. Although this network structure has been arrived at in a methodical and purely logical manner, it is still hard to believe that

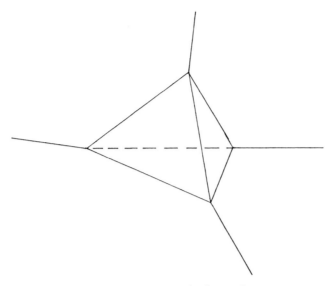

Fig. 3.12 Network connected in diamond structure.

this structure provides a lower communication overhead than that of the North–South East–West connection of the array shown in Fig. 3.4. A quick check, however, using the array in Fig. 3.4, shows that a signal passing from a transputer at a corner of the conventional array to the transputer at the opposite corner of the array has to pass along at least

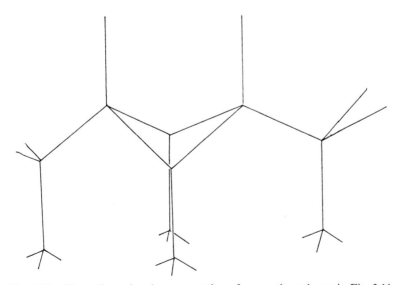

Fig. 3.13 Three-dimensional representation of connections shown in Fig. 3.11.

Fig. 3.14 Sixteen interconnected transputers.

six links. In the array shown in Fig. 3.14, the signal only requires three links to pass between the processors in the same relative positions. In fact three is the maximum number of links used to connect any two processors in this network.

It would be tempting to repeat this pattern to yet higher levels, building up networks of 64, then 256 transputers, and so on. Unfortunately the wiring would quickly become a major problem and the inter-processor links would soon exceed their 400 mm limit. However, 16 transputers form a very useful size of cluster. If 16 T425s can be fitted onto a single circuit board the cluster becomes evern more practical.

Two-dimensional transputer networks in which each processor is connected to its four nearest neighbours, as shown in Fig. 3.4, can in fact be quite useful for implementing algorithms involving matrix manipulation. This array is also applicable to many image processing tasks where the transputers can be used either to process an incoming image or to generate graphics, with each processor being allocated a number of pixels to control. Some image processing algorithms require that each modelling process communicates with its eight nearest neighbours rather than four. This does not require a particularly novel architecture, just that it would be preferable for each processor to have eight links rather than four so that all diagonals could be interconnected.

Joining two transputers using one link from each produces a dual processor with six available links:

$$(2 \times 4) - 2 = 6$$

Having six links allows cubic transputer networks to be constructed in three dimensions. Connecting three transputers in a linear structure provides a triple processor with eight spare links. This allows a four-dimensional network to be constructed. Multi-dimensional 'hyper-cubes' are not imaginary network structures, they can actually be built. However, the multi-layer printed circuit board tracking problems created by actually trying to build one can become a nightmare. In theory, an n-dimensional hypercube can be constructed from clusters containing $n - 1$ transputers and having $2n$ links each, where n can be any number. In practice it would seem to be far more sensible to wait until transputers with six, eight or ten links are manufactured. Building three-dimensional networks is worth considering, particularly where three-dimensional processes are being modelled, but the practicality of building hypercubes must be questioned. Small-sided hypercubes may well find uses as superclusters to host a closely coupled subsystem. For example, a four-dimensional cube of side 2 would contain $2^4 = 16$ nodes, with each node containing three transputers. Such a super-cluster, or mini-hypercube, may well find practical uses, but interconnecting 48 transputers in such a complex architecture is not a trivial task.

The argument for hypercubes is that they reduce communication latency. Consider two networks, each containing 48 transputers; a 6×8 two-dimensional array and a $2 \times 2 \times 2 \times 2$ triple transputer noded hypercube. Taking the worst case of trying to communicate between transputers at opposite corners of each network, on the two-dimensional array the message is relayed by 11 transputers, on the four-dimensional network it can be relayed by anything from two transputers to ten, depending on the orientation of each node. On average, therefore, communication within a hypercube is faster.

Deadlock prediction on such a structure, however, will be impossible until an automatic deadlock analyser is developed.

3.11   Future developments

We have seen that the generic architecture of the transputer allows a whole family of components to be developed, each having its own area of specialist application. The transputer's unique characteristics offer many other exciting possibilities. Many designs for two-dimensional arrays of transputers look remarkably similar to the way in which the chips are laid out on the silicon wafer on which they are manufactured. It seems a great waste of time, effort and money to split these wafers, package up the individual chips and to design and manufacture a printed circuit board so that the chips can be interconnected in the same layout in which they were manufactured. It would seem far more sensible to connect the transputers to their neighbours while they are still on the wafer. Wafer scale integration, as this is known, has already being tried out with memory devices, which like the transputer can be connected in regular networks.

Wafer scale integration has two major problems to overcome. First, the yield of working chips from a silicon wafer is rarely 100%. Simply connecting each transputer to all its neighbours would almost inevitably include faulty transputers in the network. Second, there are the problems of getting electrical power in and getting heat out. Power must be routed to each chip and the one watt of heat generated by each transputer must be removed.

Obviously, on the first point, every effort must be made to improve production techniques to achieve the maximum possible yield of correctly working chips. In the longer term, however, software could be developed to configure the arrays to bypass faulty chips. If the software could dynamically configures the networks and continually monitor the condition of each processor, chips which failed in operation could also be bypassed. The long term solution to the power problem is to develop new semiconductors which require less power. As an added bonus, these materials may present a lower impedance which would allow signals to be passed around the chips more quickly, thereby increasing the performance of each individual processor.

The short term solution to achieving wafer scale integration of transputer arrays would be to identify all occurrences of two-by-two arrays of working chips on a wafer. This process could be carried out by a computer aided device which had been fed with the position of all the working chips by the automatic testing equipment. Slicing the chip to cut out an irregular pattern of two-by-two arrays may be more difficult but should still be possible. It may also be possible to package the working chips in these two-by-two arrays.

Again in the longer term, connection of processors across the wafer would probably be by some form of parallel link, probably 32-bits wide, which would considerably increase the wafer's internal bandwidth. For the first wafer scale transputer products, the standard serial links would provide a simple means of connecting processors, without the need to modify their internal architecture.

Having two-by-two arrays of transputers on each wafer would reduce the problems of getting power to each processor, as all four would be accessible from the edge of the wafer. Waste heat might present a more difficult problem and some way of cooling the chip would be required, possibly by integrating heat pipes and heat sinks into the wafer's packaging. As these problems are gradually overcome, it will be possile to produce larger and larger arrays of integrated transputers. A wafer just 10 cm square, using 1985 technology, could operate at one billion operations per second and would also incorporate 100K of fast memory.

For those designers requiring more than four links on their transputers, the quad T425 wafer scale integrated package could well provide the answer to their problems. In addition to a performance rating of 60 MIPS, a quad T425 would have eight serial links with a total bandwith of 160 Mbit/s. In addition to the performance advantage, it may actually be that a quad T425 could be developed in a shorter timescale than a single transputer with eight links.

It should at this point be made perfectly clear that all these ideas for future products are, at the moment, pure speculation. Various representatives from Inmos have mentioned the possibility of wafer scale products, but there is no actual commitment to develop these devices. Their development, like that of the individual devices in the transputer family, will depend on demand, investment in research and development and on being able to overcome the large number of technical problems which will inevitably be encountered.

What is certain is that as the transputer is used in more and more real applications, the need for many variations of the device will emerge. The transputer is the most significant development since the microprocessor. This microprocessor-sized device, with the power of a small mainframe computer, provides us with a building block to replace most of today's machines. General purpose processors, array processors, supercomputers and machines which have not been possible until now, such as the fifth generation machines, can all be assembled from transputers. Most importantly, the transputer exists here and now. In developing new products from this device, we are limited only by our imaginations.

References

1. *Transputer Instruction Set – A Compiler Writer's Guide*, Inmos, Prentice-Hall Int., 1988.

Further reading

The Occam Programming Manual, Prentice-Hall Int., 1982.
System Development, Jackson, M. A., Prentice-Hall Int., 1983.
Towards the Fifth-generation Computers, Simons, G. L., NCC Publications, 1983.
Transputer Reference Manual, Inmos, 1985.
Kung, S. Y., IEEE ASSP magazine, July 1985.
Transputer Reference Manual, Inmos, Prentice-Hall Int., 1988.
Occam 2 Reference Manual, Inmos, Prentice-Hall Int., 1988.

CHAPTER 4
Intel's 80386 and 80486 Families

I. R. WHITWORTH
Royal Military College of Science, UK

4.1 Introduction

The world of the mainstream complex instruction set 32-bit micro-processor is one which has evolved from that of the 'industry standard' 16-bit processors. Indeed, the lineage of the 80386 can be traced right back to Intel's first 8-bit processor, the 8080; by the same rationale that Intel's first 16-bit processor, the 8086, maintained compatibility with the 8080, so the 80386 maintains compatibility with the 8086. The designers of the 80386 had to look both forwards, towards the newest fabrication and architectural techniques, and backwards, towards the existing architectures of the 8086 family.

The requirements for a processor, like the 80386, are summarised as follows:

(1) Compatibility with 8086 and 80286. The 16-bit 80286 addresses the problem of direct 8086 compatibility by having two modes of operation, the Real Address mode, which allows 8086 binary code to run without modification, and the Protected Virtual Address mode (Protected mode) which exploits the features of the 80286. The 80386 follows the same route, with a Real Address mode similar to the 8086 environment, and a Protected Virtual Address mode, like that of the 80286; a mode within Protected mode, the Virtual 86 mode, allows 8086 code to be run as a task in a protected multi-task environment.

(2) Exploitation of modern fabrication technology.

(3) Architectural improvements i.e. a more regular register set, better instruction orthogonality, within the constraints of compatibility.

(4) Improvement of bus bandwidth, by the use of full-width 32-bit buses, non-multiplexed buses, bus pipelining, a bus cycle definition which allows a good compromise between bandwidth and the use of inexpensive memory and interface devices.

(5) Improvement of execution unit throughput by the use of cache

memory (supported externally to the processor), internal pipelining and prefetch, and on-chip memory address translation.

(6) Use of an on-chip Memory Management Unit (MMU). Following the example of the 80286, this would support protection, segmentation, paging, address translation (via a Translation Lookaside Buffer (TLB) which itself has a cache structure).

(7) Good co-processor and interface support. The 80386 is supported by:

- 80387DX and SX Numeric Co-processors (IEEE Standard Floating Point).
- 82380 Advanced DMA Controller.
- 82385 External Cache Memory Controller.

(8) Standard bus support. No processors have an exact correspondence between their component level bus signals and the bus signals of one of the standard backplane buses which exist. Backplane (system) buses are usually designed to allow multiple-processor operation and processor independence, and require some interface logic between the bus and processor. The 80386 family has a number of chip sets which allow easy interfacing to a number of standard buses, e.g. Multibus (I, II), EISA (Extended PC-AT bus) and Microchannel (MCA).

(9) Multiprocessor system support.

(10) Good High Level Language (HLL) and real-time operating system support, e.g. stack frames, procedure Enter and Leave instructions, fast context switching and multi-tasking support.

(11) Built-in Test (BIT) and debugging features.

At the time of its release, the 80386 was a giant. Although nowadays, the one-million transistor chip is with us, in 1985, the 275 000 transistor 80386 represented the state-of-the-art in fabrication technology. It is manufactured using Intel's proprietary CHMOS III process (1.5 μm), and packaged as a 132-lead Pin-Grid Array (PGA). Power consumption is around 2 W.

The 80386 family possesses several variants, all based around a 32-bit core, but with different speeds and bus widths. They are:

(i) The original 80386, now known as the 80386DX, with 32-bit, non-multiplexed external buses, and 132-pin PGA package. It is available in speeds of 16, 20, 25 and 33 MHz.

(ii) The 80386SX, a less expensive version which has a 24-bit address bus, a 16-bit data bus, is non-multiplexed and is available as a 16 MHz part. The smaller bus sizes mean that the package does not need to be as large as that for the 80386DX; to keep costs down, a 100-

pin plastic quad flatpack package is used.

(iii) The 80376, a processor targeted at embedded control applications. Like the 80386SX, it has a 24-bit address bus, a 16-bit data bus and is available as a 16 MHz part. It differs from the other members of the family by having reduced the memory management facilities – an embedded processor is unlikely to need virtual memory support and paging, so these features are not provided in the 80376. Compatibility with the 8086 is reduced. Like the 80386DX, the 80376 is available as a 100-pin plastic quad flatpack, and is also available as an 88-pin PGA.

The 80486 is Intel's second generation, one million transistor, 32-bit processor. It is designed to be 100% binary-compatible with the 80386, but to run at between twice and four times the speed of the 80386DX. Whilst the 80386 supports an entirely external cache memory (making the design of the cache a system design issue), the 80486 has a single internal cache for both instructions and data. Although the internal cache (8K) is smaller than a typical external 80386 cache, the wide internal data path (128 bits) between the cache and instruction prefetcher and instruction decoder make the equivalent cache speed very high indeed. The external bus feeding the cache has a fast Burst Mode so that the cache is not bound by bus bandwidth.

Like the 80386 family, the 80486 has internal memory management and address translation, but also has an on-chip floating point unit, compatible with the 80387 numeric co-processor. Multiprocessor facilities, the self-test and debugging features are enhanced.

4.2   Basic 80386 architecture

The internal structure of the 80386 is shown in Fig. 4.1. Internal 6-stage pipelining allows the six functional blocks to operate in parallel. The six functional blocks of Fig. 4.1 are:

- Bus Interface Unit (BIU)
- Code prefetch unit
- Instruction decode unit
- Execution unit
- MMU segmentation unit
- MMU paging unit

Like the 8086 architecture, the 80386 uses queues in the instruction stream, as First In, First out (FIFO) buffers between the code prefetch unit and instruction decode unit, and between the instruction decode unit and execution unit. Whilst the 8086 used an instruction prefetch

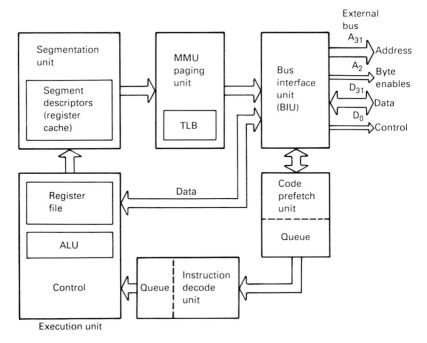

Fig. 4.1   80386 block diagram.

queue of 6 bytes (claimed to be optimal for the 8086 instruction set), the equivalent queue in the 80386 is longer at 16 bytes to match the faster cache memory fetches which might be used, and the internal pipelining. The instruction queue feeding the execution unit holds microcode instructions created by the decoder (three deep).

The execution unit contains the microcode memory and sequencer which form the control unit for the CPU, an Arithmetic and Logic Unit (ALU) which includes hardware multiply/divide and a 64-bit barrel shifter, to allow multi-place shifts in a single cycle, and a file of eight general purpose 32-bit registers.

The BIU communicates between the external bus of the 80386 and the Instruction Prefetch Unit (IPU) (code fetchers) and execution unit (data transfers). Internally generated requests to the BIU for code fetchers or data transfers are prioritised. This automatically gives data transfers a higher priority than code prefetches, so that prefetch operations never hold up instruction execution, and with zero memory cycle wait states, there is no conflict between the two.

Whenever the BIU is not fetching data, and the bus would otherwise be idle, the IPU requests the BIU to perform a code fetch. The IPU maintains a linear address pointer (the prefetch instruction pointer) and a segment prefetch limit register for checking address violations; requests to the BIU are made via the paging unit of the CPU. Code is prefetched sequentially from the instruction stream in memory whenever the prefetch queue is partly empty and no other bus cycle has been requested, or whenever a branch or exception causes a transfer of control within the code. The prefetch queue feeds instructions to the instruction decoder which has its own queue feeding the execution unit. Whenever the instruction queue is partly empty, the unit fetches instructions from the prefetch queue, and decodes them to microcode words which need no further decoding in the execution unit, and which are added to the instruction queue.

The execution unit, as might be expected from its name, contains the ALU which supports hardware integer multiply and divide, like the 8086 and 80286 and, in addition, is equipped with a barrel shifter. The barrel shifter of the 80386 is a 64-bit register which is capable of performing multi-place shifts in a single CPU clock cycle. For many years, barrel shifter logic has been used in programmable Digital Signal Processing (DSP) hardware to give rapid powers-of-two scaling; the speed advantage it brings is now being exploited by general purpose processors, such as the 80386. Associated with the ALU is a register file of eight, 32-bit, 'general purpose' registers; whilst they may be freely specified for many operations, some are still used implicitly for certain operations.

Control of the execution unit is exercised by the control unit, which contains the microcode and sequencer (or micro engine). This is a highly efficient unit which makes extensive use of operation overlaps to achieve a high execution speed. As well as controlling the ALU, the control unit also controls another part of the execution unit, the protection test unit. This unit is responsible for checking for static segment violations.

The memory management facilities of the 80386 are split between two units which are part of the CPU address generation system. The 80386 uses three address spaces:

(1) Logical (or virtual) addresses which consist of a selector value (contents of a segment register), and an offset value (the effective address computed from the addressing mode of the instruction). The virtual address space is the one visible to the program code. In Protected mode, the 16-bit segment registers hold 14-bit selector index values which can be used, in conjunction with 32-bit offset values, to give a total logical address space of 64 terabytes (46 bits). The remaining two (least significant) bits of the segment registers make up

the Requestor Privilege Level (RPL), which is the privilege level of the original supplier of the selector. In Real Address mode, and VM86 mode, a 16-bit segment register is regarded in the same way as a segment register in the 8086.

(2) Linear addresses, which are produced by translation from logical addresses in the segmentation unit. The 32 bits used give a total linear address space of 4 Gbytes.

(3) The 32-bit physical address, which appears at the CPU pins, corresponds to the linear address if the paging unit is not enabled. In Real Address mode, the paging unit is not used anyway. If the paging unit is enabled, it performs a translation between linear and physical address spaces.

The segmentation unit takes logical addresses used by the execution unit, and translates them to linear addresses, checking for any bus-cycle segmentation violations. The translation process depends on the CPU mode.

In Real mode (directly compatible with the 8086), the segmentation unit shifts the segment address four places left and adds the result to the offset to form the 32-bit linear address..8086 code normally uses a 16-bit segment register, shifted four places left and added to a 16-bit offset value, to generate a 20-bit address; any carry generated by the addition is ignored. The same code running on the 80386 will generate a 21-bit linear address (carry is included) in the range 00000000H to 0010FFEFH. Segments in this mode are a uniform 64K in length.

In Protected mode, the segmentation unit uses the upper field of a 16-bit segment register as a 14-bit selector value. The selector value is used as an index into a segment descriptor table, translated via the table to a segment base address, and added to the offset address to form a 32-bit linear address. Segment limits and attributes checking may be performed by the segmentation unit in this mode. In Protected mode, segments may be of a specified length, depending upon the values of a limit field and a granularity field in the segment descriptor. If segment lengths are required to be specified to the nearest byte, the maximum length of a segment is 1 Mbyte; the alternative is to specify segment lengths to the nearest 4K, to a maximum segment length of 4 Gbytes.

The paging unit uses the linear address produced by the segmentation unit as a virtual address, interpreted as three fields – an index into a directory table, an index into a page table selected by the indexed entry in the directory table, and an offset, or index, into the fixed size 4K page selected. A combination of the offset field and the selected entry in the selected page table gives the required physical address. The directory table and page table entries have attribute and protection bits which are checked by the paging unit. To speed up the mechanism of address translation, and to avoid constant access of directory and page tables, a 32-entry Translation Look-aside Buffer (TLB), operated as a four-way set-associative cache, is used with the paging unit, and performs direct linear-to-physical address translation for the most used resident pages.

4.3   The 80386 bus signals and timing

The 80386DX pinout is shown in diagrammatic form in Fig. 4.2. (Physically, the device pins are laid out in multiple rows parallel to all four sides of the PGA package.) The clock CLK2 applied to the CPU has a frequency which is twice the CPU speed (40 MHz for a 20 MHz 80386, etc.) and is divided internally to the correct rate. The shortest time unit, or 'state', for a bus cycle is one CPU clock period, which is two CLK2 periods. Each bus cycle is made up of at least two bus states, T1 and T2, and so takes at least four CLK2 cycles.

The address bus is a non-multiplexed 30-bit bus, A31-A2, which carries word addresses for the 32-bit words of the system. The data bus is a 32-bit bus, D31-D0. Internally, physical addresses are generated as

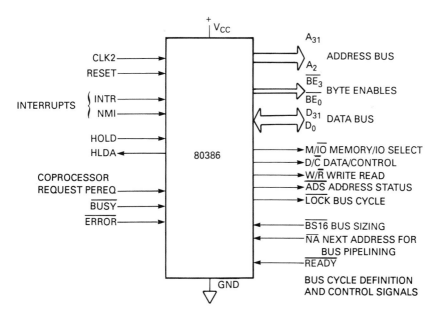

Fig. 4.2   80386 CPU external signals.

32-bit byte addresses – the two least significant two bits of address are the 'byte specifier'. These are decoded to individual byte enable signals BE0# to BE3#, which allow the bus to support 8-bit, 16-bit and 32-bit transfers. All 4 byte enables are asserted for a full 32-bit transfer; only the relevant ones are asserted for 8-bit and 16-bit transfers. BE0# corresponds to the byte on data pins D0 to D7, BE1# corresponds to D8 to D15, etc.

4.3.1   BUS CYCLES

Each bus cycle is defined by a set of 'bus cycle definition' signals:

(1) W/R# Write-read indication.
(2) D/C# Data-control indication. When low, indicates memory code read (instruction fetch), HALT, SHUTDOWN or interrupt acknowledge. When high, indicates memory or I/O data read or write.
(3) M/IO# Memory-I/O cycle.
(4) LOCK# Bus Lock (used for shared-bus, multiple processor systems). Asserted automatically when the processor is acknowledging interrupts, manipulating descriptors and some page-table bits, and executing the XCHG instruction (used as the 80386's indivisible test-and-set instruction). Asserted under program control by using the instruction prefix LOCK before bit test and change instructions, before certain one-operand and two-operand arithmetic or logical instructions.

Control and timing of the bus transfer is handled by:

(i) ADS# Address Status
(ii) BS16# Bus Size 16 (bits). Allows dynamic bus sizing, controlled either by logic associated by the bus itself, or by an interface device. Since the bus width is determined individually for each bus cycle, the CPU may be connected to buses of both 16 and 32 bits. Data is transferred on the lower 16 bits of the data bus; if the instruction being executed requires a 32-bit transfer when BS16# is asserted, an extra cycle is automatically introduced by the CPU.
(iii) READY# Transfer complete. The signal gives a positive indication of a transfer, and ends a bus cycle.
(iv) NA# Next Address, an input to the CPU which causes the CPU to assert address and status signals for the next bus cycle before the current bus cycle has completed. This feature supports bus pipelining.

The 80386 uses seven types of bus cycle:

- Read from memory space
- Locked read from memory space
- Write to memory space
- Locked write to memory space
- Read from I/O space or co-processor
- Write to I/O space or co-processor
- Interrupt acknowledge
- Indicate HALT or SHUTDOWN.

A 'bus idle' state is entered if no bus cycles are required by the BIU; it is signalled by ADS# remaining high after the last bus cycle has terminated, signalled by READY# being taken low. Bus cycles may be non-pipelined or pipelined, with or without wait states.

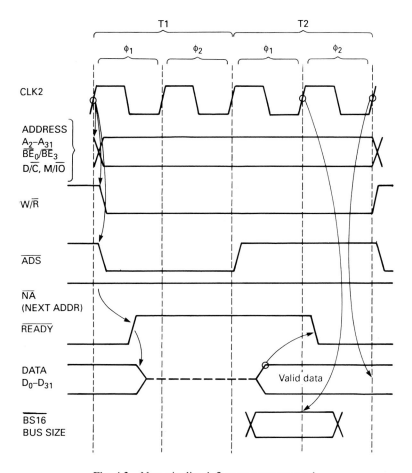

Fig. 4.3 Non-pipelined, 2-state memory read.

4.3.2 NON-PIPELINED BUS CYCLES

For fast memory (usually the fast static memory selected for the external cache), a two-state non-pipelined bus cycle is appropriate, as shown in Fig. 4.3. State T1 is initiated by CLK2 phase 1 which causes ADS# to be driven low, and the address bus A31-A2 byte enables BE3#-BE0#, and bus state signals D/C#, W/R#, M/IO#, LOCK# to become active. ADS# terminates at the end of bus state T1, but the other signals remain active for the duration of the bus cycle. In bus state T2, the bus size is read by the rising edge of CLK2 phase 2, and at the end of T2, READY# is sampled. If READY# is low, indicating that data is on the data bus, the data is read and the cycle terminates. The equivalent two-state memory write cycle is shown in Fig. 4.4.

In the memory read cycle, if READY# is still high at the end of T2,

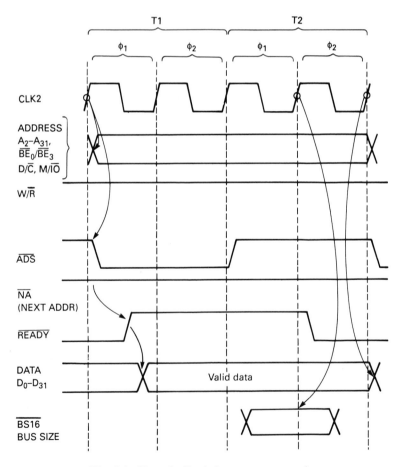

Fig. 4.4 Non-pipelined, 2-state memory write.

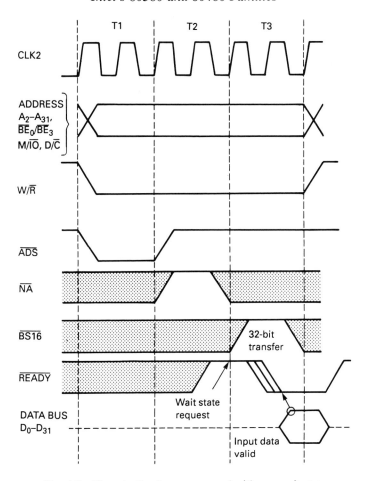

Fig. 4.5 Non-pipelined, memory read with one wait state.

wait states are added to the bus cycle (identical to state T2), with the READY# pin sampled at the end of each wait state. As soon as READY# is sampled low, the data is read and the bus cycle terminates (see Fig. 4.5.). Action is similar in the write cycle.

For a 20 MHz 80386, with worst case timings, but no bus buffer delays, required memory access time for a no-wait-state read cycle will be:

Bus cycle time – A2-A31 valid delay – D0-D31 read set up time
100 ns   –   30 ns max   –   11 ns min   = 59 ns

With 5 ns (FAST logic) address and data buffer delays, this is reduced to 49 ns. For the 33 MHz part, the required memory access time for no-wait-state operation falls even further. Although static memory with access times of 25–45 ns is readily available, it is more costly than slower dynamic memory, and is unlikely to form the basis for main 80386 memory. Use of such static memory for a cache of, for example, 64K, is economically viable, and is used in a large number of 80386-based pc systems, supported by non-pipelined, no-wait-state bus cycles.

4.3.3   PIPELINED BUS CYCLES

Address pipelining is available on the 80386, invoked by the 'Next Address' (NA#) input signal. Pipelining allows a longer time between the address and bus state signals becoming active, and data being read or written, achieved by overlapping bus cycles. A pipelined memory read cycle is shown in Fig. 4.6.

NA# is asserted by logic in the system outside the CPU to indicate that the address bus information is no longer required by the bus cycle

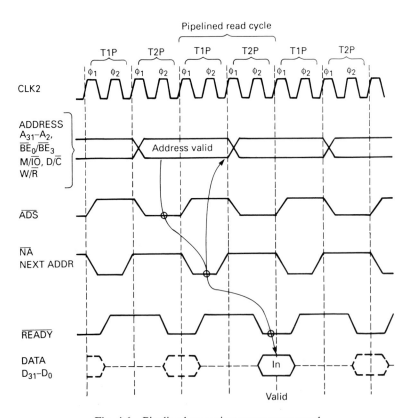

Fig. 4.6   Pipelined no-wait-state memory read.

in progress. NA# is sampled by the 80386 by the rising edge of phase 2 of any clock cycle. In Fig. 4.6, where no-wait-state operation is required, NA# is asserted in state T1 of the current bus cycle and sampled by phase 2 in the middle of state T1. At the end of the state, the current address is removed from the bus and replaced by the next memory address required. Address Status ADS# is asserted at the same time to indicate that a new address is on the bus. State T2 of the current bus cycle proceeds, and is terminated by READY# going low at the end of T2. The next cycle is entered with a new state, T1, which does not alter the address bus but may cause LOCK# to be asserted if the new cycle requires the bus to be locked.

If NA# is reasserted during this T1 state, the address will be removed from the address bus at the end of T1, and replaced by a new address, continuing the pipelining process. Other bus signals will remain active during the second state of this bus cycle, T2, which, for no-wait-state operation, will be terminated by READY# at the end of T2 when data may be read from the data bus.

The effect of pipelining is to insert at least one state time in the required access time for memory. For a 20 MHz 80386, this will add 50 ns to the minimum access time. If memory can be structured so as to allow consecutive pipelined accesses without wait states, the bus throughput will be the same as in the no-wait-state, non-pipelined case. A conventional singly-addressed memory system will not allow this, since it cannot begin decoding a second address before dealing with data appropriate to the first address. If the memory is interleaved, however, so long as pipelined addresses are consecutive, full bus transfer rates can be maintained. With a doubly-interleaved memory (i.e. two banks of memory for alternate addresses), one memory bank can be latching a new address whilst the other bank, latched with the previous address, is still delivering its data. If addresses become non-consecutive, wait states may have to be inserted where the current bus cycle requires access to the same memory bank as the previous one.

4.3.4   TRANSITION BETWEEN PIPELINED AND NON-PIPELINED BUS CYCLES

The type of bus cycle may be selected on a cycle-by-cycle basis using NA#. To move from pipelined to non-pipelined operation is easy, i.e. the last pipelined cycle is allowed to terminate without assertion of NA# which, for pipelined cycles, is always sampled during state T1 of the cycle. The cycle which follows will automatically be non-pipelined.

To move from non-pipelined to pipelined operation is a little more

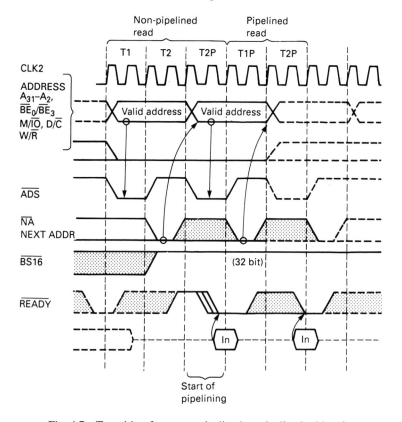

Fig. 4.7 Transition from non-pipelined to pipelined addressing.

complex; a non-pipelined bus cycle samples NA# during state T2. To allow pipelining to begin, the non-pipelined cycle must be extended by the addition of a wait state (a second T2 state) so that the address is phased correctly (see Fig. 4.7).

It is worth noting that the first bus cycle following a bus idle state is always non-pipelined.

4.3.5 BUS ARBITRATION

Two signals are provided for bus arbitration used by DMA controllers and other peripherals which may require bus mastership. Bus hold request (HOLD) is a synchronous input, level sensitive, which must be held asserted for as long as the requesting device requires the bus.

When HOLD is asserted whilst the bus is active, it must be asserted no later than READY# is asserted to terminate the bus cycle, for a non-pipelined bus cycle, or in the same bus state as NA# is asserted, for a pipelined bus cycle. At the end of the cycle, so long as LOCK# is not asserted, a hold acknowledge cycle is initiated. At the beginning of the hold acknowledge cycle HLDA is asserted, and the following pins are taken to a floating (high impedance) state:

- Address   A31–A2
- Byte enables   BE3#–BE0#
- Address status   ADS#
- Bus lock   LOCK#
- Data   D31–D0

Inputs NA#, BS16# and READY# are ignored in the hold state.

HOLD may also be asserted in the bus idle state, and will be acknowledged when the idle state terminates.

4.3.6   INTERRUPTS

The interrupt inputs of the 80386 consist of a maskable interrupt input INTR, a non-maskable interrupt input NMI, and RESET.

When interrupts are enabled, an interrupt request on INTR causes interrupt acknowledge action when the current bus cycle terminates. This action consists of two successive interrupt acknowledge cycles, separated by four idle bus states, to ensure timing compatibility with Intel's 8259A Interrupt Controller. The first acknowledge cycle consists of a bus read with byte enables BE3#–BE1# set to 1, BS0# set to 0 and all address signals set to 0 except for A2, which is set to 1. LOCK# is asserted and the bus cycle definition signals indicate read, control and I/O. ADS# is asserted during T1 state of the cycle. The cycle is terminated by READY# like a normal bus read cycle; no valid vector data is passed during this first cycle. LOCK# is held asserted during the subsequent idle states and the second interrupt acknowledge cycle. The second interrupt acknowledge cycle is identical to the first except that, this time, A2 is set to 0. The interrupting device may put vector data on the data bus lines D0–D7, and assert READY# when this acknowledge cycle is recognised. As usual, READY# terminates the bus cycle and the CPU reads the vector data.

Non-maskable interrupts invoke no interrupt acknowledge cycle, and are automatically assigned vector number 2.

RESET forces termination of all execution and bus activity, and will hold the CPU in this state for as long as the signal is asserted. RESET causes some of the internal CPU registers to be set to defined values: all segment registers except the Code Segment (CS) register are set to 0, the CS register has base address set to FFFF0000H, limit set to

0FFFFH, and the Instruction Pointer (IP) register is set to 0000FFF0H. When RESET is released, between 350 and 450 CLK2 periods elapse before the 80386 starts executing instructions near the top of memory at FFFFFFF0H.

4.3.7   CO-PROCESSOR INTERFACE SIGNALS

The 80386 is provided with three co-processor signals:

- PEREQ   Co-processor Request. Indicates a co-processor request for data to be transferred. The 80386 controls the transfer of data between co-processor and memory, using the co-processor opcode to determine memory address and direction of transfer.
- BUSY#   Co-processor Busy. When asserted, it indicates that the co-processor is unable to handle another instruction.
- ERROR#   Co-processor Error. Indicates that an error, which has not been masked by the co-processor's error register, has occurred. The 80386 may generate an exception 16 in response to this error signal.

4.4   External cache memory

The timing of 80386 bus signals demands fast memory for no-wait-state operation. Economics dictate that if a system requires a reasonable size of main memory, that memory will usually be dynamic, and require wait states. Even with interleaved memory, it may be necessary to introduce one or more wait states in each bus cycle and, in any case, wait states will be introduced whenever one bank is accessed by consecutive bus cycles. The bus throughput will be reduced, and the processor performance impaired.

One solution is to build a small amount of fast static memory which will work without wait states, and use it to cache data and instructions transferred from the slower large memory. Caches rely on code and data being reused often enough that most memory access may use the cache without the need to generate slow bus cycles. The optimum size of a cache depends upon program code statistics and may differ between processors with different instruction sets.

The 80386 puts cache design in the hands of the system designer. It supports an external cache by adjusting the length of bus cycles to accommodate cache accesses as two-state, non-pipelined bus cycles, and main memory accesses as pipelined or non-pipelined accesses with wait states inserted. The difference between cache and main memory (apart from size, speed and cost) is the way they handle addresses. Main memory is directly addressed; an address uniquely locates a single memory location. A cache memory stores at least part of the address (the 'address tag') with its associated data, and locates that data by comparing the appropriate field of the address issued by the CPU with the address tag. This feature allows a cache memory to be small yet, at the same time, store data items which are associated with widely separated addresses.

4.4.1   BASIC CACHE OPERATION

This operation is illustrated in Fig. 4.8.

In a bus read cycle (from memory), the CPU issues a memory address, and logic associated with the fast cache memory performs the address tag comparison. If the instruction or data addressed as in the cache, a match is found, data from the cache memory will be allowed onto the data bus, and the bus cycle initiated by the CPU will be terminated in two states, using READY#. Signals generated in the cache control logic indicate a 'cache hit'.

If an address tag match is not found, the cache control logic indicates a 'cache miss', and the bus cycle is extended by inserting wait states to accommodate reading the addressed data or instruction from slower main memory. When data is available on the bus, it is read by the CPU and, simultaneously, written to the cache, along with its associated address tag. The bus cycle is terminated by READY# as usual. If the instruction or data is reused, and it is still in the cache when it is required for a second time, a cache hit will cause a fast bus read from cache.

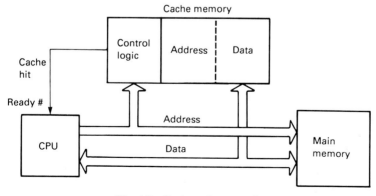

Fig. 4.8   Basic cache operation.

The cache architecture determines how data read from memory on a cache miss may be written to the cache memory.

If the cache is to be used only for code – an instruction cache – the cache is only written during a bus read cycle. No explicit write to the cache will be made by the CPU.

If the cache is to be used for data – a data cache – some strategy must be evolved for handling a CPU write to a cached location. Three possible strategies are:

(1) Write-through. When the CPU performs a memory write to alter data in the cache, it generates a bus write cycle long enough to accommodate main memory, and performs a simultaneous write to cache (some of the cache memory always reflects the contents of those main memory locations which are cached). Since timing of the write cycle is the same as that of main memory, the cache offers no performance improvement for writes.

(2) Buffered write. The cache is written to as quickly as possible, and the written data and address stored in a buffer so that the processor can proceed to the next bus cycle without being held up. Writing to main memory will occur as soon as the bus is available; it may be possible to overlap a write to main memory with a read from cache. Usually only a single level of buffering is allowed – if two consecutive writes occur, the second one is held up whilst the first completes.

(3) Deferred write. The cache is written to as quickly as possible and the entry flagged to indicate that it is no longer the same as the corresponding entry in main memory. The data item is used from the cache until the entry is replaced, when it is written back to main memory, before replacement.

Both (2) and (3) require additional logic and increase the cost of the cache system. In practice, most 80386 cached systems use a 'write-through' cache.

4.4.2   CACHE ARCHITECTURE

A structure for holding data with an associated address tag may take many forms, ranging from the flexible but complex fully associative memory, to the inflexible but simple direct mapped cache. Combinations of the two two-way and four-way set-associative memories attempt to compromise between them.

The fully associative cache is shown in diagrammatic form in Fig. 4.9. Each entry in the cache, or 'cache row', consists of a data item, its full address, and fields which indicate the validity and maybe use of the

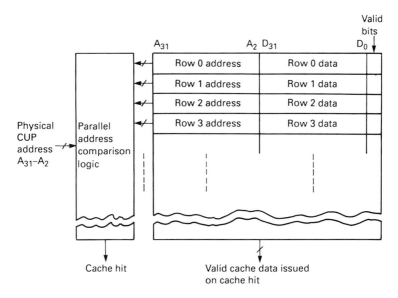

Fig. 4.9   Fully associative cache memory.

entry. A row can be written anywhere in the cache memory; conventional addressing concepts do not apply. When the CPU issues an address, the address field of every cache row must be simultaneously checked against it for a match. When data is written to the cache on a memory read following a cache miss, some algorithm is required which will select the cache entry to be replaced. Selecting the 'least recently used' cache entry for replacement is a commonly used strategy (the LRU algorithm). The high complexity of the fully associative cache will compromise the cache speed in a practical system.

The direct mapped cache is shown in Fig. 4.10. It consists of two conventional memories, the data memory and the address tag memory. The address signals to each memory are common, so that a single address selects corresponding locations in each memory; this address is derived simply by taking the lower bits from the address bus. If the data memory in the cache is 16K × 32 bits (64K), the low 14 bits (A2–A15) of the 80386 address bus would be used to locate a cache entry. To allow entries in the cache to be associated with any location in the 4 Gbyte 80386 address space, the upper bits of the CPU address (in this case A16–A31) are stored as the address tag in the cache tag memory location corresponding to the cache data memory location. For each entry in a 64K address space in main memory, the cache will have a unique location defined by the low address bits. There is no flexibility in locating data in a direct mapped cache – if a second data

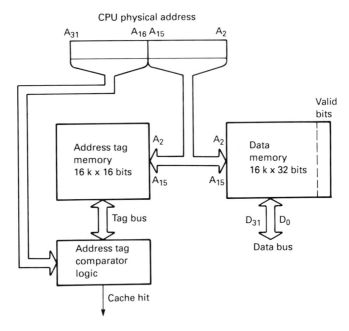

Fig. 4.10 Direct mapped cache.

item is read from main memory, at an address 64K away from an entry already in the cache, the cache entry will be overwritten. If this happens repeatedly 'cache thrashing' occurs, and the efficiency of the cache deteriorates. So long as code or data forms frequently used modules less than 64K in extent, cache replacement will occur only infrequently, and cache efficiency will not be impaired.

Increasingly, with very large programs becoming the norm, cache thrashing is a problem. Introducing just a little associativity into a direct mapped cache, to give a choice of locations for replacement, is usually worthwhile. A two-way set associative cache for the 80386 is shown in Fig. 4.11. Two banks of each memory and two address comparators are required. Cache control logic, typically a Programmable Logic Device (PLD) controls cache hit/miss signals and cache entry replacement.

As the 80386 has an on-chip MMU, and any caching is external to the chip, it is the physical addresses which are cached. Cache accesses are protected by the MMU in the same way as normal memory accesses. With a system with an external MMU, the MMU address translation could slow down cache accesses (typical external MMU chips take an extra clock cycle to perform address translation). With the 80386, the internal MMU translation may be pipelined to eliminate

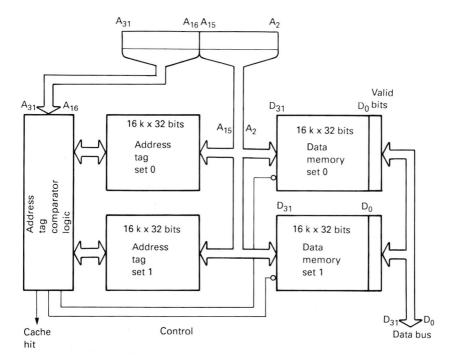

Fig. 4.11   Two-way set associative cache.

the effect of translation delay, and no speed penalty suffered.

To help with cache management, Intel has produced a monolithic cache controller for the 80386, the 82385. The 82385 operates in the full 32-bit physical address space of the 80386, can control a cache data memory of 8K × 32 bits, and can support either a direct mapped, or a two-way set associative organisation. It implements a 'posted write-through' (form of buffered write) policy to give effectively zero-wait-state writes. It will also protect the cache when it is operating in th presence of other bus masters and DMA. In such circumstances, it would be easy for the cache and main memory to lose coherency. This is detected by 'bus snooping' which invalidates a cache entry if it has detected a write to that location in main memory by another bus master.

4.5   Interfacing

An advanced processor like the 80386 can use those interface devices designed for its predecessors. Indeed, we have already seen that the 80386 interrupt acknowledge bus cycles have been specifically designed to maintain compatibility with the 8259A interrupt controller. Any of the devices designed for Intel's mainstream 8-bit and 16-bit processors can be used with the 80386, but it is inevitable that wait states will have to be inserted into the I/O bus cycles to allow for the relatively slow response times. There are a number of devices produced by Intel as 'high integration' interfaces with high functionality and speed commensurate with that of the 80386 bus. Examples are:

- 82830　　　　　　　　32-bit DMA controller with integrated system support peripherals
- 82786　　　　　　　　Graphics co-processor
- 80387　　　　　　　　Numeric co-processor
- 82335, 82230, 82231　PC-AT bus chip set
- 82350　　　　　　　　EISA chip set
- 82320　　　　　　　　Microchannel (MCA) chip set.

4.5.1　82830 32-bit DMA CONTROLLER

This DMA controller provides direct support for 16 MHz and 20 MHz 80386 CPUs. It has eight independently programmable DMA channels, capable of supporting transfer rates of 32 Mbytes/s (at 16 MHz) and 40 Mbytes/s (at 20 MHz). It can transfer any combination of bytes, 16-bit words, and 32-bit double words, and can perform assembly and disassembly of data using an internal DMAC register. DMA may be performed between memory locations, between I/O locations, and between memory and I/O locations. There are both chaining and auto-initialisation modes which reduce time overheads in DMA set up and execution.

As well as DMA, the 82830 supports interrupt control using an 8259A compatible structure. It has 15 external interrupt inputs and can generate a further five interrupts internally. Each interrupt can be independently set up with its own interrupt vector. By cascading 8259A controllers on to the external request inputs, a total of 120 external interrupt request inputs may be supported.

Four 16-bit programmable interval timers, compatible with the 82C54 PIT, share a common clock which may be independent of the system clock. Three of the timers have specific functions, whilst the fourth timer is a general purpose one.

A programmable wait state generator can be used to generate wait states in both CPU and DMA generated bus cycles (1–16 wait states in non-pipelined cycles, 0–15 wait states in pipelined cycles).

DRAM refresh support is also fitted onto the chip, with a 24-bit refresh address counter, and bus size programming for 8, 16 and 32 bits.

4.5.2 82786 GRAPHICS CONTROLLER

This device is designed to work with all Intel's microprocessors, but may be of particular use to 80386 systems. It integrates onto one chip and three modules (a display processor, a graphics processor and a bus interface unit which includes a video RAM controller). The display processor generates the serial video bit stream and CRT timing for a display resolution up to 2000 × 2000 × 8 bits. The graphics processor uses high level commands (read from a graphics control block in memory) and updates the bit-map memory used by the display processor. The command set supports a number of existing graphics standards, i.e. Graphics Kernel System (GKS), NAPLPS, Colour Graphics Interface (CGI) and Graphics Device Interface (GDI). It gives hardware support of windows. Typical performance of the 82786, executing graphics primitives, is given below.

- Line, polyline, polygon   2.5   Mpixels/s
- Circle, arc   2   Mpixels/s
- Character drawing   25K   characters/s
           (for 16 × 16 pixel characters)
- Bit block transfer (bitblt)   24   Mbits/s
- Fill (horizontal line fill)   30   Mbits/s

4.5.3 80387 NUMERIC CO-PROCESSOR

The 80387 implements ANSI/IEEE Standard 754-1985 for binary floating point arithmetic. It is compatible with its predecessors, the 8087 and 80287 and, like them, implements an internal 80-bit 'temporary real' format to guarantee accuracy of single precision and double precision IEEE standard results. It extends the 80386 instruction set to include arithmetic, trigonometric, logarithmic and exponential operations for a range of numeric data types. Internally, it operates from a register file of eight 80-bit registers which can be used as a stack, or as explicitly designated registers. Each register has an associated 2-bit tag field which allows the 80387 to distinguish which registers are being used.

The structure of the 80387 is shown in Fig. 4.12(a) and its connection to an 80386 CPU is shown in Fig. 4.12(b). It shares the bus with its parent 80386 and can operate with either pipelined or non-pipelined addressing. Instruction types supported are:

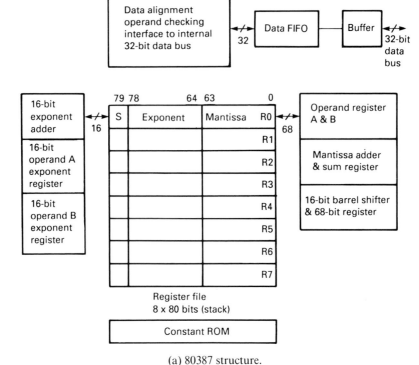

(a) 80387 structure.

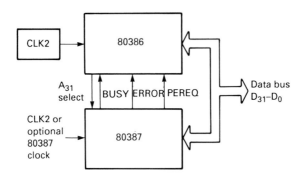

(b) 80386/80387 combination.

Fig. 4.12

- Data transfer: Load, store, exchange, store-&-pop
- Compare: Compare, compare-&-pop, compare-&-pop-twice, unordered compare.
- Constants: Load 0.0, 1.0, pi, log(base 2)10, log(base 2)e log(2), 1n(2).

- Arithmetic: Add, subtract, multiply, divide, absolute value, change sign, round, remainder and square root.
- Transcendental: Sine, cosine, partial trangent, partial arctangent, various log and exponent expressions.
- Processor control: Initialise, load & store control, status, environment, save and restore state, manipulate stack pointer, clear exceptions.

4.5.4   CHIP SETS

There are currently three sets of chips aimed at easing the job of designing the 80386DX and 80386SX into standard architecture and standard bus sytems.

The AT-compatible chip set consists of three chips which are intended for use with the 80386SX and 80387SX. The 82335 supports high-speed local memory, using page-mode DRAMs with up to four-way interleaving, and the 82230 and 82231 support interfacing to an AT expansion bus, running at up to 8 MHz.

The Extended Industry Standard Architecture (EISA) defines a PC-AT compatible bus, with 8-bit, 16-bit and 32-bit data transfers and 4 Gbyte address range on both memory and I/O. The bus is synchronous, with burst transfers at up to 33 Mbytes/s. Fast DMA is provided over the full address range with 8, 16 and 32-bit transfers; up to seven DMA channels with fixed or rotating arbitration, and with burst operation up to 33.3 Mbytes/s. Up to 14 bus masters are allowed, with centralised arbitration. The interrupt structure of EISA may have interrupts independently programmed for edge- or level-triggered operation, and cascaded interrupts to give a total of 15 bus interrupt levels.

EISA boards are arranged to be software-configurable, with a product identification mechanism, resources assigned at configuration time, and I/O addresses reserved for configuration information.

The 82350 EISA peripherals chip set consists of four chips which ease construction of an EISA-bus based system. The chips themselves are highly integrated, with multiple functions:

(1) 82358 EISA Bus Controller (EBC). Generates signals for a range of EISA bus cycles, supports 8–, 16–, and 32-bit DMA transfers, with byte assembly, disassembly for transfers, EISA refresh cycles. Interfaces to 16, 20, 25, 33 MHz 80386, and 25, 33 MHz 80486 processors, generates system resets, supports I/O recovery mechanisms and interface to the 8235 cache controller (80386 systems only).

(2) 82352 EISA Bus Buffers (EBB). Multiple address and data swap latch buffer/drivers with or without parity support.

(3) 82355 Bus Master Interface Controller (BMIC). Supports 32-bit address and data paths, and EISA burst transfers between bus master and bus main memory. Provides all necessary control, data, and address signals for an EISA master to interface to the EISA bus.

(4) 82357 Integrated System Peripheral (ISP). Provides DMA functions, i.e. seven independent channels, timing signal generation, bus arbitration and refresh address generation. In addition, five programmable 16-bit counter/timers, and logic for NMI generation and control are provided.

The 82311 micro channel compatible peripheral chip set does the same for Micro Channel Architecture (MCA) system designs. MCA allows for memory addressing in a 4 Gbyte or 16 Mbyte range (32 or 24 bits), and an I/O address range of 64K (16 bits). It allows up to eight DMA channels with 24-bit addressing, at a two cycle 'flow-through' transfer rate of 5 Mbytes/s. Single cycle, memory I/O 'fly-by' transfers are not permitted. To support multiple-processor operation, MCA has an 18-level pre-emptive priority scheme with central arbitration. Fifteen level-sensitive interrupt requests are provided, eight of them cascaded. Programmable Option Select (POS) allows card ID to be read during Power-on Self-test (POST) and cards to be configured by software.

The chip-set consists of:

(i) 82303 Local Channel Support Chip (LIO). This provides an integrated parallel port and card set-up port, peripheral bus address latches and supports system board set-up.

(ii) 82304 Local Channel Support Chip (LIO). Gives I/O peripheral support to the keyboard/mouse controller, Real Time Clock (RTC), the configuration RAM, serial and parallel ports, and local channel VGA controller.

(iii) 82307 DMA and MCA Arbiter (DMA/CACP). Supports eight channels of flow-through DMA, the bus Central Arbitration Control Point (CACP), refresh address generation and timing, and the numeric co-processor interface.

(iv) 82308 MCA Bus Controller (BC). Generates MCA bus control signals, supports parity, motherboard I/O, 82385 cache controller and bus data transfers.

(v) 82309 Address Bus Controller (ABC). Decodes motherboard address space and provides for shadow ROM BIOS, DRAM refresh, page mode and RAS/CAS generation.

A further device, the 82077 Floppy Disc Controller (FDC), provides a single chip, PC-AT and MCA compatible interface.

4.6 80386 programmer's model

The 80386 is a complex processor with many software support features. The instruction set is extensive with multi-function instructions and a variety of addressing modes which support access to data structures used by high level languages.

4.6.1 80386 REGISTER SET

The 'applications register set' is shown in Fig. 4.13(a). The eight general registers of the 80386 may be used as 32-bit registers, their low halves as 16-bit registers, and the low pairs of bytes of four of them as byte registers:

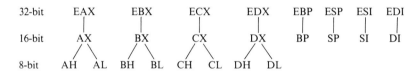

The register set is more general than the registers in the 8086 or 80286, but compatibility with these processors is maintained. The registers may all be used for address calculations, with one minor exception – the ESP (stack register) may be used as a base register but not as an index register. They may also be used to hold data operands, and may be specified freely for many arithmetic operations, although some arithmetic operations use dedicated registers (e.g. multiply and divide).

The 16-bit segment registers are used by the segmentation unit of the MMU to generate the linear addresses which may correspond with the physical addresses issued by the CPU, or which may be used by the paging unit of the MMU. Four of the segment registers, CS, SS, DS and ES correspond exactly with their counterparts in the 8086 and 80286; to improve flexibility, the set of 'data segment' registers (DS, ES in the 8086, 80286) has been expanded by the addition of two more registers, FS and GS. The total of four data segment registers makes for efficient access of different types of data structure and eases compiler construction.

Two additional registers complete the model: the 32-bit Instruction

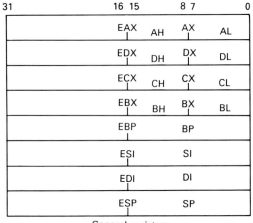

General registers

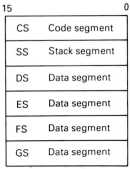

Segment registers

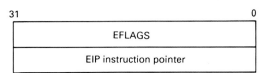

(a) Applications register set.

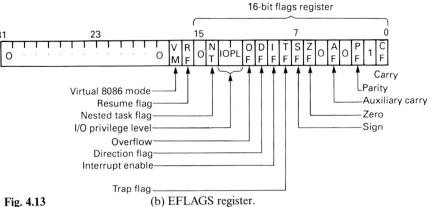

Fig. 4.13   (b) EFLAGS register.

Pointer, EIP, and the 32-bit Extended Flags register, EFLAGS. To maintain compatibility with the 8086 and 80286, the EIP may have only its low 16 bits used, and be referred to as IP. The EFLAGS register uses only some of its 32 bits for single-bit flags (see Fig. 4.13(b)); the status flags (Carry CF, Parity PF, Auxiliary Carry AF, Zero ZF, Sign SF, Trap TF and Overflow OF) are arranged in the low 16 bits of EFLAGS, together with Interrupt Enable IF, Direction DF, IO Privilege Level IOPL (2 bits) and Nested Task Flag NT. This block is called FLAGS and treated as a single entity. To allow easy compatibility with previous processors, there are a number of flag register manipulation instructions, i.e. LAHF, SAHF (load, store five status flags from/to AH), PUSHF, POPF (low 16-bits or FLAGS), PUSHFD and POPFD (32-bit EFLAGS).

4.6.2 ADDRESSING MODES

The general registers described in the previous section may be used to source data for effective address generation. The effective address is the offset into a segment, calculated by combining specified register contents, perhaps scaled, and any displacement directly specified in an instruction. Memory reference instructions usually use a byte field which follows the opcode in the instruction word, called mod R/M. Mod R/M specifies whether the addressed operand is in memory or a register. If it is in memory, the address is computed as an effective address, combined with the appropriate segment register contents.

Certain memory reference instructions use implied addressing modes which depart from this convention:

- Stack operations use implicit addressing via SS:ESP.
- String operations use DS:ESI (source index and data segment)
  ES:EDI (destination index and extra segment)
- Some short forms of MOV implicitly use EAX and an offset specified in the instruction.

Use of the mod R/M field allows specification of base, index and displacement components used to calculate an effective address; the components are optional – any may be specified as null. To allow for addressing data elements of varying size, 1, 2, 4, 8 bytes, a scale factor may be specified which is applied to the index value (the index component must be specified in this case). The overall address is calculated as:

Segment	+	Base	+	(Index	×	Scale)	+	Displacement
Code CS		Null		Null		1		None
Stack SS		EAX		EAX		2		8-bit
Data DS		EBX		EBX		4		16-bit
Extras ES		ECX		ECX		8		
Data FS		EDX		EDX				
Data GS		ESP		EBP				
		EBP		ESI				
		ESI		EDI				
		EDI						

Various address components are used to support different data objects (see Table 4.1).

Table 4.1   Data objects to be accessed and address components to be used

Data object to be accessed	Address components to be used
Statically allocated scalar operand, beginning of static array	Displacement alone
Indirect address	Base alone
Index into static byte array, access item of record	Base + Displacement
Index into static array of elements of size 2, 4, 8 bytes	(Index × Scale) + Displacement
Two-dimensional byte array, array of records	Base + Index + Displacement
Two-dimensional array of elements of size 2, 4, 8 bytes	Base + (Index × Scale) + Displacement

Associated with addressing issues, the 80386 possesses a BOUND instruction which verifies that the signed value in a specified register lies between two signed limit values (upper bound and lower bound), occupies adjacent memory locations and is specified by an effective relative address. Whilst the BOUND instruction cannot check the final computed effective address of an operand, it can be used to check offset addresses from the start of an array or record.

4.6.3   DATA TYPES

The operand addressing modes described in the previous section, which use register index values, allow a size of operand to be specified by a scale factor of 1, 2, 4 and 8 bytes. The 80386 supports a number of different data types which fit these sizes. Types are:

- Byte integer: 8-bit, 2's complement
- Word integer: 16-bit, 2's complement
- Doubleword integer: 32-bit, 2's complement
- Byte ordinal: 8-bit, unsigned
- Word ordinal: 16-bit, unsigned
- Doubleword ordinal: 32-bit, unsigned
- Bit field: up to 32 bits
- Near pointer: 32-bit logical address; offset within segment
- Far pointer: 48-bit logical address; 16-bit segment address, 32-bit offset value
- String: Continuous sequence of characters (bytes), words and doublewords; up to 4 Gbytes
- Bit string: Contiguous sequence of up to 4 Gbits
- Binary Coded Decimal (BCD): A single decimal digit in the range 0 to 9, coded in the low 4 bits of a byte.
- Packed BCD: Two decimal (0 to 9) digits in one byte.

No word or doubleword alignment with memory addresses is needed; if, however, a data element is misaligned, more than one bus cycle is needed to access the complete operand, and the memory reference instruction invoking the access executes more slowly than if it had been aligned.

4.6.4 APPLICATION INSTRUCTION SET

The application instruction set consists of those instructions which may be used by the programmer when writing application software to run on the 80386 in Protected Virtual Address mode. They may be grouped into categories:

(1) Data Movement:	MOVe	Register <--> memory
		Register <--> register
		Immediate data --> register
		Immediate data --> memory
		(No memory <--> memory or segment register <--> segment register)
	XCHG	Exchange two register operands or a register operand with a memory operand. Bus LOCK asserted automatically when used with a memory operand
(2) Stack:	PUSH	Memory, immediate, register operands on stack addressed by ESP

	PUSHA	Push all (eight) general purpose registers onto the stack addressed by ESP. Includes the old (initial) value of ESP
	POP	From stack
	POPA	From stack; does not restore ESP to its old value

(3) Conversion:	CWD	Convert word in AX to doubleword in DX:AX
	CDQ	Convert doubleword in EAX to quadword in EDX:EAX
	CBW	Convert byte in AL to word in AX
	CWDE	Convert word in AX to doubleword in EAX
	MOVSX	Move with sign extension 8 bit --> 16, 16 bit --> 32
	MOVZX	As MOVSX, but with zero extension

(4) Arithmetic:	ADD	Integer add
	ADC	Add with carry
	SUB	Integere subtract
	SBB	Subtract with borrow
	INC	Increment (by 1)
	DEC	Decrement (by 1)
	CMP	Compare
	NEG	Negate (reverse sign of operand)
	MUL	Unsigned integer multiply:

$$8\text{-bit source} \times AL \quad --> SX$$
$$16\text{-bit source} \times AX \quad --> DX:AX$$
$$32\text{-bit source} \times EAX --> EDX:EAX$$

| | IMUL | Signed integer multiply |
| | DIV | Unsigned integer divide: |

$$16\text{-bit } AX / 8\text{-bit source} \qquad --> AL$$
$$\text{remainder} --> AH$$
$$32\text{-bit } DX:AX / 16\text{-bit source} \quad --> AX$$
$$\text{remainder} --> DX$$
$$64\text{-bit } EDX:EAX / 32\text{-bit source} --> EAX$$
$$\text{remainder} --> EDX$$

	IDIV	Signed integer divide
	DAA	Decimal adjust after addition of two pairs of BCD operands in AL
	DAS	Decimal adjust after subtraction
	AAA	ASCII adjust after addition (in AL)
	AAS	ASCII adjust after subtraction (in AL)
	AAM	ASCII adjust after multiplication (in AH, AL)
	AAD	ASCII adjust before division

(5) Logical:	AND	Two register operands, register operand
	OR	with memory operand, or immediate
	XOR	operand with either register or memory operand
	NOT	Invert bits in operand

	BT	Bit test
	BTS	Bit test and set
	BTR	Bit test and reset
	BTC	Bit test and complement
	BSF	Bit scan forward (lsb to msb), 16 or 32-bit operand for a '1' bit and store the index of the first bit set in a register
	BSR	Bit scan reverse (msb to lsb)
(6) Shifts and Rotates:	SAL	Shift arithmetic left: byte, word, doubleword by specified number of places
	SHL	Shift logical left (as SAR)
	SAR	Shift arithmetic right (signed)
	SHR	Shift logical right
	SHLD	Shift left double
	SHRD	Shift right double
	ROL	Rotate left
	RCL	Rotate left through carry
	ROR	Rotate right
	RCR	Rotate right through carry
(7) Conditional:	SET	byte on condition:: 1 if true, 0 if false
	TEST	Logical AND two operands, set flags, but no result returned
	JMP	Unconditional jump:
		Direct near – relative to EIP, signed displacement in instruction
		Indirect near – absolute address from register, memory
		Indirect far – indirect via far pointer
	Jc	Jump on condition, relative to EIP
	LOOP	whilst ECX nonzero
		Decrements ECX before test
	LOOPE	As LOOPZ, loop while zero
	LOOPNE	As LOOPNZ, loop while non-zero
	JCXZ	Jump if ECX zero
	INT n	Software interrupt
	INTO	Interrupt on overflow (INT 4)
(8) String Handling:	MOVSB	Move string byte (pointed by ESI to the location pointed by EDI)
	MOVSW	Move string word
	MOVSD	Move string doubleword
	CMPSB	Compare string bytes
	CMPSW	Compare string words
	CMPSD	Compare string doublewords
	SCASB	Scan a string byte (for value in AL)
	SCASW	Scan a string word (for value in AX)
	SCASD	Scan a string doubleword (for value in EAX)
	LODSB	Load string byte into AL
	LODSW	Load string word into AX

LODSD	Load string doubleword into EAX
STOSB	Store string byte (from AL)
STOSW	Store string word (from AX)
STOSD	Store string doubleword (from EAX)
XLAT	Translate in place in AL (byte operands only)

The string instructions are all primitives which need the addition of a repeat prefix and a direction flag value to make them work for multi-byte, word, or doubleword strings.

- Repeat Prefix:

REP	Repeat while ECS non-zero
REPE	Repeat while equal
REPZ	Repeat while zero
REPNE	Repeat while not equal
REPNZ	Repeat while non-zero

- Direction Set:

CLD	Clear direction flag (DF)
SLD	Set direction flag (DF)

The repeat prefix specifies that the string primitive must be repeated using the source and destination index registers, and that the source and destination registers must be automatically decremented (DF = 1) or incremented (DF = 0). ECX may be used as a count register (string length)

(9) Subroutines and Procedures:

CALL	Procedure (address in general register or memory)
RET	Return from procedure
IRET	Return from interrupt
CALL	Pushes both CS and EIP on the stack (far call)
RET	Restores CS:EIP (far return)
ENTER	Procedure and create stack frame
LEAVE	Procedure and discard stack frame

(10) Co-processor:

ESC	Prefix for co-processor instructions which signals to the main CPU that the instruction which follows is destined for the co-processor
WAIT	For co-processor operation completion

(11) Segmentation:

MOVe	Segment register
PUSH	Segment register
POP	Segment register

(12) Pointers:

LDS	Load pointer from a memory operand into specified general register, with segment selector loaded into DS
LES	As LDS, except segment selector loaded into ES
LFS	As LDS, except segment selector loaded into FS

LGS	As LDS, except segment selector loaded into GS
LSS	As LDS, except segment selector loaded into SS. Allows change of SS:ESP in one uninterrupted instruction
LEA	Load effective address from memory to general register

An application instruction which does not fit into the above categories is NOP (No Operation). The application instruction set assumes that applications will be written to run in a protected, virtual memory environment. In addition to the application set, the 80386 possesses a set of privileged instructions (which affect system data structures and can only be run by the highest priority procedures) and 'sensitive' instructions, such as I/O (which possess a priority of their own, IOPL).

4.6.5 OTHER FEATURES

Other features of the 80386 programming model include the facilities for memory management and protection, interrupts, and I/O. These are of sufficient complexity to warrant separate sections of their own.

4.7 Memory management

The 80386 offers the software engineer a selection of memory management models: 'flat' addressing, segmented addressing, and paged addressing (actually a combination of segmentation and paging). The segmentation unit and the paging unit provide the necessary support to implement these schemes.

The logical address generated by the CPU takes the form of a 32-bit offset address, and a 16-bit 'selector', held in the appropriate segment register. The segmentation unit translates this to a 'linear address', which may be used as the physical address if the paging unit is turned off. If the paging unit is turned on, the linear address is translated using a paging model to give the physical address for the memory. At each stage, checks can be performed by the MMU hardware for segment and page validity.

4.7.1 LOGICAL-TO-LINEAR ADDRESS MAPPING

The mechanism for logical-to-linear address mapping is shown in Fig. 4.14(a). The 16-bit selector value, held in one of the segment registers, has its upper 12 bits used as the index into one of two segment

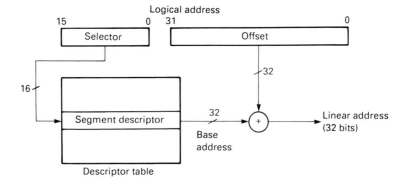

(a) Logical-to-linear address mapping.

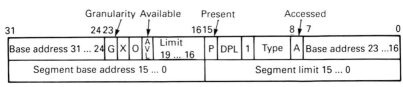

Applications code and data segment descriptor

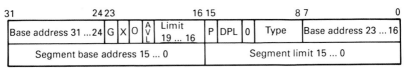

System segment descriptor

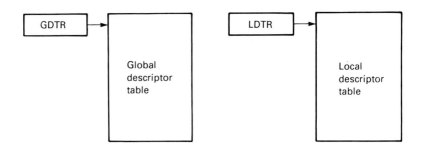

(b) Segment descriptors.

Fig. 4.14

descriptor tables. The two descriptor tables each hold 4096 segment descriptors of 8 bytes each (Fig. 4.14(b)). The Global Descriptor Table (GDT) holds segment descriptors which are available to all tasks in the system. The Local Descriptor Table (LDT) may specify segment descriptors which are local to a particular task, and may be changed when tasks are swapped. Two pointer registers (GDTR, LDTR) hold the base addresses for their respective tables. Bit 3 of a selector indicates which table is to be used. The remaining bits of the selector indicate the requested privilege level, and are used by the protection mechanism built into the CPU.

The 8 bytes of each segment descriptor contain the following information:

- The segment base address (32 bits).
- The segment limit (20 bits), which is interpreted in conjunction with the segment granularity bit.
- Segment granularity bit, G. If G is clear, the 20-bit limit field specifies the segment size in bytes (up to 1 Mbyte). If G is set, the limit field specifies the segment size in units of 4K (up to 4 Gbytes).
- The Descriptor Privilege Level (DPL), 2 bits, used by the CPU protection system.
- A 4-bit type field, which identifies segment attributes for data and code segments, and the specific type of segment, for system segments.
- Segment present, and available bits.

The segment type field for a data segment contains bits which indicate how its limit should be interpreted, whether it is writable or not, and whether it has been accessed.

In an executable (code) segment, the same type field descriptor is used to indicate whether the segment is conforming (adopts a privilege level the same as the current CPU level) or not, whether the segment is readable, and whether it has been accessed.

In a system segment, the segment type field indicates whether the segment is one of a number of types which are appropriate to task, call and interrupt handling. Segments may be identified as available and busy Task State Segments (TSS), interrupt, trap and call gates, compatible with either the 80286 or the 80386.

The segment registers are not totally visible to the programmer. As well as a 16-bit visible selector field, each segment has an 'invisible descriptor' field, inaccessible to the programmer. When the visible part of a segment register is loaded with a selector value, the CPU automatically loads the invisible descriptor part of the register from the relevant segment descriptor table. The contents of the base address field are taken from the invisible descriptor and added to the offset part of the logical address, to form the linear address, whenever the CPU issues a logical address using a selector in one of the segment registers. No time overhead is incurred in generating the linear address.

Using just the linear address, the 80326 can adopt a 'flat' address architecture, by loading the segment registers with selectors which point to descriptors which encompass the whole 32-bit address space. These selectors need never be changed during subsequent operation.

4.7.2   PAGING UNIT

80386 paging is based around 4K pages; the 32-bit linear address space potentially contains rather more than 1 million pages, aligned to 4K address boundaries. Paging is controlled using the three 80386 control registers, CR0, CR2 and CR3, shown in Figure 4.15. (CR1 is currently 'reserved' by Intel, and not used in the 80386). CR0 contains single-bit command flags, used not only for paging, but also for co-processor control, protection and task control.

The bits used by the 80386 are:

- EM, ET: Indicate presence or absence, and type, of co-processor
- MP   : Controls WAIT (for co-processor) instruction
- PE   : Protection Enable
- PG   : Set to invoke paging, otherwise the linear address is used as a physical address
- TS   : Task Switched flag

CR2 is used to store the linear address of the instruction which caused a page fault. CR3 is the Page Directory Base Register (PDBR),

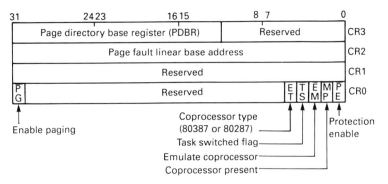

Fig. 4.15   80386 control registers.

which points to the page table directory for the current task (physical address).

The page directory occupies a single page of 4K and contains up to 1024 entries, each of which points to a page table. Each page table is itself a page of 4K, and contains up to 1024 page specifier (32-bit) entries. The 32-bit linear address generated by the segmentation unit is interpreted as shown in Fig. 4.16(a), split into three fields: the Directory table index (DIR), Page table index (PAGE) and Offset into the page (OFFSET). Both the directory table and the page table have 32-bit entries of the same format (Fig. 4.16(b)). The upper 20 bits of each entry are used as the page frame address which identifies the 4K

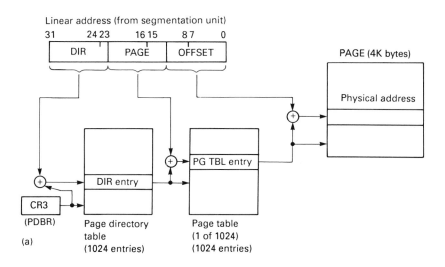

(a) Translation of linear address by paging unit.

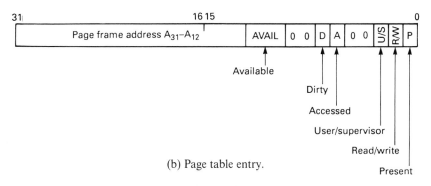

(b) Page table entry.

Fig. 4.16

page address boundary. Bits in the lower part of the entry denote the page attributes: P (present), R/W (read/write), U/S (user/supervisor), A (accessed), D (dirty (page written to by CPU without the page image on disk being written to update it)). P, A and D are used to implement virtual memory; R/W, U/S are used for protection. These attributes are checked automatically when a page is first referenced.

To speed up address translation, by avoiding multiple table accesses every time a linear address is issued, a 32-entry page translation cache (or Translation Look-aside Buffer (TLB)), is included as part of the paging unit. When a linear address is issued, and paging is enabled, if the translation cache generates a cache hit, the page frame address is acquired directly from the cache, and no time penalty is incurred in generating the corresponding physical address. On a cache miss, the tables in memory must be accessed to acquire the page frame address, and the page translation cache is updated at the same time.

Using paging, virtual memory may be implemented; the 'A' (Accessed) bit of the page descriptor can be used to support a 'Least Recently Used' (LRU) style of page-swap strategy; the 'D' (Dirty) bit can be used to control page write-back to disk. If a page is not available in memory at the time of attempted access, a 'page fault' will be generated by the paging unit. Action of the 80386 on a page fault is to generate a 'special' interrupt, INT14. This exception automatically places an error code on the stack which gives some details of the circumstances of the exception – whether it was caused by an attempt to access a non-resident page, or by an access rights violation, whether the CPU was in user or supervisor mode at the time, and whether the attempted access was a read or write. The linear address of the attempted access which caused the page fault is stored in CR2.

When a page fault occurs, an entry is made to the operating system of the processor running at the most privileged level; the page is located on disk, and swapped with one of the pages currently resident in memory. Upon a return from the operating system to the instruction which caused the page fault, that instruction is re-executed.

4.7.3   PAGED ARCHITECTURES

Using the paging unit in conjunction with the segmentation unit, a number of paged address schemes are possible.

When a segment is larger than the 4K extent of a page, it is divided into a number of pages, and virtual memory may be implemented in a manner invisible to the programmer.

When segments are smaller than the page size, they may be allocated one page per segment or, more economically, segments which share the same access rights and attributes may be clustered in a single page.

A simple management strategy can be adopted if each segment descriptor is allocated its own page directory entry. Since the Local Descriptor Table (LDT) may be changed with each task, each task may use up to 1024 segments (as many entries as are in the page directory). Each segment descriptor, page directory entry and page table may be manipulated together by the operating system.

Although there is no restriction on the relative placement of segments and pages, the memory allocation function of the operating system will be made easier if segments are allocated only in integral units of one page, and if page and segment boundaries are aligned.

4.8   Operating system considerations

To support operating system functions, particularly for real time systems, the 80386 provides protection and privilege levels, and task and task-switching support. The 80386 differs from many of its competitors in supporting four privilege levels, rather than simply user and system modes. The protection model of the system is shown in Fig. 4.17. The highest privilege level, level 0, is reserved for the operating system kernel and the lowest privilege level, level 3, is the applications

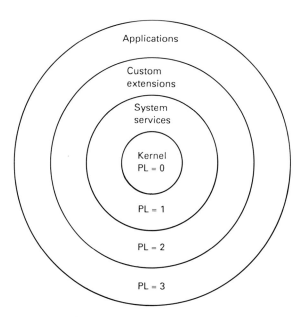

Fig. 4.17   80386 privilege levels.

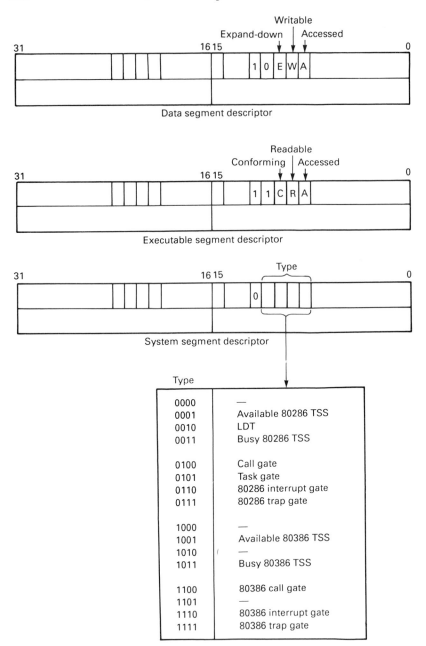

Fig. 4.18 Segment descriptor types.

code level. In between, level 1 is intended for system services, and level 2 for custom extensions. If a simple two-level system is used (levels 0 and 3), the CPU behaves as though it has system and user modes. Segment descriptors carry privilege level and other protection information.

The three segment descriptor types are shown in Fig. 4.18. Their protection fields differ, although some attributes are shared. The protection bits, and their use with segment type, are detailed below in Table 4.2.

Table 4.2 Protection bits and their use with segment type

	Protection field	Data segment	Executable segment	System segment
A	= Accessed	*	*	
AVL	= Available	*	*	*
B	= Big	*		
C	= Conforming to CPU privilege level		*	
D	= Default		*	
DPL	= Descriptor Privilege Level	*	*	*
E	= Expand Down	*		
G	= Granularity	*	*	*
P	= Present	*	*	*
R	= Readable		*	
W	= Writable	*		

The B, E and G bits control the way in which the segment size is checked. The A and P bits may be used by memory management. C and DPL control privilege. The segment descriptor fields are used for segment type and limit checking, for restricting the addressable domain, for controlling access to procedure entry points, and for restriction of the CPU instruction set. Instructions may be unprivileged (the application set), 'sensitive' to privilege (I/O instructions) and 'privileged', or operating system only (privilege level 0). The privileged instructions are those which can be used to critically alter the CPU status and which must be used by only the most trusted code. Such instructions include LGDT, LIDT, LLDT (Load Descriptor Table register), LTR (Load Task Register), LMSW (Load Machine Status Word), HLT (Halt CPU), CLTS (Clear Task Switched flag) and MOVe to or from a control, debug or test register.

Protection is invoked at both segment and page translation levels, before a memory cycle has started; any violation causes an exception.

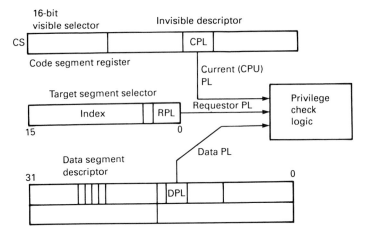

Fig. 4.19   Data segment privilege checking.

4.8.1   DATA SEGMENTS

The data segment registers DS, ES, FS, GS and SS have accesses checked for privilege as shown in Fig. 4.19. The hidden part of the code segment register contains a two-bit field which is set to reflect the Current Privilege Level (CPL); when a target segment selector is loaded, it has its own Requestor Privilege Legel (RPL), and when a linear address is acquired via the segment descriptor table, the data segment descriptor too has a Descriptor Privilege Level (DPL).

Interpretation of the privilege levels is as follows: an instruction attempting to access a data segment, running at a CPL, and with a target segment selector RPL, may only do so if the DPL of the segment is numerically greater than or equal to the maximum of CPL and RPL. Since privilege levels run in reverse numerical order, this means that the DPL must be lower than or equal to either the current privilege level or RPL. A program can only access data of the same or a lower privilege level.

4.8.2   EXECUTABLE SEGMENTS

Code segments can be protected in a similar way. To enter a code segment requires a control transfer, which may be accomplished using instructions JMP, CALL and RET, or by exceptional conditions INT and IRET. If a JMP, CALL or RET is of the 'near form' (within the same code segment), the only protection applied is the segment limits check.

If a JMP, CALL or RET is of the 'far form' (between segments), there are two ways of implementing the transfer – the direct way, where the descriptor of another executable segment is selected, and the gated way, where a call gate descriptor is selected. With a direct transfer, the privilege checks require that CPL is equal to the target segment DPL, or that the target segment is a conforming one, and DPL of the target is less than or equal to CPL. (Conforming code segments adopt the privilege level of the CPU, and allow shared code to be called from

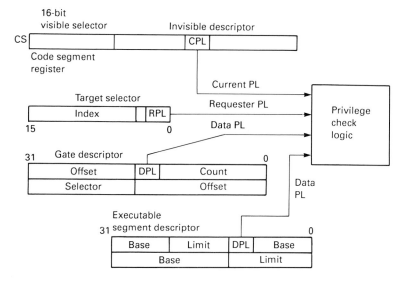

Call gate privilege check

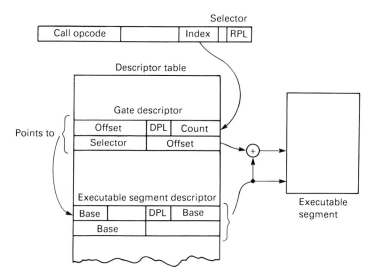

Fig. 4.20 Call gate operation.

different privilege levels, but to run at the privilege level of the calling program.)

Normally, to allow protection for control transfers between segments at different privilege levels, the gate descriptor method is used. There are four types of gate descriptor, covering call gates, trap gates, interrupt gates and task gates. A call gate, used by JMP and CALL, defines the entry point of the target code using <selector value>:<offset value>, and the associated gate privilege level. The operation of a call gate is shown in Fig. 4.20. Four privilege levels are checked: CPL, RPL, DPL of gate descriptor, and DPL of target executable segment selector.

For a JMP instruction to a non-conforming segment, the gate privilege (DPL) must be lower than or equal to the lower privilege level of CPL and RPL, and the target segment DPL must be equal to CPL.

For a CALL instruction, or a JMP to a conforming segment, the gate privilege must be lower than or equal to the lower privilege level of CPL and RPL, and the target segment DPL must be at a higher than or equal privilege level to CPL.

To allow easy system management, the 80386 supports a separate stack for each privilege level. A data structure called the Task State Segment (TSS) is used to provide initial stack pointer values for stacks which exist at privilege levels 0, 1 and 2. When an inter-privilege level call is made, the new stack is checked for size. If it is large enough, the old SS:ESP are pushed onto the new stack, a number of parameters (doublewords) specified by the 'count' field of the call gate descriptor are copied onto the stack and, finally, a return address (old CS:EIP) is pushed onto the stack.

A 'far' (inter-segment) return, RET, from a procedure can change privilege levels, but only by lowering privilege.

4.8.3   MULTI-TASKING

To support multi-tasking, the 80386 does not use special instructions, but uses the normal control transfer instructions, with the CPU Task Register (TR), Task State Segments (TSSs), TSS descriptors, and task gate descriptors. The TSS format is shown in Fig. 4.21. It takes the form of a data structure with a dynamic set of fields used to store the task environment: general registers, segment registers, flag register, instruction pointer and previous TSS selector (to allow return). It also has a static set of fields which are read-only parameters; the task LDT selector, the Page Directory Base Register (PDBR), pointers to stacks for operation at different privilege levels, a debug trap bit (for trap on

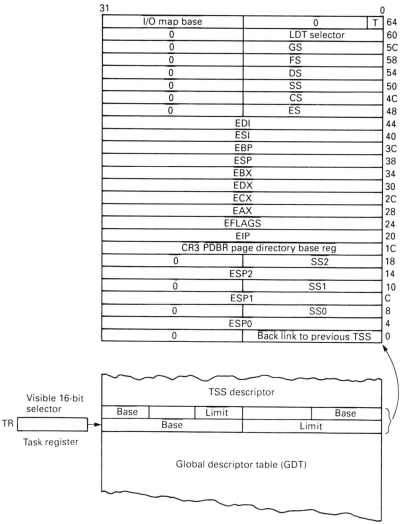

Fig. 4.21 Task state segment.

task switch) and the base for the I/O permission bit map base.

The TSS descriptor, which can only be held in the Global Descriptor Table (GDT), points to the TSS; a selector in the TR (manipulated by instructions LTR, STR) is used to index the GDT, and the base address and limit fields of the TSS descriptor are loaded into the invisible part of TR.

The task gate provides an indirect, protected reference to the TSS and contains merely a selector value (for TSS descriptor) and DPL. Task gates may be held in the LDT, or for tasks invoked by interrupts, in the Interrupt Descriptor Table (IDT).

A task switch can be invoked by a current task JMP or CALL using the TSS descriptor, or using the task gate, by an interrupt or exception which vectors to a task gate in the IDT, or by an IRET in the current task, when the CPU 'nested task' flag is set. The sequence of operations involved in a task switch is as follows:

- Check validity of the task switch (no privilege violation)
- Check that TSS descriptor of the new task indicates that it is present and that it has a valid limit
- Save the state of the current task in the current TSS
- Load TR with the selector of the new task TSS descriptor; mark TSS descriptor as 'busy', and set the 'task switched' bit of the CPU Machine Status Word (MSW)
- Load incoming task state from TSS and commence execution

4.8.4 V86 MODE

To allow 8086 code to run as a task under protected mode of the 80386, a special mode is provided. Features of this mode are provision of a virtual set of registers via the TSS, a virtual memory space of 1 Mbyte and external interface control. A flag in EFLAGS (VM) is set when this mode is required. The flag is tested when segment registers are loaded, to allow for 8086-style linear address formation.

V86 mode is entered via a task switch or IRET, and is left by an interrupt or exception which causes a task switch or entry to the operating system.

4.9 Interrupts and exceptions

Intel defines exceptions as internal events, and interrupts as external, asynchronous events. The 80386 characterises its exceptional conditions as:

- Processor-detected faults, traps and aborts
- Programmed (software interrupts)
- External interrupts (non-maskable and maskable)

The processor-detected exceptions and non-maskable interrupts have higher priority than the external maskable interrupts.

4.9.1 PROCESSOR-DETECTED EXCEPTIONS

Faults are detected during instruction execution and an exception is raised with the processor restored to a condition that allows the instruction to be restarted. The segment values CS:EIP stored on the stack point to the instruction which caused the fault. Traps are exceptions which are generated after an instruction; the segment values CS:EIP stored on the stack point to the instruction following the instruction which generated the trap, taking into account any jump target addresses. Aborts are much more severe, and do not allow a return to the program which caused the abort. Typically, an abort condition is caused by a double-fault, a co-processor segment overrun, and certain protection violations.

The processor-detected exceptions, in priority order (lowest interrupt number corresponds to highest priority) are given in Table 4.3

Table 4.3 Processor-detected exceptions (in priority order)

Interrupt number	Description
0	Divide error fault (DIV, IDIV instructions)
1	Debug exceptions – use debugging register DR6, DR7 conditions – single-step trap – instruction-address breakpoint – data-address breakpoint – task switch breakpoint
3	Breakpoint trap (invoked by instruction INT3)
4	Overflow trap (enabled by INTO instruction)
5	Bounds check fault (invoked by BOUND)
6	Invalid opcode fault
7	Co-processor not available fault (invoked by use of ESC prefix or WAIT instruction)
8	Double-fault abort
9	Co-processor segment overrun abort (ESC-prefixed instruction which overlaps the end of a segment)
10	Invalid ISS fault (invoked by JMP, CALL, IRET, interrupt)
11	Segment not present fault (invoked by any instruction which modifies the contents of a segment register)
12	Stack exception fault (invoked by any stack instruction)
13	General protection fault or abort (invoked by any memory reference)
14	Page fault (invoked by any memory reference)
16	Co-processor error fault (invoked by ESC-prefixed instruction or WAIT)

4.9.2 SOFTWARE INTERRUPTS

Software interrupts are traps, invoked by a two-byte instruction of the form INT n, where n is an integer in the range 0 to 255.

4.9.3   EXTERNAL INTERRUPTS

External interrupts are vectored, using a vector supplied by the interrupting device when it detects an interrupt acknowledge bus cycle. All interrupts and exceptions are handled using an Interrupt Descriptor Table (IDT), pointed by an internal CPU IDT register (16-bit IDT limit parameter, 32-bit IDT base address). The interrupt number (vector) is used to index this table and locate the relevant entry or IDT descriptor. The IDT descriptor contains a 16-bit selector value which can be used to locate a segment descriptor in the LDT or GDT. For an interrupt or trap, the segment descriptor will point to the linear base address of an executable segment; the offset value of the IDT descriptor will locate the code entry point in the segment. Fig. 4.22 illustrates the way in which a linear address is produced.

Two CPU inputs are provided for external interrupt signals. One input is specifically for Non-maskable Interrupts (NMI) which are fixed at interrupt number 2 in the IDT. The general interrupt input, INTR, is used for vectored, maskable interrupts in the range INT32 to INT255. (Whilst the current set of exceptions only occupy numbers INT0 to INT16, the remaining interrupt numbers INT17 to INT31 are reserved for future expansion.)

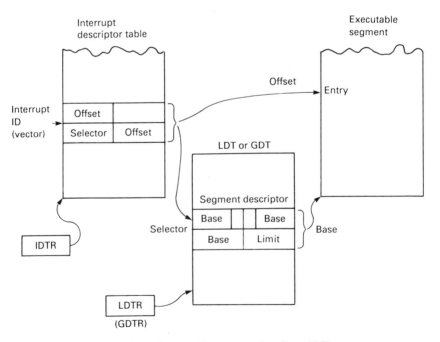

Fig. 4.22   Linear address generation from IDT.

Maskable interrupts may be controlled by the processor Interrupt Flag (IF) and associated instructions CLI (clear IF) and STI (set IF). These instructions can critically affect the state of the CPU and are considered privileged. The IDT registers may be manipulated with LIDT (load linear limit: base address) and SIDT (store).

4.10   Input/output

Input/output (I/O) on the 80386 may either use a separate I/O space, and specific I/O instructions, or may be memory-mapped and enjoy protection via the MMU.

4.10.1   SEPARATE INPUT/OUTPUT

The I/O address space uses 16-bit port addressing with port data widths of 8, 16 or 32 bits. Addresses may be sourced as 8-bit immediate operands, addressing just a fraction of I/O address space, or as full 16-bit addresses via register DX. The style of addressing is given in Table 4.4.

Table 4.4   Style of addressing

Field size	*8-bit ports*	*16-bit ports*	*32-bit ports*
Immediate (8-bit)	0, 1, . . . 255	0, 2, 4, . . . 254	0, 4, 8, . . . 252
Via DX (16-bit)	0, 1, . . . 65535	0, 2, 4, . . . 65534	0, 4, 8, . . . 65532

For port access in a single bus cycle, 16-bit and 32-bit ports should be aligned to even addresses, and to addresses evenly divisible by 4, respectively.

'Sensitive' I/O instructions are IN, OUT and INS, OUTS (string).

In 80386 protected mode, and in V86 mode, protection may be applied to I/O operations in two ways:

(1) The IOPL field in EFLAGS defines the privilege level to use I/O-related instructions. (CPL must be <= IOPL.)

(2) An I/O permission bit-map may be held in the TSS which defines which ports in I/O space may be used. Each bit in the field corresponds to an I/O port byte address; since many applications will only use a small part of the I/O space, a 'map limit' parameter allows only the useful part of the I/O bit map to be included in the TSS.

4.10.2   MEMORY-MAPPED I/O

Memory-mapped I/O allows the use of general purpose operand manipulation instructions. The only constraints are that the I/O device should behave like a memory location if, for example, bit manipulation instructions are used. Access protection is available in the same way as for memory.

4.10.3   CO-PROCESSOR AND MULTIPROCESSOR INTERFACE FEATURES

The 80386 is designed to support a numeric co-processor such as the 80387 or its predecessor, the 80287. In the CPU control register CR0, bits are provided for this support, i.e. ET defines the type of co-processor in the system (80287/387); EM is the emulation flag which traps co-processor instructions (Exception 7) to allow software emulation of co-processor functions; MP monitors the co-processor; TS, the task switched flag, allows detection of a CPU task switch which has occurred during a WAIT (for co-processor) instruction.

The co-processor-specific part of the 80386 instruction set consists of the ESC prefix which identifies co-processor instructions and the WAIT instruction (while the co-processor is busy).

For general multiple-processor, shared bus systems, the LOCK prefix allows certain instructions to exclude any pre-emption of the bus during the instruction cycle, for example, manipulating resource-control semaphores in shared memory.

4.11 Debugging

A complex processor like the 80386, designed as a real time, multi-tasking system, would make life very difficult for the system software developer if it did not have hardware support for debugging code. The debug features of the 80386 provide facilities at the machine code level which can be used with sophisticated software debugging tools to provide a realistic development environment.

Associated with the CPU and its memory management functions are a total of eight debug registers, of which six are used (see Fig. 4.23). Registers BP0 to BP3 allow linear addresses to be specified which can be monitored by the CPU. The debug control and debug status registers, DR7 and DR6, are used in conjunction with these linear address registers to qualify the breakpoints and to specify data sizes. Using them, a debug exception (INT1) may be invoked on execution of an instruction at a given address, read or write of data as a byte, word

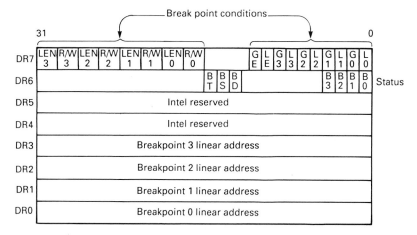

Fig. 4.23 Debug registers.

or doubleword at a given address, or data writes only at a given address.

A debug instruction may be placed in code, as a software interrupt INT3; the T-bit (trap) may be set in a task's TASS to invoke debugger software upon a task switch to a specific task. The single-step trap flag, TF, in EFLAGS, may be used to cause a break to the debug software at every instruction execution.

Some self-test features are also built in to the CPU to test the translation unit cache (TLB) used in paging. The TLB is a four-way, set-associative memory, which may be tested using the test command register, TR6, and data register, TR7. Using the registers together, individual blocks of the TLB may be written with test data, and the address translation functions checked against known data.

4.12 The 80486

The 80486 represents an evolutionary development of the 80386 architecture. It consists of an 80386 core, with complete binary compatibility with the 80386, and a compatible MMU. In addition, the 80486 possesses the following features:

(1) An on-chip Floating Point Unit (FPU) compatible with the 80387 co-processor
(2) An on-chip cache memory, for data and code, of 8K, with support for a second-level, external cache, and with consistency checking
(3) A bus interface unit which supports burst-mode bus transfers at up to 106 Mbytes/s.

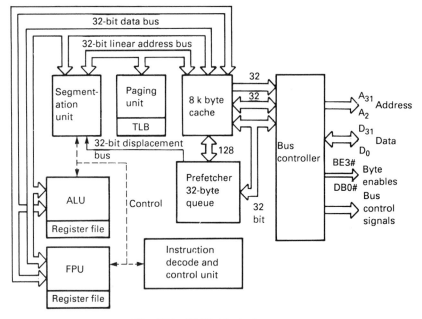

Fig. 4.24   80486 block diagram.

Following RISC practice, the most frequently used instructions are designed to execute in one clock cycle, ensuring a performance well in excess of that of the fastest 80386.

The 80486 is packaged in a large 168-pin ceramic Pin Grid Array (PGA) package and is available with clock speeds of 25 and 33 MHz. A block diagram of the device is shown in Fig. 4.24. Parity checking is provided on the component level data bus of the CPU – one bit per data byte, with the result of parity checks signalled on a pin PCHK#. Other additional signals are PLOCK# (pseudo-lock) which indicates a multi-bus cycle instruction execution, bus burst-transfer control signals, cache control signals and FPU error reporting signals. Unlike the 80386 CLK2 signal, the clock input to the 80486 is the same frequency as the internal clock rate. Internally, some of the data paths are 128 bits wide, communicating with the cache and FPU to avoid internal bottlenecks.

The base architecture of the 80486 is identical to that of the 80386, described elsewhere in this chapter; it is the added features of the 80486 that will be described in Sections 4.13 to 4.16.

4.13   80486 CPU signals

The signals issued by the 80486 are shown grouped by function in Fig.

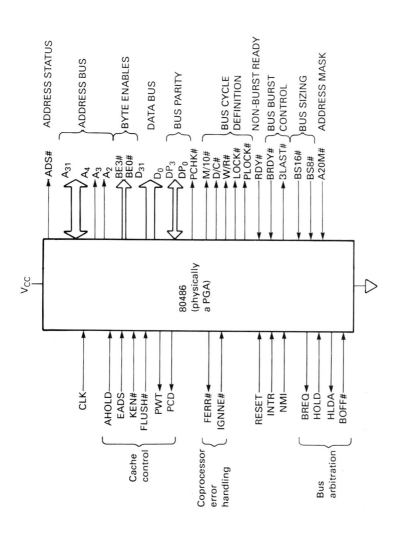

Fig. 4.25 80486 signals.

4.25. The address bus is much the same as that for the 80386, except that lines A31 to A4 are bi-directional, to allow interaction with the on-chip cache. Byte enable signals BE3# to BE0# perform the same functions as before. The data bus, D31 to D0, is the same as the bus on the 80386, but signals DP3 to DP0 have been added, to give data parity on a byte basis; even parity is used, and read cycles from memory automatically check that parity is correct. Incorrect parity on a read cycle does not affect instruction execution, but causes the parity status signal, PCHK#, to be asserted after any READY signal has been returned.

The bus cycle definition signals are largely the same as those on the 80386, i.e. M/IO#, D/C#, W/P# and LOCK#. LOCK# is used to indicate that the CPU is performing a read–modify–write cycle, where the bus must not be pre-empted between read and write cycles. LOCK# works with single instructions, as an opcode prefix, and hence will only cover transfers of up to 32 bits on the bus. A new signal, PLOCK#, has been added to cover transfers of more than 32 bits, and to indicate that the current operations on the bus require more than one bus cycle to complete. PLOCK# will remain asserted until the last bus cycle address has been issued. Bus size control signals, BS16# and BS8#, allow dynamic bus sizing to be used.

Bus control signals allow the bus to be operated in burst mode or non-burst mode. RDY# input indicates that the current bus cycle in non-burst mode is complete, and that the addressed device has responded to the bus transaction (read or write). The equivalent input signal when the bus is operated in burst mode is BRDY#. BRDY# operates to indicate each transfer of a burst cycle; the end of the burst is signalled from the CPU using BLAST# (burst last output) – when BLAST# is asserted, the burst cycle is complete as soon as the next BRDY# signal is returned.

Interrupts follow the same pattern as those of the 80386. The 80386 bus arbitration signals, HOLD and HLDA, are augmented by two more signals. The CPU generates BREQ to indicate that there has been an internal request for the bus issued. Input BOFF# (back-off) may be used to force the 80486 to float its buses within one clock cycle, without asserting HLDA. The CPU remains with its buses floating until the BOFF# signal is removed. When BOFF# is de-asserted, the processor restarts the bus cycle which was abandoned when BOFF# was first asserted. This contrasts with the HOLD request which forces the 80486 to float its buses at the end of the current bus cycle.

Cache signals form an important group of 80486 CPU signals. Since the 80486 has an internal cache, some access is needed from the CPU pins which will control operation of the cache. AHOLD (address hold request) allows another master access to the address bus for a cache invalidation cycle. No hold acknowledge signal is returned, since the response to AHOLD is immediate. EADS# is used to signal that a valid external address is present on the CPU address pins; this address will be checked against current cache address tags, and any area with an address that matches one of the cache address tags will be immediately invalidated.

KEN# (cache enable inpout) is used to signal whether data input to the CPU is cachable. Cache Flush, FLUSH#, forces a complete flush of the internal CPU cache. Bit PCD in the page table entry provides a cachable/non-cachable indication for each page; bit PWT in the same entry is used to indicate write-back.

Two additional floating point co-processor signals are provided, i.e. FERR# (floating point error output) and IGNNE# ignore numeric error input). The address bit 20 mask A20# input is used to force the 80486 to mask A20 before accessing cache or main memory. The effect is to emulate the 1 Mbyte address limit and wrapround of the 8086.

Dynamic bus sizing control is expanded over the 80386, with BS16# augmented by BS8#.

4.14   The 80486 FPU

The FPU is designed to be compatible with the 80387 co-processor; it fully conforms with ANSI-IEEE Standard 754-1985 for floating point arithmetic. Software written for the 80386–80387 combination will execute directly on the 80486 without modification.

4.14.1   FPU REGISTER SET

The register set of the FPU is shown in Fig. 4.26. Like the 80387, it has eight 80-bit registers arranged as a stack; each has a 1-bit sign field, a 15-bit exponent field and a 64-bit mantissa, or significant field. A tag word register contains a 2-bit tag field associated with each register; the position of a tag field does not correspond directly with a particular register. Instead, the logical top of the stack is located using the 'top' field of the FPU status register and associated with the appropriate tag field. The 3-bit 'top' field identifies the top of the stack directly: 000 = Register 0 is top of stack; 001 = Register 1 is top of stack, etc. The tag values allow optimisation of the FPU stack handling by identifying register states as given in Table 4.5.

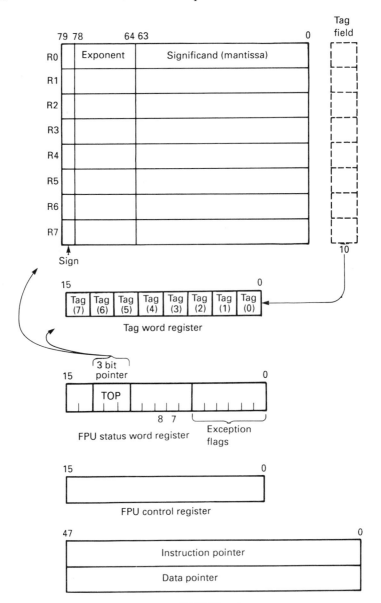

Fig. 4.26   80486 FPU register set.

The status word carries Busy flag (B) (for 80387 compatibility), Top Of Stack indication (TOP), Error Summary status (ES), Stack Flag (SF) (which indicates invalid operations due to stack underflow or overflow), and Exception flags for Precision (PE), Underflow (UE), Overflow (OE), Zero Divide (ZE), Denormalised Operand (DE) and Invalid Operation (IE).

Table 4.5   Tag values and register contents

Tag values	Register contents
00	Valid
01	Zero
10	QNaN, SNaN, infinity, denormalised, and unsupported formats
11	Empty

The FPU control word allows exception flag masking, and rounding and precision control. The 2-bit precision control field allows a choice of mantissa (or significant) precision – 24 bits (single precision); 53 bits (double precision); 64 bits (extended precision). The 2-bit rounding control field allows a choice of the way in which numbers are adjusted to fit the size constraints: round to nearest or even number; round down (towards – infinity); round up (towards + infinity) or truncate (chop least significant bits).

To allow for the FPU operating in parallel with the 80486 CPU, it is necessary to provide facilities for identifying FPU errors which may occur some time after the floating point instruction in error has been fetched. The FPU uses two pointer registers which indicate the address of the floating point instruction in error, and the address of any numeric operand it may possess. Whenever the processor decodes a new floating point instruction, it saves the instruction, including any prefixes, the address of any operand and the opcode. To allow error handling routines access to this information, the pointer registers are accessed using instructions FLDENV (load environment), FSTENV (store environment), FSAVE (save state) and FRSTOR (restore state). Information is transferred to or from memory in a format which depends upon the CPU mode (real address or protected) and operand size (32-bit or 16-bit). The four formats are shown in Fig. 4.27.

4.14.2   FPU INSTRUCTION SET

The FPU instruction set is compatible with that of the 80387, outlined in Section 4.5.3.

4.15   The 80486 internal cache

The 80486 contains an on-chip 8K cache memory which works with physical addresses and is used as a combined instruction and data cache. The cache organisation is four-way, set-associative, with a line

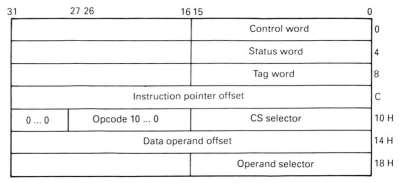

32-bit protected mode format

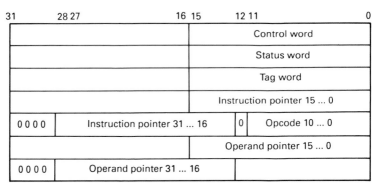

32-bit real address mode format

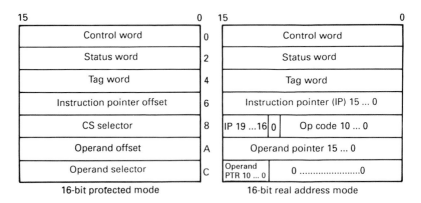

16-bit protected mode   16-bit real address mode

Fig. 4.27   FPU instruction and data pointer images.

size of 16 bytes. A block diagram of the cache is shown in Fig. 4.28. Each 2K data block is organised as 128 lines; each line is associated with a 21-bit tag and a single 'line valid' bit.

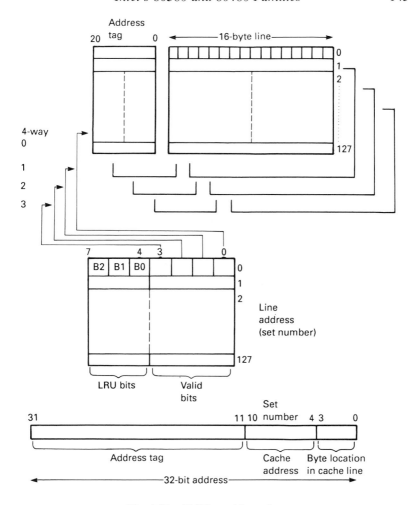

Fig. 4.28 80486 on-chip cache.

The valid bits are organised into 128 words, each of which contains a valid bit for the corresponding line in each block, together with a 3-bit 'LRU' field which allows a 'pseudo-least-recently-used-algorithm' to be used to determine cache line replacement strategy.

A data cache needs to allow cache writes, and a strategy is needed to ensure consistency between cache and main memory contents (see Section 4.4.1). The 80486 designers have chosen the simplest strategy: the cache is 'write-through' (simultaneous write to cache and main memory on a cache bit) with no cache write (just a main memory write) on a cache miss.

4.15.1   CACHE CONTROL

Cache control is exercised via the processor's Control Register CR0. The following bits have been added to this register:

- Bit CE   Enables and disables the cache
- Bit WT   Controls memory write-through and cache line invalidation.

Together, these two bits define four cache operating modes given in Table 4.6.

Table 4.6   Cache operating modes

CE	WT	Cache mode
0	0	Cache fills disabled. Cache write-through and line invalidation disabled. Any information in the cache remains static ('frozen'), and the cache may be used as a fast static memory by pre-loading data. If this mode is selected, and the cache is flushed, the effect of the cache is completely disabled.
0	1	Cache fills disabled. Cache write-through and line invalidation enabled. The cache can be used, and will remain valid, but there will be no replacement of cache lines.
1	0	Invalid combination of bits which will cause a fault exception.
1	1	Normal cache operation.

4.15.2   CACHE OPERATIONS

Cache operations may be classified as line fills, line replacement, line invalidation and flushing.

Memory can be categorised as cachable or non-cachable, using the hardware control KEN# during a memory access, or by software control, using the PCD bit in the page table entry. If a cache miss occurs on a memory read or instruction prefetch cycle, a bus read request is generated. If the target of the request is a cachable area of memory, the 80486 initiates a cache line fill, and a 16-byte line will be read into the CPU and cache. The cache fill will be at its most effective if burst bus cycles are used (see Section 4.16). Cache fills will only occur on read cycles; a cache hit on a write cycle will cause the line to be updated; a cache miss on a write cycle will not affect the cache at all.

When a cache miss occurs on a read cycle, and a cache line needs to

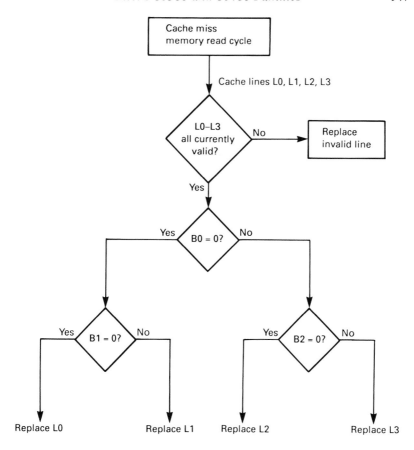

Fig. 4.29

be put into the cache, a choice needs to be made as to which of the four cache blocks is used. If a line in the set is invalid, that line will be selected as the destination for the cache fill. If all lines in the cache are set valid, the line to be replaced is selected using a 'pseudo-least-recently-used' replacement algorithm. This algorithm is shown in diagrammatic form in Fig. 4.29. If the lines are labelled L0, L1, L2, L3, this will be the order of checking the valid bits, and the order of the cache line fills after reset or flush, which clear all the valid bits; if all four valid bits are set, three bits, defined for each of the 128 sets in the cache, B0, B1, B2, are used to locate the line to be replaced. These LRU bits are updated for every cache hit or replacement as follows.

If the most recent access to the set was to L0 or L1, then B0 = 1; if it was to L2 or L3, then B0 = 0.

If the most recent access to the pair L0 and L1 was to L0, B1 = 1; if it was to L1, B1 = 0.

If the most recent access to the pair L2 and L3 was to L2, B2 = 1; if it was to L3, B2 = 0.

The decision tree of Fig. 4.29 will locate the line to be replaced.

Line invalidation is necessary if a device external to the CPU, e.g. a DMA unit, is allowed to change the contents of memory, where some lines of the cache correspond to the original values of the memory area. The action of DMA will cause those cache lines to no longer reflect the values in memory. A mechanism called 'bus snooping' will allow any inconsistency between memory and cache contents to be detected at the time of memory write (DMA), by looking for any cache address hits on DMA write, and the relevant lines of the cache can be flagged invalid (to be more precise 'no longer valid').

Cache flushing is normally invoked by either hardware or software. The action of a cache flush is to clear all the valid bits for the whole of the cache. The FLUSH# input to the 80486 forces a cache flush, and must be asserted by external logic. Two instructions also flush the cache. INVD causes the cache to be flushed regardless of its contents; WBINVD causes the cache to be flushed after any dirty lines have been written back to memory.

4.15.3   PAGE CACHABILITY

Cache control bits PWT and PCD are included in the page and directory table entries, and generate external control signals on CPU pins of the same names. PWT exercises control of the write policy for external cache (write-through or write-back) – the on-chip cache is only write-through. PCD controls cachability as individual pages are accessed. When a page is accessed, and has the PCD bit in the page table entry set, signal PCD is asserted. External logic returns the signal KEN# to indicate that the page is cachable.

4.15.4   PAGE TRANSLATION CACHE

Like the 80386, the 80486 contains a page translation cache, or Translation Look-aside Buffer (TLB), of 32 entries. The TLB has been redesigned so that the 'same pseudo-LRU' algorithm can be used as is used for the on-chip instruction and data cache.

4.16   80486 burst mode bus cycles

Multiple bus transfer requests may be originated internally by the CPU, or externally by the memory system. CPU requests may, for example, be for 8-byte floating point operands, or for 16-byte prefetches. External requests may be used when external memory can only support 8-bit or 16-bit transfers at each bus cycle.

The advantage of burst mode is one of speed. Whilst the fastest normal (non-burst) bus transfer will take two clock cycles, in burst mode, the first transfer will take two clock cycles and, subsequently, transfers can be made at the rate of one per clock cycle. To implement burst mode, it is necessary for the data to reside in a 16-byte aligned area (the area used by a cache line fill). Aligned 16-byte areas run between hex addresses XXXXXXX0 and XXXXXXXF.

A burst cycle (see Fig. 4.30) starts just like a conventional bus cycle, with the CPU placing a memory address on the bus and asserting ADS#. BLAST# is used to signal the requirement for a burst transfer by holding it de-asserted during the second clock cycle of the instruction. External memory must respond by returning BRDY# before the cycle turns into a burst-mode one. The non-burst 'ready' signal, RDY#, is not used when BRDY# is being used.

Whilst BLAST# remains de-asserted, second and subsequent bus cycles can proceed at every clock cycle until BLAST# is asserted. When BLAST# is asserted, during the last transfer of a burst, the cycle terminates, and the multiple transfer is complete. ADS# is asserted

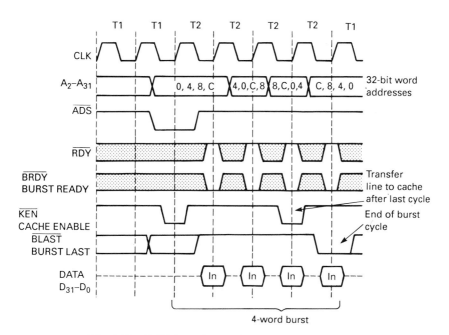

Fig. 4.30   80486 burst bus cycle (read) – cachable data.

only once during a burst cycle to signal the first issue of an address at the beginning of the cycle.

With RAM components becoming faster and tailored for multiple consecutive addresses, it is to be expected that burst transfers will be easy and inexpensive to support, and afford a worthwhile performance improvement.

4.17   The future for 80X86 processors

The future development path for 80X86 processors is 'more of the same'; Intel has a policy of upward compatibility, and it is to be expected that this will be maintained. Improvements in fabrication technology will allow ever-increasing functionality. It has been suggested that the 80586 may be available by 1993, with 5 million transistors, and maybe the 80786 (!) by 1999, running at 250 MHz clock rate and delivering 2000 MIPs.

CHAPTER 5
The Motorola MC68020 and MC68030

JOHN RALSTON
Motorola Semiconductors, UK

5.1 Introduction

This chapter contains an insight into the MC68020 and MC68030 which are the 32-bit members of Motorola's M68000 family of microprocessors. Descriptions of the support co-processors for memory management (MC68851) and floating point support (MC68881 and MC68882) are also included. Figure 5.1 shows the M68000 family of microprocessors and co-processors currently available at the time of print.

5.2 The MC68020

The MC68020 is the first 32-bit microprocessor based on Motorola's M68000 family. It is implemented with 32-bit registers and data paths, 32-bit addresses, a rich instruction set, and versatile addressing modes.

The MC68020 is object code compatible with the other members of the M68000 family (the MC68000, MC68008, MC68010 and the MC68012). It has the added features of an on-chip instruction cache, high level language support via new addressing modes, and a flexible co-processor interface. In addition, the MC68020 supports a dynamic bus sizing mechanism that allows it to determine port size on a cycle-by-cycle basis.

Sections 5.3 to 5.12 will first cover the processing technology and the architecture of the MC68020, followed by a discussion on data organisation. Next, the addressing capabilities, instruction set and hardware signals will be examined. Then, some of the special features of the MC68020 will be detailed, including the dynamic bus sizing mechanism, the on-chip instruction cache, and the co-processor interface. Next, memory management, development system support, software support and performance will be examined.

5.3 Processing

The MC68020 is a product of 60 man-years of design effort. The

Device	Description	Operating Frequency (MHz)								
		8	10	12.5	16.67	20	25	33.3	40	50
MC68000 MPU	16-Bit Data Bus, 16MByte Address Space	X	X	X	X					
MC68HC000 MPU	HCMOS version of MC68000	X	X	X	X					
MC68008 MPU	8-Bit Data Bus, 1MByte Address Space	X	X							
MC68010 MPU	16-Bit Data Bus, 16MByte address Space, Supports Virtual Memory	X	X	X						
MC68020 **MPU**	32-Bit Data Bus, 4GByte Address Space, Instruction Cache, Coprocessor Interface			X	X	X	X	X		
MC68030 **MPU**	32-Bit Data Bus, 4GByte Address Space, Instruction and Data Caches, Memory Management Unit, Coprocessor Interface				X	X	X	X	X	X
MC68851 PMMU	32-Bit Logical to Physical address translation			X	X	X				
MC68881 FPCP	IEE 754 Standard, 67-Bit arithmetic unit, 8, 16, or 32 bit data bus			X	X	X	X			
MC68882 EFCP	All features of the MC68881 with enhanced performance				X	X	X	X	X	

Fig. 5.1 M68000 microprocessor and co-processor family.

processor is manufactured using a High-density Complementary Metal Oxide Semiconductor (HCMOS) process which provides an important combination of high speed performance and low power consumption. The processor consists of 200 000 actual transistors in a die 0.375 × 0.350 in and is packaged in a 114-pin grid array.

5.4   Architecture

Figure 5.2 shows a functional block diagram of the MC68020. The processor can be divided into three main sections: the bus controller,

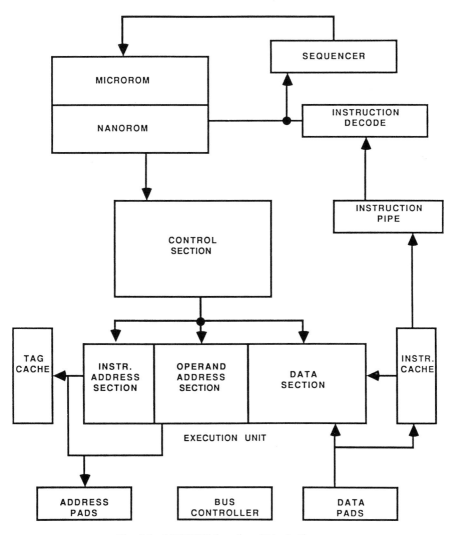

Fig. 5.2   MC68020 functional block diagram.

the micromachine, and the miscellaneous area. These major sections operate in a completely autonomous fashion.

The bus controller comprises the address and data pads and the multiplexors necessary for dynamic bus sizing support. In addition, the bus controller contains the instruction cache and associated control circuitry, a macro bus controller and two micro bus controllers. The macro bus controller schedules bus cycles on a priority basis, while the two micro bus controllers control the bus cycles; one for instruction accesses and the other for operand accesses.

The micromachine consists of an instruction pipe, decode PLAs, ROM control store, an execution unit, and miscellaneous control stores. The execution unit contains an instruction address section, an operand address section, and a data section. The ROM control store comprises the microrom and the nanorom, which provide microcode control. The decode PLAs are used to provide the information necessary to sequence through the microcode. The instruction pipe consists of three stages (see Fig. 5.3) and provides for decode of instructions. Instructions that have been prefetched from either the on-chip cache or from external memory are loaded into stage B. The instructions are then sequenced from stage B to stage D. Stage D contains a fully decoded instruction ready for execution. If the instruction had contained an extension word, it would be available in stage C at the time the op code would be in stage D.

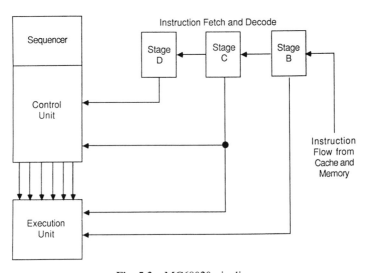

Fig. 5.3   MC68020 pipeline.

5.5 Data organisation

5.5.1 OPERANDS

The MC68020 supports seven basic data types: bits, bit fields, BCD digits, byte integers, word integers, long word integers, and quad word integers. A bit field consists of from 1 to 32 bits, a byte is 8 bits, a word is 16 bits, a long word is 32 bits and a quad word is 64 bits wide. In addition, the MC68020 supports variable byte length operands necessary for the co-processor interface (i.e. co-processors can define operand lengths required for its particular application).

5.5.2 PROGRAMMING MODEL

As with the other processors in the M68000 family, the MC68020 operates in one of two modes – user or supervisor. The user mode is intended to provide an environment for application programs. The supervisor mode has access to additional instructions, registers and privileges and is intended to be used by the operating system.

The user and supervisor programming models for the MC68020 are shown in Fig. 5.4(a) and (b) respectively. The user programming model features eight 32-bit data registers, eight 32-bit address registers, one of which (A7) is used as the user stack pointer, a 32-bit program counter, and an 8-bit condition code register. In addition to the above registers, the supervisor programming model also includes two 32-bit supervisory stack pointers (one called *master* and the other called *interrupt*), a 16-bit status register (the low byte of which is the condition code register mentioned above), a 32-bit vector base register, two 3-bit alternate function code registers, a cache control register, and a cache address register. A description of each of these registers is given in the following paragraphs.

The eight data registers (D0–D7) are used for bit, bit field, BCD, byte, word, long word, and quad word operations. In general, operations on data registers affect the condition codes, but do not cause the result in the register to be sign extended to the full 32 bits. The seven address registers (A0–A6) and the user, master and interrupt stack pointers can be used as software stack pointers, as base address registers and for word or long word operations. In general, operations on address registers do not affect the condition codes (CMPA is an exception to this statement) and cause the result to be sign extended to the full 32 bits. In addition, both data and address registers (D0–D7 and A0–A7) can be used as index registers.

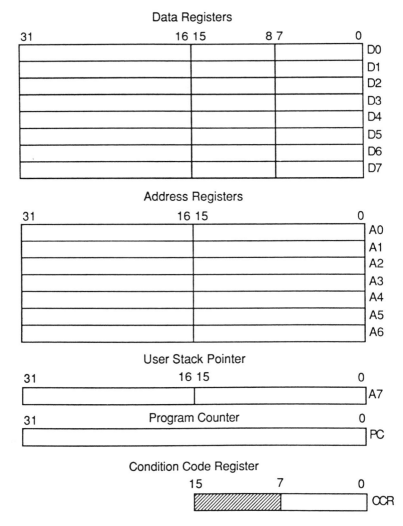

Fig. 5.4   (a) User programming model.

The Status Register (SR) contains two bytes: the user byte (condition code register) and the system byte. The system byte is accessible only in the supervisor mode. The user byte contains bits for the following conditions: extend (X), negative (N), zero (Z), overflow (V), and carry (C). The system byte has two trace mode bits that allow tracing on every instruction or only on change of program flow, an S bit that indicates whether the processor is in the user or supervisor mode, an M bit that indicates whether the supervisor is using the master or interrupt stack, and three interrupt priority mask bits. These bits cause the

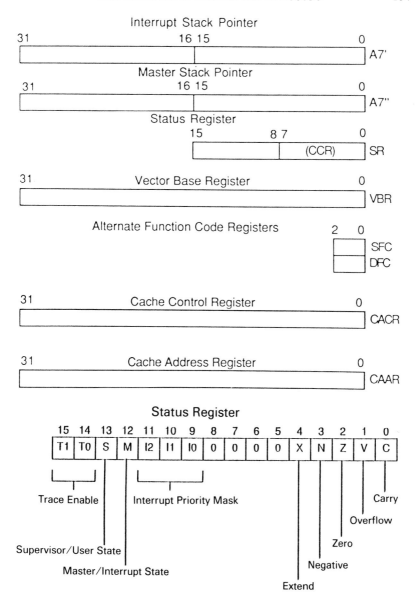

Fig. 5.4 (b) Supervisor programming model supplement.

MC68020 to ignore all interrupt requests with equal or lower priority than that of the interrupt mask.

The MC68020 has three stack pointers: user, master and interrupt. Only one of these is active at any given time, depending on the state of the M and S bits in the status register. The User Stack Pointer (USP) operates in the same way in the MC68020 as it does for other M68000 family processors. It is active only when the S bit in the status register is cleared. If both the S bit and M bit are set to 1, the Master Stack Pointer (MSP) is the active stack. If the S bit is set to 1 and the M bit is cleared, the Interrupt Stack Pointer (ISP) is the active stack. This final scenario corresponds to the supervisor mode in the MC68000, MC68008, MC68010 and MC68012. The master and interrupt stacks interact with each other during interrupts. If both the M and S bits in the status register are set (master stack operation) and an interrupt is recognised, the exception vector offset, program counter, and the status register are saved on the master stack. In addition, the M bit will be cleared and a copy of this stack frame (called a *throwaway stack frame*) is created on the interrupt stack. If any other interrupts occur while processing this interrupt, the corresponding state information will be stacked only on the interrupt stack. Thus, the two stack pointers work very well in multi-tasking environments. Each task can have its own master stack pointer and exceptions that apply only to that task stacked there. If an interrupt occurs, the information is stacked on both the master stack and the interrupt stack because it may apply to both the task and the operating system (as in the case of a task switch). The information for interrupts that occur while processing this interrupt would be stacked only on the interrupt stack because it would apply only to the operating system.

The Vector Base Register (VBR) contains the base address of the 1K exception vector table and is used to relocate the vector table anywhere within the 4 Gbyte address space of the MC68020. As a result, the MC68020 supports multiple vector tables such as might be required in a multi-tasking environment. Upon reset, the vector base register is set to zero.

The two alternate function code registers (source SFC and destination DFC) allow the supervisor to access any address space (see Section 5.5.4) and are used only with the MOVES instruction. In some earlier members of the M68000 family, namely the MC68000 and the MC68008, the alternate function code registers were not implemented. Thus, all supervisor accesses were made to either supervisor program or data space. When a MOVES instruction is executed on the MC68020, the contents of the alternate function code registers are put on the function code lines (FC0–FC2) for either the source or destination operand. This allows the supervisor to have access to other address spaces. The MOVES instruction is privileged, thus prohibiting the user from accessing supervisor space.

The two cache registers (control, CACR and address, CAAR) are provided to allow software manipulation of the on-chip instruction cache. The cache control register contains bits for clearing the cache, freezing the cache, enabling the cache, and clearing a specific entry in the cache. When clearing a cache entry, the address of the entry is contained in the cache address register.

5.5.3 MEMORY ORGANISATION

As with all members of the M68000 family, memory for the MC68020 is organised so that the lower addresses correspond to the higher order

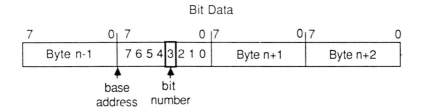

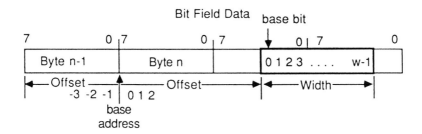

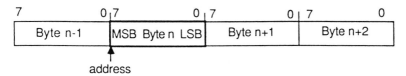

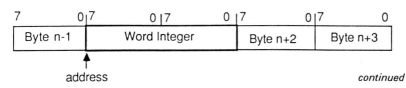

continued

Fig. 5.5 Memory data organisation.

Long Word Integer Data

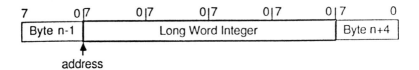

Packed Binary-Coded Data

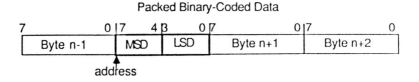

Unpacked Binary-Coded Data

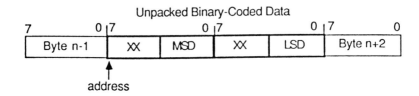

XX = User-Defined Value

Fig. 5.5   Memory data organisation continued.

bytes. For example, the addressN of a long word is also the address of the most significant byte of the higher order word. Thus, the address of the least significant byte of the lower order word is N + 3.

Figure 5.5 shows how the data types supported by the MC68020 are organised in memory. These data types can be accessed on any byte boundary. The MC68020 does not require that data operands be on even byte boundaries. This feature is called *misalignment* and will be discussed in Section 5.9.2. However, maximum performance is achieved whenever data is aligned to the same byte boundary as its operand size. Instructions are not allowed to be misaligned. All instructions must always be aligned to even byte boundaries. The MC68020 forces an address error exception any time the program counter contains an odd address.

5.5.4   PROGRAM AND DATA REFERENCES

Memory is divided into two classes in the MC68020: program and data. Program references are references to that part of memory that contains instructions. Data references are references to that part of memory tha contains data. In general, operand reads are from the data space and all operand writes are to the data space, except when caused by the MOVES (move address space) instruction.

5.6 Addressing capabilities

5.6.1 EFFECTIVE ADDRESSING MODES

The location of an operand used in the execution of an instruction can be specified in one of three ways. First, the location (or address) can be contained in a register. Second, the instruction, by definition, can imply the use of a specific register that contains the location of the operand. Third, the address of the operand can be specified by one of the remaining addressing modes. These types of addressing will be discussed in this section.

5.6.1.1 *Register direct modes.* These effective addressing modes specify that the operand is contained in one of the 16 general purpose registers (A0–A7, D0–D7) or in one of the six control registers (SR, VBR, SFC, DFC, CACR and CAAR).

(1) Data register direct. The operand is found in the data register specified by the register field of the operation word.

(2) Address register direct. The operand is found in the address register specified by the register field.

5.6.1.2 *Register indirect modes.* These effective addressing modes specify that the operand is located at a memory address based on the contents of an address register.

(1) Address register indirect. The address of the operand is contained in the address register specified by the register field.

(2) Address register indirect with postincrement. The address of the operand is contained in the address register specified by the register field. The contents of the address register are then incremented by 1, 2 or 4 depending on whether the operand size is a byte, word or long word. An exception to this is when the address register is the stack pointer and the operand size is a byte. In this case, the stack pointer will be incremented by two to keep the stack pointer aligned on an even byte boundary.

(3) Address register indirect with predecrement. The address

register specified by the register field is first decremented by 1, 2 or 4 depending on the size of the operand. This decremented value is then used as the address of the operand. Stacks are handled as in 2 above with decrement substituted for increment.

(4) Address register indirect with displacement. The address of the operand is the sum of the contents of the address register specified by the register field and a sign extended 16-bit displacement. This displacement is contained in an extension word following the op word.

5.6.1.3 *Register indirect with index modes.*   These addressing modes specify that the address of the operand is derived from a calculation involving an address register, an index register and a displacement. The format of the index operand is 'Xn.SIZE*SCALE'. Xn can be any data or address register. SIZE specifies the index size and can be either word or long word. SCALE allows the contents of the index register to be multiplied by 1, 2, 4 or 8. Index operands and displacements are always sign extended to 32 bits before being used in the calculation.

(1) Address register indirect with index (8-bit displacement). The address of the operand is the sum of the contents of the address register specified by the register field, the sign extended contents of the index register (sized and scaled), and a sign extended 8-bit displacement. This mode requires one word of extension that specifies the index register and the 8-bit displacement.

(2) Address register indirect with index (base displacement). The address of the operand is the sum of the contents of the address register specified by the register field, the sign extended contents of an index register, and a sign extended 16- or 32-bit displacement. Note that with this addressing mode, a 'data register indirect' addressing mode can be obtained by using a data register as the index register and not specifying an address register.

5.6.1.4 *Memory indirect addressing modes.*   These addressing modes use four user-specified values in determining the value of the operand. They are: an address register to be used as a base register; a base displacement, which is added to the base register; an index register; and an outer displacement that is added to the address operand. These addressing modes call for intermediate addresses to be fetched from memory before continuing with the effective address calculation. The index operand can be added in after the intermediate address fetch (post-indexed) or before the intermediate address fetch (pre-indexed).

All four user-specified values are optional. The base and outer displacement may be null, word or long word values. If a displacement is null (or an element is suppressed), its value is taken as zero in the effective address calculation.

(1) Memory indirect post-indexed. An intermediate indirect memory address is calculated by adding together the base register and the base displacement. This address is used for an indirect memory access of a long word. This long word is then added to the index operand (Xn.SIZE*SCALE) and the outer displacement, if any, to yield the effective address.

(2) Memory indirect pre-indexed. The index operated (XN.SIZE*SCALE) is added to the base register and the base displacement. This intermediate sum is then used for an indirect access of a long word. The outer displacement, if any, is then added to this long word to yield the effective address.

5.6.1.5 *Program counter indirect with displacement mode.* The address of the operand is the sum of the address in the Program Counter (PC) and a sign extended 16-bit displacement. The displacement is contained in an extension word following the op code. The value in the program counter is the address of the extension word. All references that use this addressing mode are classified as program references.

5.6.1.6 *Program counter indirect with index modes.* These addressing modes are analogous to the register indirect with index modes described earlier, with the PC used as the base register. As before, the index operand (sized and scaled) and a displacement are used in the calculation of the effective address. Once again, displacements and index operands are always sign extended to 32 bits prior to being used in the effective address calculation.

(1) PC indirect with index (8-bit displacement). The address of the operand is the sum of the address in the program counter, the sign extended integer in the lower order 8 bits of the extension word, and the sized and scaled index operand. The value in the PC is the address of the extension word. The user must specify the displacement, the PC and the index register when using this addressing mode.

(2) PC indirect with index (base displacement). The address of the operand is the sum of the address in the program counter, the sized and scaled contents of the index register, and the sign extended base displacement. This addressing mode requires additional extension words that contain the index register indication and the 16- or 32-bit displacement. All three parameters are optional in this mode.

5.6.1.7 *Program counter memory indirect modes.*   These addressing modes are analogous to the memory indirect addressing modes described earlier, with the program counter being used as the base register. The intermediate memory access can be either post-indexed or pre-indexed. All four user-specified values are optional.

(1) Program counter memory indirect post-indexed. An intermediate indirect memory address is calculated by adding the PC (used as a base register) and a base displacement. This address is used for an indirect access of a long word, followed by the addition of the index operand (sized and scaled) with the fetched address. Finally, the outer displacement, if any, is added to yield the final effective address.

(2) Program counter memory indirect pre-indexed. The sized and scaled index operand is added to the program counter and the base displacement. This sum is used for an indirect access of a long word. The outer displacement, if any, is then added to yield the final effective address.

5.6.1.8 *Absolute address modes.*   These addressing modes specify the address of the operand in the extension words.

(1) Absolute short address. The address of the operand is contained in the extension word. The 16-bit address is sign extended to 32 bits before it is used. This mode requires one word of extension.

(2) Absolute long address. This addressing mode requires two words of extension. The address of the operand is obtained by the concatenation of the extension words. The first extension word contains the higher order part of the address and the second extension word contains the lower order part.

5.6.1.9 *Immediate data.*   This addressing mode requires one or two words of extension, depending on the size of the operation.

(1) Byte operation. Operand is in the lower order byte of the extension word.
(2) Word operation. Operand is in the extension word.
(3) Long word operation. Operand is in two extension words; high order 16 bits are in the first extension word; low order 16 bits are in the second extension word.

5.7 Instruction set summary

This section contains an overview of the MC68020 instruction set. The instructions can be categorised as follows:

Data movement	Bit field manipulation
Integer arithmetic	Binary coded decimal arithmetic
Logical	Program control
Shift and rotate	System control
Bit manipulation	Multiprocessor control

The following sections describe the MC68020 instruction set by categories.

5.7.1 DATA MOVEMENT

The basic means of accomplishing address and data transfer and storage is through the move (MOVE) instruction. Data movement instructions allow byte, word and long word operands to be transferred from memory to memory, memory to register, register to memory, and register to register. Address movement instructions (MOVE and MOVEA) allow word and long word operand transfers on legal address boundaries. In addition to the move instruction, there are several special data movement instructions: move multiple registers (MOVEM), move peripheral data (MOVEP), move quick (MOVEQ), exchange registers (EXG), load effective address (LEA), push effective address (PEA), link stack (LINK), and unlink stack (UNLK).

5.7.2 INTEGER ARITHMETIC OPERATIONS

The integer arithmetic instructions consist of the four basic operations of add (ADD), subtract (SUB), multiply (MULT) and divide (DIV) as well as clear (CLR), negate (NEG) and arithmetic compare (CMP, CMPM). Both data and address operations can be performed with the ADD, SUB and CMP instructions. Address operations are limited to legal address size operands (16 or 32 bits), while data operands can accept all operand sizes. The CLR and NEG instructions may be used on all data operand sizes.

The MC68020 has a multiply and divide instruction for both signed and unsigned integers. Multiplying word size operands results in a long word product and multiplying long word operands results in either a long word or quad word product. A long word dividend with a word divisor produces a word quotient with a word remainder, and a long word or a quad word dividend with a long word divisor produces a long word quotient with a long word remainder.

The MC68020 has a set of extended instructions to accomplish multi-precision and mixed size arithmetic operations. They are: add extended (ADDX), subtract extended (SUBX), sign extend (EXT) and negate binary with extend (NEGX).

5.7.3 LOGICAL OPERATIONS

The logical operation instructions include AND (AND), inclusive OR (OR), exclusive OR (EOR), and one's complement (NOT). These instructions may be used with all sizes of data operands. A similar set of immediate instructions (ANDI, ORI and EORI) performs the logical operations on all sizes of immediate data. The test instruction (TST) arithmetically compares the operand with zero. The result is reflected in the condition codes.

5.7.4 SHIFT AND ROTATE OPERATIONS

The MC68020 can perform shifts in both directions via the arithmetic shift (ASL and ASR) and the logical shift (LSL and LSR) instructions. In addition, the processor also has four rotate instructions (with and without extend): ROR, ROL, ROXR and ROXL.

All shift and rotate instructions can be performed on either a data register or memory. Register shifts and rotates support all operand sizes and allow a shift count to be specified in the instruction operation word or in another register. Memory shifts and rotates operate on word operands only and allow only single-bit shifts and rotates.

The last instruction in the shift and rotate category is the swap register halves instruction (SWAP). This instruction exchanges the upper and lower words of a data register.

5.7.5 BIT MANIPULATION OPERATIONS

The bit manipulation instructions are bit test (BTST), bit test and change (BCHG), bit test and clear (BCLR), and bit test and set (BSET). All bit manipulation instructions can be performed on either a data register or memory with the bit number being specified in either the immediate field of the instruction or in a data register. Register operands are always 32 bits wide while memory operands are 8 bits wide.

5.7.6 BIT FIELD OPERATIONS

The bit field instructions include four that are analogous to the bit manipulation instructions discussed in Section 5.7.5, namely, bit field test (BFTST), bit field test and change (BFCHG), bit field test and clear (BFCLR), and bit test and set (BFSET). In addition, there is a bit field insert instruction (BFINS) that inserts a value in a bit field; bit field extract, signed and unsigned (BFEXTS and BFEXTU), which extracts a value from a bit field; and bit field find first one (BFFFO) which finds the first bit that has been set in a bit field. These instructions operate on bit fields of variable length up to 32 bits.

5.7.7 BINARY CODED DECIMAL OPERATIONS

Multi-precision arithmetic operations on Binary Coded Decimal (BCD) numbers are accomplished through the following instructions: add decimal with extend (ABCD), subtract decimal with extend (SBCD), and negate decimal with extend (NBCD). The pack (PACK) and unpack (UNPK) instructions are used for conversion of byte encoded numeric data, such as ASCII or EBCDIC strings, to BCD and *vice versa*.

5.7.8 PROGRAM CONTROL OPERATIONS

Program control operations are accomplished using a set of conditional and unconditional branch instructions and return instructions. The conditions on which a branch can occur are:

- carry clear
- carry set
- equal
- never true
- greater or equal
- greater than
- high
- less or equal
- low or same
- less than
- minus
- not equal
- plus
- always true
- overflow clear
- overflow set

In addition, this category includes branch always (BRA), branch to subroutine (BSR), call module (CALLM), jump (JMP), jump to subroutine (JSR), return and deallocate parameters (RTD), return from module (RTM), return and restore condition codes (RTR), and return from subroutine (RTS).

5.7.9 SYSTEM CONTROL OPERATIONS

System control operations are accomplished via privileged instructions, trap generating instructions, and instructions that use or explicitly modify the condition code register. The privileged instructions perform ANDing, exclusive ORing, and ORing of immediate data to the status register (ANDI, EORI and ORI, respectively) as well as moving information to and from the status register, the user stack pointer and the control registers. Another version of the MOVE instruction, MOVES, uses the source and destination function code registers to determine which addresss space to move data into or out of. Other privileged instructions are RESET (which causes the RESET* line to assert), RTE (return from exception), and STOP (which causes the MC68020 to stop processing information). Included in the trap generating instruction category are the BKPT (breakpoint), CHK (check), CHK2 (check 2), ILLEGAL, TRAP, TRAPcc, and TRAPV. The BKPT instruction causes the MC68020 to execute a breakpoint acknowedge cycle, during which the processor latches data bits D31 through D24 and uses the value as the op word. The CHK and CHK2 instructions compare a register value against some specified upper and/or lower bounds and either generate an exception or continue instruction execution based on the results of the compare. The ILLEGAL and TRAP instructions force the MC68020 to generate an illegal instruction exception or a trap exception, respectively. TRAPcc and TRAPV cause the MC68020 to take a trap if the condition is true (TRAPcc) or if an underflow occurred (TRAPV). The instructions affecting the condition code register are ANDI, EORI, ORI and MOVE. The first three instructions either AND, exclusive OR, or OR immediate data with the condition code register, while the last instruction moves data into and out of the register.

5.7.10   MULTIPROCESSOR CONTROL OPERATIONS

Multiprocessor support is provided in the MC68020 via the TAS, CAS and CAS2 instructions. These three instructions execute indivisible read–modify–write bus cycles. To indicate this to the external world, the RMC* signal is asserted throughout the execution of the instruction (see Section 5.8).

The Test And Set (TAS) instruction is used to support semaphore operations. It first reads a byte from memory and checks the most significant bit of that operand, setting the condition codes accordingly. Then it sets the most significant bit of that byte in memory, regardless of its previous state. The program can then execute a conditional branch based on the state of the condition codes. If the bit has been set previously, this indicates that another processor owns that semaphore and this processor must wait before it can attempt to use the resource associated with that semaphore. If the bit has been cleared then the processor executing the TAS instruction has already claimed ownership by setting the most significant bit. The Compare And Swap (CAS and CAS2) instructions are used to update system counters, history information and globally shared pointers. Three operands are defined within the CAS instruction: the effective address of the operand, the compare register and the update register. The operand specified by the effective address is first read and compared to the value in the compare register. If the values are equal, then the value contained in the update register is written to the effective address. If the values are not equal, then the operated value is loaded into the compare register. The CAS2 instruction works in exactly the same way, except that it uses two sets of three operands each. This instruction is handy for manipulating doubly-linked lists.

The co-processor instructions are also included in the multiprocessor operation category. These instructions will be discussed in detail in Section 5.11.

5.8 Signal description

This section contains a brief description of the input and output signals on the MC68020. It is organised by signal function as shown in Fig. 5.6. The term 'assert' is used to indicate that a signal is active, regardless of whether or not that level is represented by a high or low voltage. In the same manner, the term 'negate' is used to indicate that a signal is inactive.

5.8.1 FUNCTION CODE SIGNALS (FC0–FC2)

These three-state output signals are used to identify the processor state (supervisor or user) and the address space of the bus cycle currently executing as described in Table 5.1.

5.8.2 ADDRESS BUS (A0–A31)

During the execution of all bus cycles except CPU-space references, these three-state outputs provide the address for a bus cycle. During CPU-space references, the address bus provides CPU related information. The MC68020 can linearly address 4 Gbytes (2^{32}) of data.

5.8.3 DATA BUS (D0–D31)

These three-state, bi-directional signals provide the data path between

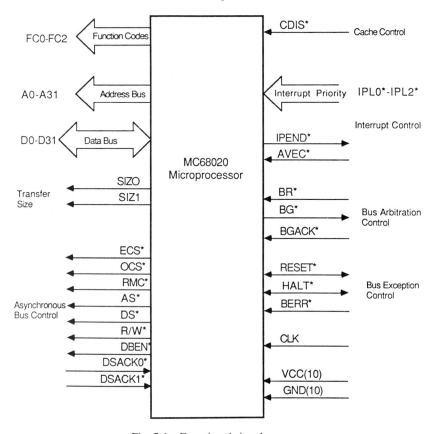

Fig. 5.6   Functional signal groups.

Table 5.1   Function code assignments

FC2	FC1	FC0	Cycle Type
0	0	0	(Undefined, Reserved)*
0	0	1	User Data Space
0	1	0	User Program Space
0	1	1	(Undefined, Reserved)*
1	0	0	(Undefined, Reserved)*
1	0	1	Supervisor Data Space
1	1	0	Supervisor Program Space
1	1	1	CPU Space

*Address Space 3 is reserved for user definition,
while 0 and 4 are reserved for future use by
Motorola.

the MC68020 and the other devices in the system. The data bus can transmit and accept data using the dynamic bus sizing capabilities of the MC68020.

5.8.4   TRANSFER SIZE (SIZ0, SIZ1)

These three-state outputs indicate the number of bytes of an operand that remain to be transferred in a given bus cycle. These outputs are used with the dynamic bus sizing capabilities of the MC68020.

5.8.5   ASYNCHRONOUS BUS CONTROL SIGNALS

Paragraphs 1 to 8 below describe the asynchronous bus control signals on the MC68020.

(1) External cycle start (ECS*). This output provides an early indication that the MC68020 is starting a bus cycle. It is asserted during the first one-half clock cycle of every bus cycle. This signal must be qualified later with AS* to ensure a valid MC68020 bus cycle, since the MC68020 may start an instruction fetch and then abort the access if the instruction word is found in the on-chip cache. The MC68020 drives only the address bus, function code signals and the size outputs when it aborts a bus cycle due to a cache hit.

(2) Operand cycle start (OCS*). This output signal is asserted only during the first bus cycle of an operand transfer and has the same timing as the ECS* signal.

(3) Read–modify–write cycle (RMC*). This three-state signal is asserted for the duration of a read–modify–write cycle. It should be used as a bus lock to insure the integrity of instructions that use read–modify–write cycles.

(4) Address strobe (AS*). This three-state signal is used to indicate that valid addresses, function code, size and read/write information is on the bus.

(5) Data strobe (DS*). During a read cycle, this three-state signal indicates that the selected peripheral should drive the data bus. During a write cycle, this signal indicates that the MC68020 has placed valid data on the data bus.

(6) Read/write (R/W*). This three-state signal is used to indicate the direction of data transfer. A high level indicates that a read cycle is in progress and a low level indicates that a write cycle is being executed.

(7) Data buffer enable (DBEN*). This three-state signal provides an enable to external data buffers. It allows the R/W* line to transition

without causing external buffer contention. This signal is not necessary in all systems.

(8) Data transfer and size acknowledge (DSACK0*, DSACK1*). These inputs indicate to the MC68020 that a data transfer is complete and the amount of data that the external device has accepted or provided. During a read cycle, when the MC68020 recognises the assertion of DSACKx*, it latches the data and terminates the bus cycle. During a write cycle, upon recognition of DSACKx*, the processor terminates the bus cycle. Further explanation of the DSACKx* encodings can be found in Section 5.9.

5.8.6   CACHE DISABLE (CDIS*)

This input signal dynamically disables the on-chip cache. The cache will be disabled internally after the CDIS* signal has been asserted and synchronised internally. Similarly, the cache will be enabled after the CDIS* line has been negated and this condition internally synchronised. See Section 5.10.2 for more information.

5.8.7   INTERRUPT CONTROL SIGNALS

Paragraphs 1 to 3 below describe the interrupt control signals for the MC68020.

(1) Interrupt priority level (IPL0*–IPL2*). These inputs indicate the priority level of the device requesting an interrupt. Level 7 has the highest priority and is non-maskable; level 0 indicates that no interrupt is requested.

(2) Interrupt pending (IPEND*). This output is used to indicate that the priority level on the IPL2* through IPL0* lines is higher than the priority level in the interrupt mask of the status register, or that a non-maskable interrupt has been recognised.

(3) Autovector (AVEC*). This input may be asserted during an interrupt acknowledge cycle, indicating that an interrupt vector number should be generated internally.

5.8.8   BUS ARBITRATION SIGNALS

Paragraphs 1 to 3 below describe the pins used in determining when other devices in a system may become the bus master.

(1) Bus request (BR*). This input is asserted by a device indicating that it wishes to become the bus master. This signal should be wire-O Red with the other request signals from all other potential bus masters.

(2) Bus grant (BG*). This output signal indicates that the MC68020 will relinquish the bus at the end of the currently executing bus cycle.

(3) Bus grant acknowledge (BGACK*). This input signal indicates to the MC68020 that some other device has assumed ownership of the bus. The device must keep this signal asserted until it has completed its transactions. This signal should not be asserted until the following conditions have been met:

(i)   BG* has been received.
(ii) AS* has been negated, indicating that the MC68020 is not running a bus cycle.
(iii) DSACK0* and DSACK1* are negated, indicating that no other device is currently driving the bus.
(iv) BGACK* is negated, indicating that no other bus master has the bus.

5.8.9   BUS EXCEPTION CONTROL SIGNALS

Paragraphs 1 to 3 below describe the exception control signals for the MC68020.

(1) Reset (RESET*). This bi-directional, open-drained signal is used as the system reset signal. If asserted as an input, RESET* causes the processor to enter reset exception processing. As an output, the MC68020 asserts RESET* (in response to executing the RESET instruction) to reset external devices but is not affected internally.

(2) Halt (HALT*). This bi-directional, open-drained signal indicates whether the processor is in the halted or run state. When HALT* is asserted as an input, the MC68020 stops all bus activity at the end of the currently executing bus cycle and places all control signals in their inactive state. The processor will, however, continue to drive the function code lines and the address bus.

The MC68020 asserts HALT* as a result of a double bus fault condition to indicate to the other devices in the system that it has stopped executing instructions.

(3) Bus error (BERR*). This input signal is used to indicate to the MC68020 that there is a problem with the currently executing bus cycle. These problems could be the result of:

(i)   Non-responding devices.
(ii) Failure to acquire an interrupt vector.
(iii) Illegal accesses as determined by a memory management unit.
(iv) Other application dependent errors.

The BERR* signal interacts with the HALT* signal to determine if the current bus cycle should be re-run or aborted.

5.8.10 CLOCK (CLK)

This TTL-compatible signal is internally buffered to generate the internal clocks required by the MC68020. It should not be gated off at any time.

5.8.11 SIGNAL SUMMARY

Table 5.2 provides a summary of the MC68020 signals discussed in the previous sections.

Table 5.2 Signal summary

Signal Function	Signal Name	Input/ Output	Active State	Three- State
Function Codes	FC0-FC2	Output	High	Yes
Address Bus	A0-A31	Output	High	Yes
Data Bus	D0-D31	I/O	High	Yes
Size	SIZ0-SIZ1	Output	High	Yes
External Cycle Start	ECS*	Output	Low	No
Operand Cycle Start	OCS*	Output	Low	No
Read-Modify-Write Cycle	RMC*	Output	Low	Yes
Address Strobe	AS*	Output	Low	Yes
Data Strobe	DS*	Output	Low	Yes
Read/Write	R/W*	Output	High/Low	Yes
Data Buffer Enable	DBEN*	Output	Low	Yes
Data Transfer/Size Acknowledge	DSACK0-1*	Input	Low	-
Cache Disable	CDIS*	Input	Low	-
Interrupt Priority Level	IPL0-IPL2*	Input	Low	-
Interrupt Pending	IPEND*	Output	Low	No
Autovector	AVEC*	Input	Low	-
Bus Request	BR*	Input	Low	-
Bus Grant	BG*	Output	Low	No
Bus Grant Acknowledge	BGACK*	Input	Low	-
Reset	RESET*	I/O	Low	No*
Halt	HALT*	I/O	Low	No*
Bus Error	BERR*	Input	Low	-
Clock	CLK	Input	-	-
Power Supply	VCC	Input	-	-
Ground	GND	Input	-	-

*Open Drain

5.9   Operand transfer mechanism

5.9.1   DYNAMIC BUS SIZING

The MC68020 supports an operand transfer mechanism called *dynamic bus sizing* that allows it to determine port size (8, 16 or 32 bits) on a bus cycle by bus cycle basis. During a bus cycle, a port will signal its data bus width and transfer status (complete or not complete) to the MC68020 via the DSACK0* and DSACK1* input lines. These DSACKx* inputs perform the same function as the DTACK* input of the other M68000 family processors, as well as indicating port size. Table 5.3 describes the DSACKx* encodings and their meanings.

As an example, if the MC68020 is attempting to read a 32-bit value from a port, it need not know the port size before it initiates the transfer. If the port responds with a DSACK1*/DSACK0* = 00, indicating that it is a 32-bit wide port, the MC68020 will latch in all 32 bits of the data bus and complete the transfer (i.e. negate the address and data strobes and control signals). If the port indicates that it is 16 bits wide (DSACK1*/DSACK0* = 01), the processor will latch the 16 bits on D31–D16 and begin another bus cycle. When the port asserts DSACKx*, the MC68020 will again latch the data on D31 through D16, thus picking up the full 32 bits. Similar events would occur if the port were 8 bits wide, except that four bus cycles would be required to latch in four bytes on D31 through D24.

In order to locate valid data, the MC68020 makes certain assumptions about where the ports are located with respect to its data bus. 32-bit ports should reside on D31 through D0, 16-bit ports on D31 through D16, and 8-bit ports on D31 through D24. Having the ports aligned in this manner minimises the number of bus cycles required to transfer data.

Table 5.3   DSACK codes and results

$\overline{\text{DSACK1}}$	$\overline{\text{DSACK0}}$	Result
H	H	Insert wait states in current bus cycle
H	L	Complete cycle - Data bus port size is 8 bits
L	H	Complete cycle - Data bus port size is 16 bits
L	L	Complete cycle - Data bus port size is 32 bits

Table 5.4   SIZE output encodings

SIZ1	SIZ0	Size
0	1	Byte
1	0	Word
1	1	3 Byte
0	0	Long Word

The MC68020 contains an internal multiplexor that allows it to route the four bytes of the data bus to their correct position. This multiplexor provides the mechanism by which the MC68020 supports dynamic bus sizing and operand misalignment. For example, the most significant byte of an operand, OP0, can be routed to bits D31 through D24, as in normal (aligned) operation, or it can be routed to any other byte position in order to support misalignment. The same applies to the other operand bytes. The byte position the operand occupies is determined by the size lines (SIZ0 and SIZ1) and the two least significant address lines (A1 and A0).

The SIZ1 and SIZ0 lines indicate the number of bytes remaining to be transferred during the current transaction. The number of bytes that are actually transferred depends on port size and operand alignment and will be less than or equal to the value indicated by the SIZx lines. Table 5.4 shows the SIZx output encodings.

The address lines A1 and A0 also affect the operation of the multiplexor. During an operand transfer, A31 through A2 give the

Table 5.5   Address offset encodings

A1	A0	Offset
0	0	+0 Bytes
0	1	+1 Byte
1	0	+2 Bytes
1	1	+3 Bytes

long word base address of the operand to be accessed and A1 and A0 give the byte offset from that address. Table 5.5 shows the address offset encodings.

Table 5.6 describes the use of the SIZ0, SIZ1, A0 and A1 lines in defining the transfer pattern from the MC68020's internal multiplexor to the external data bus. For example, suppose the MC68020 needs to move the value $01234567 to the 8-bit port located at address $8000. When the processor begins to execute this instruction, it does not know to which size port it is sending the information, so it attempts to write

Table 5.6   MC68020 internal to external data bus multiplexor

Transfer Size	Size		Address		Source/Destination External Data Bus Connection			
	SIZ1	SIZ0	A1	A0	D31:D24	D23:D16	D15:D8	D7:D0
Byte	0	1	x	x	OP3	OP3	OP3	OP3
Word	1	0	x	0	OP2	OP3	OP2	OP3
	1	0	x	1	OP2	OP2	OP3	OP2
3 Byte	1	1	0	0	OP1	OP2	OP3	OP0
	1	1	0	1	OP1	OP1	OP2	OP3
	1	1	1	0	OP1	OP2	OP1	OP2
	1	1	1	1	OP1	OP1	OP2	OP1
Long Word	0	0	0	0	OP0	OP1	OP2	OP3
	0	0	0	1	OP0	OP0	OP1	OP2
	0	0	1	0	OP0	OP1	OP0	OP1
	0	0	1	1	OP0	OP0	OP1*	OP0

* On write cycles, this byte is output; on read cycles, this byte is ignored.
x = don't care

the full operand, in this case 32 bits, during the first bus cycle. The size lines are both low to indicate that a long word is to be transferred and A1 and A0 are low to indicate that the long word is aligned. The 8-bit port will latch bits D31 through D24 and assert a DSACK1*/ DSACK0* of 10, first to indicate that it has received the data, and second, to tell the MC68020 that it is only an 8-bit port. As a result of this '8-bit DSACK', the MC68020 initiates another bus cycle with the next most significant byte of data multiplexed to the uppermost byte of its data bus (D31–D24). The size lines indicate that three bytes remain to be transferred and A1 and A0 are incremented by one to indicate that the next byte in the memory map is being addressed. Again the port latches in the data on D31 through D24 and signals back an 8-bit DSACK. This process continues until the long word transfer is complete.

5.9.2 OPERAND MISALIGNMENT

The MC68020 also supports misaligned data operand transfers. The transfer of an operand to/from memory is considered to be misaligned if the address does not fall on an equivalent operand size boundary. Transferring a word to an odd address or a long word to something other than a long word boundary are both examples of misaligned transfers.

The MC68020 places no restrictions on data alignment. However, some performance degradation may occur due to the extra bus cycles the MC68020 must run when word or long word accesses are not made to word or long word boundaries. Note that instructions must always reside on even byte boundaries to ensure compatibility with the other members of the M68000 family and to optimise performance for instruction prefetches. Any time an instruction prefetch is attempted from an odd word address the MC68020 forces an address error exception. This occurs any time an instruction leaves the program counter set to an odd address.

As an example of a misaligned read, suppose the MC68020 is reading a word from location $4001 and storing it in data register D0, where address $4001 corresponds to a 16-bit port. The SIZ1 and SIZ0 lines are 1 and 0 respectively indicating that a words needs to be transferred. The 16-bit port outputs the word at location $4000 ($0123) on bits 31 through 16 of the MC68020 data bus and signals back a DSACK1*/DSACK0* of 01. This encoding indicates to the processor that valid data is present on the data bus and that the port is 16 bits wide. The MC68020 latches in the data, ignores all bytes except for the one at D23–D16 and stores this byte ($23) in a temporary register. It then executes another bus cycle, with the size lines indicating a byte transfer, and the address incremented by one. The 16-bit port then outputs the word at location $4002 ($4567) and returns a 16-bit DSACK*. The MC68020 latches in the data, ignores bits 23 through 0 and stores the value on D31 through D24 ($45), along with the byte stored in the temporary register during the previous cycle, in the lower word of the data register D0.

5.9.3   ADVANTAGES OF DYNAMIC BUS SIZING

The dynamic bus sizing capability of the MC68020 gives system designers considerable flexibility; they can pick and choose the size of the ports in the system as they wish. For example, system RAM is accessed numerous times and therefore extra transfers to and from it should be minimised to obtain maximum performance. Thus, in an MC68020 system, the RAM is typically 32 bits wide. However, the same is not necessarily true for ROM. Since existing EPROMs are only 8 bits wide, 16-bit ROM ports require splitting the ROM program into odd and even bytes and 32-bit ROM ports require splitting the program into four pieces. If the ROM contains a monitor routine where execution speed is not a major factor in the performance of the system, then the designer might choose to make it only 8 bits wide. This would eliminate the need to split the routine into every two or every four bytes every time a new EPROM needed to be burned. Also, changes to the routine could be made much more easily and quickly. Programmers are relieved from any constraints imposed by the hardware. Because each size port has a unique handshake via the DSACK* lines, the system, in essence, becomes 'software independent'. In other words, the programmer can send any size data to any port in the system.

5.10   Cache

5.10.1   CACHE BASICS

A cache memory differs from main memory in a number of regards. First, a cache is smaller and has a much faster access time than main memory. Second, the processor accesses cache memory differently than it accesses main memory. When main memory is accessed by the processor, it outputs the data value contained at the specified address. Cache memory, however, first must compare the incoming address to the address (or addresses) stored in the cache. If the addresses match, then a 'hit' is said to have occurred and the corresponding data is allowed to be read from the cache. If the addresses do not match, a 'miss' is said to have occurred and an access from main memory is allowed to complete. When a miss occurs, the data retrieved from main memory is also provided to the cache so that the next time this specific address is accessed, a hit may occur in the cache.

Sections 5.10.2 and 5.10.3 describe the types of caches that are or could be implemented with the MC68020. The first section discusses the MC68020 on-chip cache and the second covers two ways of designing an external data cache for an MC68020 system.

5.10.2   ON CHIP

The MC68020 contains an on-chip instruction cache that improves the performance of the microprocessor by decreasing instruction access time and reducing the processor's external bus activity.

Instruction words that are stored in the cache are accessed much more quickly than if they had been stored in external memory. In addition, while the MC68020 is accessing the instruction cache, it can make a simultaneous data fetch on the external bus.

An improvement in bus bandwidth can be obtained using the cache. If the MC68020 finds an instruction word in the cache, it does not need to make an external access, thus freeing the bus for other bus masters in the system.

The MC68020 on-chip cache is a direct-mapped cache containing 64 long word entries. Each entry consists of a tag field, a valid bit, and instruction words (32 bits). The tag field comprises the upper 24 address bits and the FC2 value. Thus the 4 Gbyte address space of the MC68020 is partitioned into blocks of 256 bytes in size.

Whenever the MC68020 makes an instruction fetch, it begins two simultaneous accesses, the normal one to external memory (assuming the external bus is free) and the one to the cache (assuming the cache is enabled). The processor checks the cache to see if the instruction is present in the cache. To do this, a portion of the tag field is used as an index into the cache to select one of the 64 entries. Next, the remainder of the tag for that entry is compared to the address of the instruction and the FC2 line. If they agree and the valid bit is set, a 'hit' is said to have occurred. Bit A1 is used to select the appropriate word from the cache and the cycle ends. This all occurs within two clock cycles as opposed to the normal three clock cycles required for an external access. Externally, the processor may drive the address lines, size, function code, and ECS* lines before aborting the cycle due to a cache hit. Note that address strobe is not asserted if there is a hit in the cache.

If the tag of the entry does not agree with the address of the instruction or if the valid bit is cleared, a 'miss' occurs and the external cycle is allowed to complete. If the cache is not frozen (via the freeze bit in the cache control register), the new instruction is written into the cache and the valid bit set. Note that both words corresponding to that address are replaced because the MC68020 always fetches long words.

Upon reset, the processor clears the cache by clearing the valid bits for every entry. In addition, the enable and freeze bits in the cache control register are cleared.

5.10.3   OFF CHIP

An external cache can be designed for an MC68020 system to provide even more performance. The cache could be either on the logical or on the physical side of the address bus and it could be implemented as an instruction and data cache or data-only cache.

This section will discuss the important points of designing a logical data cache for an MC68020 system. It is not meant to provide the reader with a tested design, nor is it meant to imply that this is the best or only design possible. Instead, it should be used to determine what timing specifications are important when designing an external cache for an MC68020 system.

Typically, for main memory, the critical timing specification is from addresses valid to data valid. For a cache memory, the most important timing specification in order to minimise wait states is from addresses valid to decision (hit or miss) required. The decision would trigger the event that causes the bus cycle to terminate. On an MC68020 system, the event could either by DSACKx* asserted or BERR* and HALT* asserted. Each of these methods will be looked into, including timing information and advantages and disadvantages.

In the first method, the assertion of DSACKx* is delayed until it is known whether or not a hit has occurred in the cache. Thus, DSACKx* is a product of the HIT* signal of the cache circuitry. If a hit occurs, the access to main memory (which may be happening simultaneously to the cache access) must be aborted before the memory could start driving the data bus. If a miss occurs, then the cycle to main memory is allowed to complete. Figure 5.7 shows the worst case timing requirement at 16.67 MHz for a no-wait state cache design (assuming a hit) using this method. Note that the amount of time available to determine whether there will be a hit or miss is 55 ns

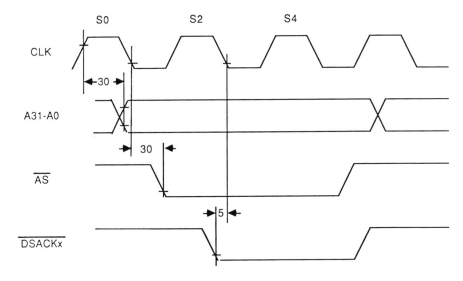

Fig. 5.7   Cache timing requirements (Case 1).

minimum (the time from addresses valid to DSACKx* asserted). If a hit does occur, data needs to be available at least 5 ns prior to the falling edge of S4. If the designer is unwilling to invest in the fast RAMs required to achieve a no-wait state cache, wait states can be added for a longer decision time at a performance degradation.

In the second method, it is assumed that the cache will always have the correct data (i.e. never incur a miss). Therefore, DSACKx* may be asserted before it is known if the desired address is available in the cache. If a hit does occur, the access will run with no-wait states. If a miss occurs, the BERR* and HALT* lines to the MC68020 must be asserted to indicate to the processor that the cycle should not be terminated normally. This is known as *late retry*. When BERR* and HALT* are negated, the MC68020 reruns the faulted bus cycle. Some external hardware is required to prevent a cache access for this second bus cycle from occurring and to handle the case where bus arbitration occurs between the two bus cycles. A smart design takes advantage of the time between these bus cycles (faulted and retry) and starts the access to main memory when it becomes obvious that the cache access is going to miss. See Fig. 5.8 for the timing requirements (assuming a miss) for this type of cache design. The only requirement for the assertion of DSACKx* is that it be present at least 5 ns before the falling edge of S2. BERR* and HALT* need to be asserted at least 20 ns prior to the falling edge of S4 in order for them to be recognised by the MC68020. Therefore, the designer has 100 ns (from addresses

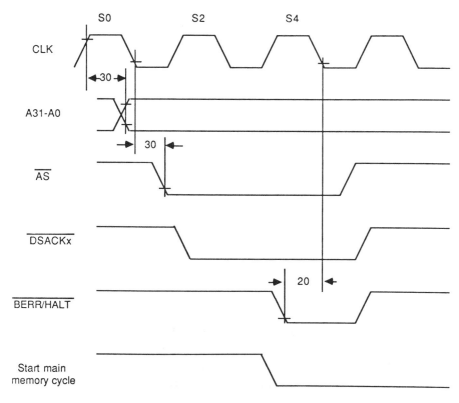

Fig. 5.8 Cache timing requirements (Case 2).

valid to BERR*/HALT* asserted) to determine if a cache hit is going to occur. If it is determined that a miss will occur, the data bus drivers from the data RAMs need to be blocked to prevent them from driving the bus and the access to main memory is started at approximately the same time the BERR* and HALT* lines are asserted.

In the first type of design, the cache requires faster RAMs in order to run with no-wait states. In the second type, slower RAMs could be used, while obtaining the same performance. The cache accesses in this second case always run with zero wait states and memory accesses due to cache misses effectively run with two fewer wait states than a normal main memory access would (i.e. no cache in the system).

5.11 Co-processors

5.11.1 CO-PROCESSOR INTERFACE

The MC68020 supports a co-processor interface that allows it to extend its functions. While a general purpose machine performs well in several different areas of application, it might not perform as well in one area as a processor designed specifically for that application. Co-processors allow a main processor to be enhanced for a particular application without losing the generality of the main processor architecture.

In addition, co-processors allow system designers to 'custom tailor' their designs by selecting only those co-processors that suit the needs of their system. This eliminates the need for designers to pay for extra hardware that they frequently have to buy in order to obtain the specific hardware that they do require.

A co-processor is defined as anything that implements the co-processor interface, whether it be one device, several devices or a whole board. It provides extensions to the main processor's programming model by adding new registers and new instructions and data types.

The co-processor implementation is completely transparent to the user. The programmer is not required to have a knowledge of the co-processor protocol. In fact, he/she need never know that the co-processor is separate from the MC68020. It appears as an extension to the MC68020 hardware.

Communication between the MC68020 and the co-processor is initiated by the MC68020 as a result of a co-processor instruction. The processor begins by writing a command to the co-processor and waiting for the response. The algorithm necessary for this communication is contained in the microcode of the MC68020. Thus, the user does not have the burden of sending out the command word and polling for a response from the co-processor. It is only necessary to use the co-processor instructions, designated by the 'ones' in the most significant bits of the op code (bits 15–12 = 1111). Figure 5.9 shows the format of a co-processor instruction word or F-line op word. Bits 11 through 9 are defined as the CP-ID (co-processor identification field). Each co-processor in a system has a unique ID. Thus, up to eight co-processors are supported in a system. When the main processor initiates communication with the co-processor, the CP-ID is placed on address lines A15–A13. While the co-processor may not necessarily decode these bits internally, they can be used within the address decode to

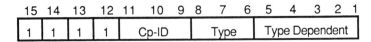

15	14	13	12	11	10	9	8	7	6	5	4	3	2	1
1	1	1	1	Cp-ID			Type		Type Dependent					

Fig. 5.9   F-line co-processor instruction operation word.

provide the chip selects for the co-processors. Bits 8 through 6 specify the type of instruction being executed: general, branch, conditional, save or restore. These instruction types will be discussed in a later section.

A co-processor can also be used as a peripheral with a microprocessor other than the MC68020, such as the MC68000, the MC68008 or the MC68010. If an F-line instruction is executed in an M68000, non-MC68020 system, the processor takes the F-line exception, thus allowing the co-processor interface to be emulated in software.

The co-processor interface operates with normal M68000 bus cycles; no special signals are required to connect the co-processor up to an M68000 processor. When running as a co-processor with the MC68020, the function code lines, along with address lines A11 through A9, are used to generate the chip select for the co-processor. All co-processor accesses are made in CPU space. When accessed as a peripheral, a chip select needs to be generated based on the address lines, just like any other peripheral. Figures 5.10(a) and (b) show a block diagram of a co-processor in an MC68020 and an MC68000 system, respectively. Note that the main processor and co-processor need not run off the same clock nor do they need to run at the same clock speed.

A processor communicates with the co-processor via the co-processor interface registers, shown in Fig. 5.11. Those with asterisks indicate the registers that are required to implement each of the instruction types. Note that all addresses are in CPU space. The following paragraphs describe the co-processor interface register set.

(1) Response register. A 16-bit read-only register by which the co-processor requests action of the main processor.

(2) Control register. A 16-bit write-only register through which the main processor acknowledges co-processor requested exception processing. In addition, the main processor uses this register to abort instruction execution.

(3) Save register. A 16-bit readable/writable register. The main processor reads this register to initiate a cpSAVE instruction. The co-processor then returns status and state frame format information to the main processor through this register.

(4) Restore register. A 16-bit readable/writable register. The main processor writes a co-processor format word to this register to initiate a cpRESTORE instruction. The co-processor then returns the format word to the main processor through this register.

(5) Operation word register. A 16-bit write-only register. The main

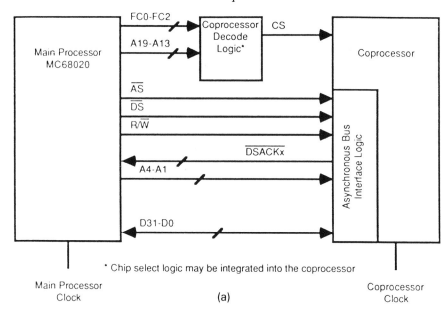

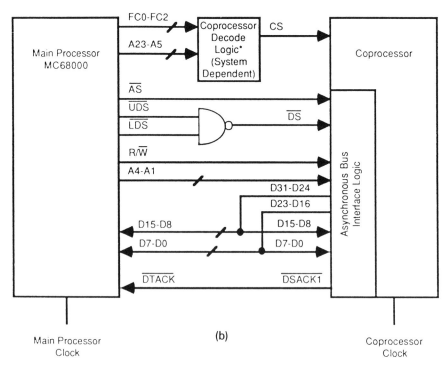

Fig. 5.10   (a) MC68020 interface to co-processor on a 32-bit data bus; (b) MC68000 interface to co-processor on a 16-bit data bus.

	31	15	0
$00	Response*	Control*	
$04	Save*	Restore*	
$08	Operation Word	Command*	
$0C	(Reserved)	Condition*	
$10	Operand*		
$14	Register Select	(Reserved)	
$18	Instruction Address		
$1C	Operand Address		

Fig. 5.11   Co-processor interface register set map.

processor writes the F-line operation word to this register in response to a transfer operation word request from the co-processor.

(6) Command register. A 16-bit write-only register through which the main processor initiates an instruction in the general instruction category (discussed later).

(7) Condition register. A 16-bit write-only register through which the main processor initiates an instruction in the co-processor conditional category.

(8) Register select register. A 16-bit read-only register. The main processor reads this register to determine which registers to transfer upon receiving a transfer register(s) request from the co-processor.

(9) Instruction address register. A 32-bit readable/writable register through which the main processor transfers the address of the instruction it is currently executing upon a request from the co-processor.

(10) Operand address register. A 32-bit readable/writable register. The transfer of an operand address is accomplished through this register upon the request of the co-processor.

There are three categories of co-processor instructions. They are general, conditional, and system control. The general class of instructions is used to describe most co-processor instructions and is defined mainly by the co-processor. For example, the floating point add, subtract and multiply instructions on the MC68881 floating point co-processor are all examples of a general instruction. The conditional instructions include both branch instructions (such as branch on condition) and other conditional instructions (such as set on condition and trap on condition). In each case, the main processor passes the condition selector to the co-processor for evaluation. The co-processor then indicates a true or false condition back to the main processor which can then continue with the execution of the instruction. The system control instructions include two instructions that permit operating system task switching. They are cpSAVE and cpRESTORE. The cpSAVE instruction causes the co-processor to pass a format word and internal state information to the main processor which then stores it in memory. The cpRESTORE instruction causes the co-processor to load its internal state with the information passed to it from the main processor. Both instructions are privileged and thus can only be executed while executing in the supervisor mode.

More information about the M68000 co-processor interface can be found in the *MC68020 Microprocessor User's Manual.*[1]

5.11.2   MC68881 FLOATING POINT CO-PROCESSOR

The MC68881 Floating Point Co-processor, processed in HCMOS, was designed primarily for use as a co-processor with the MC68020, but can also be operated as a peripheral in non-MC68020 systems. It fully supports the IEEE P754 floating point standard (draft 10.0). In addition, it provides a full set of trigonometric and logarithmic functions not defined by the IEEE standard. It performs all internal calculations to 80 bits of precision.

The MC68881 architecture appears as a logical extension of the

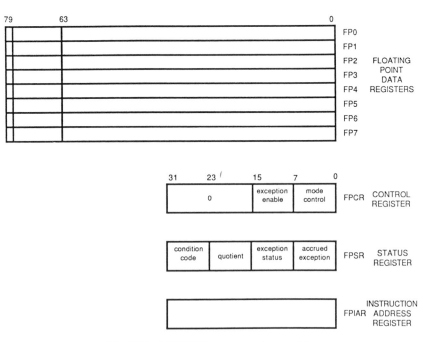

Fig. 5.12   MC68881 programming model.

M68000 architecture. When coupled to the MC68020 as a co-processor, the MC68881 registers can be regarded by the programmer as residing on the MC68020 die. Figure 5.12 shows the programmer's model for the MC68881. It contains eight 80-bit floating point registers (FP0–FP7) that are analogous to the integer data registers (D0–D7) on the MC68020, a 32-bit control register, a 32-bit status register, and a 32-bit instruction address register. The control register contains enable bits for each class of exception trap and mode bits for selecting rounding and precision modes. The status register contains floating point condition codes, quotient bits, and exception status information. The instruction address register contains the address of the last floating point instruction that was executed. This register is used for exception handling purposes.

The MC68881 supports four new data types: single precision, double precision, extended precision and packed-decimal string real, in addition to the three integer data types supported by all M68000

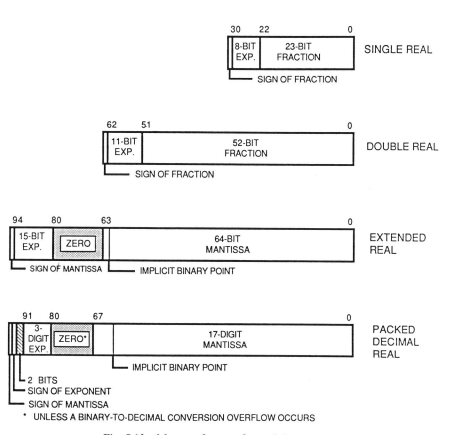

Fig. 5.13   Memory formats for real data types.

processors (byte, word and long word). Figure 5.13 shows the memory formats for the real data types.

The MC68881 supports five classes of instruction operations: data movement, dyadic operations, monadic operations, program control and system control. The data movement instructions on the MC68881 work in essentially the same way as the data movement instructions on the MC68020. They are used to move operands into, between and out of MC68881 registers. Dyadic operations require two operands and perform arithmetic functions such as add, subtract, multiply and divide. Monadic instructions provide arithmetic functions that require only one operand, such as sine, square root, negate, etc. Program control instructions affect the program flow based on conditions in the status register. These instructions include branch on condition, decrement and branch on condition, no operation, set on condition, and test operand. The system control operations are used to communicate with the operating system. The system control instructions are save state, restore state, and trap on condition.

More information on the MC68881 can be found in the *MC68881 User's Manual.*[2]

5.11.2.1 *MC68882 HCMOS enhanced floating point co-processor.*

The MC68882 floating point co-processor fully implements the IEEE Standard for Binary Floating Point Arithmetic (ANSI-IEEE Standard 754-1985) for the use with the Motorola M68000 family of microprocessors. An upgrade of the MC68881, it is pin and software compatible with an optimised MPU interface providing in excess of 1.5 times the performance of the MC68881.

5.11.3   MC68851 PAGED MEMORY MANAGEMENT UNIT

The MC68851 Paged Memory Management Unit (PMMU) is also manufactured in Motorola's HCMOS process. It was designed to support a demand paged virtual memory system. It operates as a co-processor with the MC68020 but can be used with other processors. The remaining paragraphs of this section will discuss the co-processor aspects of the PMMU, while the memory management capabilities will be discussed in Section 5.12.

Figure 5.14 shows the programmer's model for the MC68851. The CPU Root Pointer (CRP), DMA Root Pointer (DRP), Supervisor Root Pointer (SRP), Translation Control (TC), Cache Status (CS), Status (STATUS), Current Access Level (CAL), Validate Access Level (VAL), Stack Change Control (SCC), and the Access Control (AC)

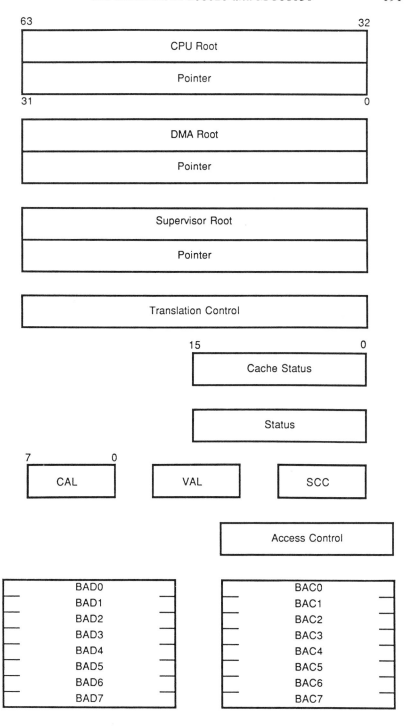

Fig. 5.14   MC68851 programming model.

registers control the translation and protection features of the PMMU. The other 16 registers, breakpoint acknowledge data (BAD7–BAD0) and breakpoint acknowledge control (BAC7–BAC0), control the breakpoint functions available with the MC68020 BKPT instructions.

The CRP register is a 64-bit register that contains the pointer to the root of the translation table tree for the current user task. The DRP is a 64-bit register that contains the root pointer to the translation table that is used when an alternate logical bus master is translating through the PMMU. The SRP is a 64-bit register whose contents point to the root of the translation table to be used for translating supervisor accesses. The TC register is a 32-bit register that contains bits that configure the translation mechanism of the PMMU. The CS register is a 16-bit read-only register that contains bits useful for maintaining a logical data cache. The STATUS register is a 16-bit register that contains bits for indicating bus error, supervisor violation, access level violation, invalid address, etc. The CAL and VAL registers are both 8 bits wide; however, only the upper three bits are implemented. The CAL register contains the access level of the currently executing routine and the VAL contains the access level of the caller of the current routine. The SCC register is an 8-bit register that determines if a stack change should occur during an MC68020 CALLM instruction. The AC register is 16 bits wide and controls access information for the PMMU (i.e. whether access levels are enabled, how many upper address bits contain access level information, etc.). The BAD and BAC registers are all 16 bits wide. The BAD registers hold op codes to be provided to the processor during a breakpoint acknowledge cycle and the BAC registers contain the enable and count functions for the breakpoint acknowledge instruction.

The MC68851 supports three classes of instructions: loading and storing of PMMU registers (PMOVE), testing access rights and conditionals (PVALID, PTEST, PLOAD, PFLUSH, PBcc, PDBcc, Scc, and PTRAPcc), and control functions (PSAVE and PRESTORE). All PMMU instructions are privileged except for the PVALID instruction.

More information on the MC68851 can be found in the *MC68851 User's Manual*.[3]

5.12 Memory management

5.12.1 MEMORY MANAGEMENT TECHNIQUES

Memory management basically has three functions: translate

addresses, provide protection for the operating system from user access, and provide write protection for some user read-only pages. Without a Memory Management Unit (MMU), an operating system would have the responsibility of handling address translation and access protection in software. Obviously, this would require an enormous amount of code. With an MMU in the system, an operating system need only set up the translation descriptors. The MMU then handles the tasks of translation and protection in hardware.

An MMU divides the system address bus, creating logical addresses and physical addresses. The logical side is the side with the main processor on it and the physical bus is used to access main memory. The MMU has two choices when it comes to translating logical addresses to physical addresses. In the first technique, the MMU adds a defined offset to the logical address to produce the physical address. In the second method, called the substitution technique, the MMU searches the translation tables to find the physical address mapping. Typically, the substitution method is preferred because physical addresses may be generated much more quickly than with the adder method.

Memory management can be implemented in one of two ways. The first implementation is called *segmented.* In this type of system, a segment descriptor contains three variables: the logical address, the length of the window or task, and the offset. The length defines a contiguous block of memory (known as a *page*) and the offset is used to generate the physical address. The second type of implementation is called *paged.* In a paged memory management system, two variables are defined, i.e. the logical address and the physical address. The length of the windows or pages are fixed. Each system has its own advantages and disadvantages.

The MC68851 discussed in Section 5.12.2 is a paged MMU.

5.12.2 MC68851

As stated in Section 5.12.1, the MC68851 PMMU supports a demand paged virtual memory environment. It supports multiple logical and/ or physical bus masters, as well as logical and/or physical data caches. The primary functions of the PMMU are to provide logical-to-physical address translation, to monitor and enforce the protection/privilege mechanism set up by the operating system, and to support the MC68020 breakpoint operation. These three topics will be discussed further in the following paragraphs.

The task of translating logical-to-physical address occupies most of the PMMU's time, and thus has been optimised in terms of speed and minimum processor intervention. The MC68851 starts an address translation by searching for the descriptor that describes the translation for the incoming logical address in the on-chip Address Translation Cache (ATC). The ATC is a very fast, fully associative, 64-entry cache that stores recently used descriptors. If the descriptor is not resident in the ATC, the PMMU aborts the bus cycle and becomes bus master in order to 'walk' the translation tables in physical memory. A translation table is a hierarchical data structure that contains the page descriptors controlling the logical-to-physical address translations. The root pointer registers discussed in Section 5.12.1 point to the top of these translation tables. When the PMMU finds the correct page descriptor, it loads it into the ATC and allows the logical bus master to retry the aborted cycle, which should now be correctly translated.

The MC68851 protection mechanism provides a cycle-by-cycle examination and enforcement of the access rights of the currently executing process. The PMMU supports eight levels of privilege in a hierarchical arrangement, which are encoded in the three most significant bits of the incoming logical address (LA31–LA29). The PMMU compares these bits with the value in the CAL register. If the priority level of the incoming address is lower than the value in the CAL register, then the bus cycle is requesting a higher privilege than it is allowed. The PMMU will terminate this access as a fault. In addition, the PMMU supports the MC68020 module call and return instructions (CALLM/RTM). Included is a mechanism to change privilege levels during module operation.

The MC68851 supports breakpoints for the MC68020 and other processors with its breakpoint acknowledge capability. When the MC68020 encounters a breakpoint instruction, it executes a breakpoint acknowledge cycle in CPU space. It reads a word from an address that is determined by the number of the breakpoint (specified in the instruction). The PMMU decodes this address and either places a replacement op code on the data bus or asserts bus error to indicate illegal instruction exception. The BAD registers contain the replacement op codes.

For more information on the memory management capabilities of the MC68851, refer to the *MC68851 User's Manual*.[3]

5.13   The MC68030

The MC68030 is an enhanced 32-bit HCMOS microprocessor that incorporates the capabilities of the MC68020 MPU, an on-chip data cache, an on-chip instruction cache, an improved bus controller, multiple internal data buses, multiple internal instruction buses, and an on-chip paged MMU structure defined by the MC68851 PMMU. The MC68030 maintains the 32-bit registers available with the entire M68000 family as well as the 32-bit address address and data paths, rich instruction set, versatile addressing modes and flexible co-processor interface provided with the MC68020. In addition, the internal operations of the integrated processor are designed to operate in parallel, allowing multiple instructions to be executed concurrently. It also allows instruction execution to proceed in parallel with accesses to the internal caches, the on-chip MMU and the external bus controller.

The MC68030 fully supports the non-multiplexed asynchronous bus of the MC68020 as well as the dynamic bus sizing mechanism that allows the processor to transfer operands to or from external devices while automatically determining device port size on a cycle-by-cycle basis. In addition to the asynchronous bus, the MC68030 also supports a fast 32-bit synchronous bus for off-chip caches and fast memories. Further, the MC68030 bus is capable of fetching up to four long words of data in a burst mode compatible with DRAM chips that have burst capability. Burst mode can reduce by up to 50% the time necessary to fetch the four long words. The four long words are used to prefill the on-chip instruction and data caches so that the hit ratio of the caches improves and the average access time for operand fetches is minimised.

The block diagram shown in Fig. 5.15 depicts the major section of the MC68030 and illustrates the autonomous nature of these blocks. The bus controller consists of the address and data pads, the multiplexers required to support dynamic bus sizing, and a macro bus controller which schedules the bus cycles on the basis of priority. The micromachine contains the execution unit and all related control logic. Microcode control is provided by a modified two-level store of microrom and nanorom contained in the micromachine. Programmed Logic Arrays (PLAs) are used to provide instruction decode and sequencing information. The instruction pipe and other individual control sections provide the secondary decode of instructions and generate the actual control signals that result in the decoding and interpretation of nanorom and microrom information.

The instruction and data cache blocks operate independently from the rest of the machine, storing information read by the controller for future use with very fast access time. Each cache resides on its own address and data buses, allowing simultaneous access to both. These caches are each organised as 64 long word entries (256 bytes) with a

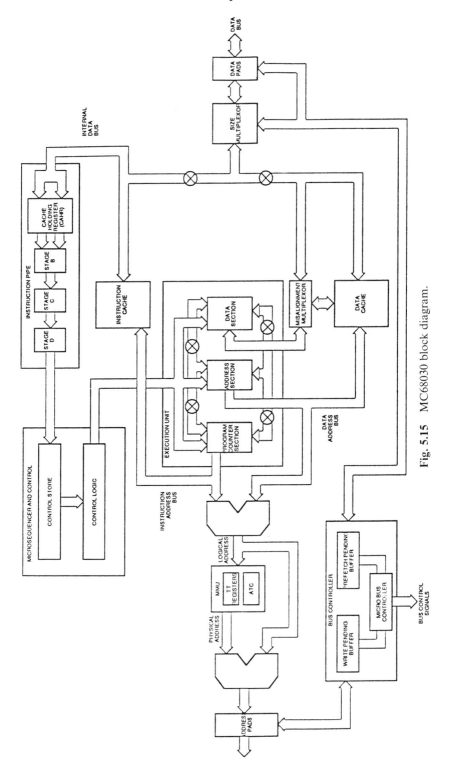

Fig. 5.15   MC68030 block diagram.

block size of four long words. The data cache uses a write-through policy with no write allocation on cache misses.

Finally, the MMU controls the mapping of addresses for page sizes ranging from 256 bytes to 32K. Mapping information stored in descriptors resides in translation tables in memory that are automatically searched by the MC68030 on demand. Recently-used descriptors are maintained in a 22-entry fully associative cache called the Address Translation Cache (ATC) allowing address translation and other MC68030 functions to occur simultaneously. Additionally, the MC68030 contains two transparent translation registers that can be used to define one to one mapping for two segments ranging in size from 16 Mbytes to 4 Gbytes each.

5.14   MC68030 data organisation

5.14.1   OPERANDS

The MC68030 supports all seven data types of the MC68020:

- Bits
- Bit fields (strings of consecutive bits, 1–32 bits long)
- BCD digits (packed: 2 digits per byte or unpacked 1 digit per byte)
- Byte integers (8 bits)
- Word integers (16 bits)
- Long word integers (32 bits)
- Quad word integers (64 bits)

As well as the above, the MC68030 also supports the co-processor interface like the MC68020 thus expanding the data types available to the programmer to include those of any co-processor connected to the MC68030. For example, connecting an MC68882 floating point co-processor will allow direct support of floating point data types.

5.14.2   PROGRAMMING MODEL

The MC68030 has exactly the same user programming model as that of the MC68020 and an expanded supervisor programming model. See Section 5.5.2 for the MC68020 user programming model description. The MC68030 supervisor programming model is shown in Fig. 5.16. The first six registers, ISP, MSP, SR, VBR, SFC and DFC, are identical to the MC68020 supervisor model.

The Cache Control Register (CACR) has been expanded to include independent control for both the data and instruction caches. The

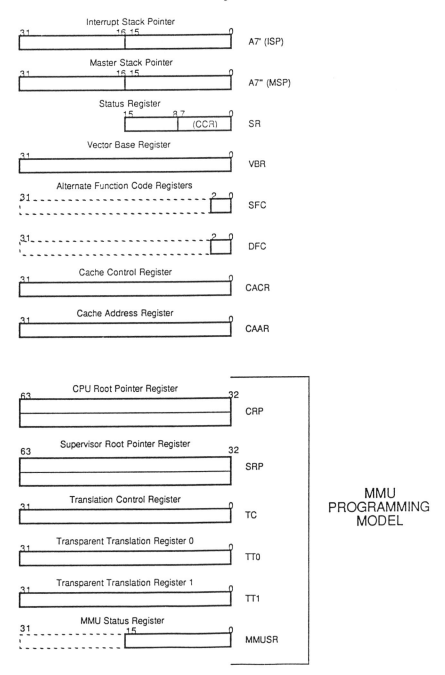

Fig. 5.16　Supervisor programming model supplement.

functions controlled are: enabling each cache, clearing each cache, freezing each cache, clearing an entry in each cache; the Cache Address Register (CAAR) is used to specify the address to be cleared in the indicated cache. There are new functions implemented in the CACR to enable the synchronous burst fillling of cache lines and to indicate if write allocation is to be used in data cache.

To support the MMU, the registers CRP, SRP, TC, TT0, TT1, and MMUSR have been included in the supervisor programming model. These registers are similar in function to those in the MC68851 (see Section 5.11.3 on memory management). The CPU Root Pointer (CRP) contains a pointer for the first descriptor to be used in the translation table search for page descriptors pertaining to the current task. If the Supervisor Root pointer Enable (SRE) bit of the Translation Control register (TC) is set, the supervisor root pointer (SRP) is used as a pointer to the translation tables for all supervisor accesses. If the SRE bit is clear, this register is unused and the CRP is used for both supervisor and user translations. The TC register configures the table look-up mechanism to be used for all table searches as well as the page size and any initial shift of logical address required by the operating system. In addition, this register has an enable bit that enables the MMU. The transparent translation registers can be used to define two transparent windows for accessing large blocks of data with untranslated addresses. Finally, the MMU Status Register (MMUSR) contains status information related to a specific address translation and the results generated by the PTEST instruction. This information can be useful in locating the cause of an MMU fault.

5.15 Memory organisation

The MC68030 supports all data types that the M68000 family support (see Section 5.5.3). Similarly, the MC68030 splits program and data references (see Section 5.5.4).

5.16 Addressing capabilities

The MC68030 has the same addressing capabilities and modes as the MC68020 (see Section 5.6).

5.17 Instruction set summary

The MC68030 is fully user object code compatible with the MC68020 and supports all the MC68020 instructions except for CALLM and RTM as these were deemed superfluous (see Section 5.7). To support the on-chip MMU, five extra instructions have been added. These perform a similar function to the instructions used by the MC68851 PMMU co-processor. The memory management instructions are:

- PFLUSHA This instruction invalidates all ATC entries
- PFLUSH   This invalidates specified ATC entries
- PLOAD   This creates an ATC entry for a given effective address
- PMOVE   Moves data to/from the MMU registers, SRP, CRP, TC and MMUSR
- PTEST   Searches the ATC or the translation tables to a specified level for the translation descriptor corresponding to the specified conditions. It reports the status of all the translation tables searched.

5.18   Signal descriptions

The MC68030 supports all of the control signals that were introduced on the MC68020 with the addition of cache control signals synchronous bus control, and emulator support (see Fig. 5.17 for functional signal groups of the MC68030). A description of the common signals between the MC68030 and MC68020 is given in Section 5.8. Sections 5.18.1 to 5.18.4 give a description of the new signals added into the MC68030.

5.18.1   BUS EXCEPTION CONTROL SIGNALS (HALT*)

The halt signal indicates that the processor should suspend bus activity or, when used with BERR*, that the processor should retry the current cycle. This is an input only signal compared to being bi-directional on the MC68020.

5.18.2   SYNCHRONOUS TERMINATION (STERM*)

This input is a bus handshake signal indicating the addressed port size is 32 bits and that the data is to be latched on the next falling clock edge of a read cycle. This signal applies only to synchronous operation.

5.18.3   CACHE CONTROL SIGNALS

Sections 5.18.3.1 to 5.18.3.4 relate to the on-chip caches.

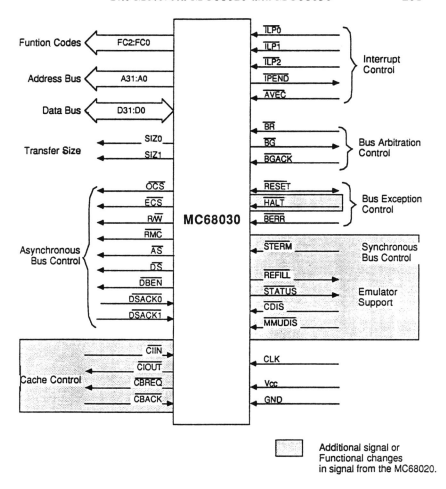

Fig. 5.17 Functional signal group for the MC68030.

5.18.3.1   *Cache Inhibit Input (CIIN*).*   This input signal prevents data from being loaded into the MC68030 instruction and data caches. It is a synchronous input signal and is interpreted on a bus-cycle-by-bus-cycle basis. CIIN* is ignored during all write cycles.

5.18.3.2   *Cache Inhibit Output (CIOUT*).*   This three-state output signal reflects the state of the CI bit in the address translation cache entry for the referenced logical address, indicating that an external cache should ignore the bus transfer. When the referenced logical address is within an area specified for transparent translation, the CI bit of the appropriate transparent translation register controls the state of CIOUT*.

5.18.3.3 *Cache Burst Request (CBREQ*).* This three-state output signal requests a burst mode operation to fill a link in the instruction or data cache.

5.18.3.4 *Cache Burst Acknowledge (CBACK*).* This input signal indicates that the accessed device can operate in the burst mode and can supply at least one more long word for the instruction or data cache.

5.18.4   EMULATOR SUPPORT SIGNALS

The signals described in Sections 5.18.4.1 to 5.18.4.4 support emulation by providing a means for an emulator to disable the on-chip caches and MMU by supplying internal status information to an emulator.

5.18.4.1 *Cache Disable (CDIS*).* The cache disable signal dynamically disables the on-chip caches to assist emulator support. The CDIS* does not flush the data and instruction caches; entries remain unaltered and become available again when CDIS* is negated.

5.18.4.2 *MMU Disable (MMUDIS*).* The MMU disable signal dynamically disables the translation of addresses by the MMU. The assertion of the MMUDIS* does not flush the address translation cache (ATC); ATC entries become available again when MMUDIS* is negated.

5.18.4.3 *Pipeline Refill (REFILL*).* The pipeline refill signal indicates that the MC68030 is beginning to refill the internal instruction pipeline.

5.18.4.4 *Internal Microsequencer Status (STATUS*).* The microsequencer status signal indicates the state of the internal microsequencer. The varying number of clocks for which this signal is asserted indicates instruction boundaries, pending exceptions, and the halted conditions.

5.19   Operand transfer mechanism

5.19.1   ASYNCHRONOUS TRANSFERS

The MC68030 supports the dynamic bus sizing mechanism of the

MC68020 for asynchronous bus cycles (terminated with DSACKx*) with two restrictions. Firstly, for a cachable access within the boundaries of an aligned long word, the port size must be consistent throughout the transfer for each long word. For example, when a port resides at address $00, addresses $01, and $03 must also correspond to byte ports. Secondly, the port must supply as much data as it signals as port size, regardless of the transfer size indicated with the size signals and the address offset indicated by A0 and A1 for cachable accesses. Otherwise, dynamic bus sizing is identical in the two processors (see Section 5.9 for description of MC68020 operation).

5.19.2 ASYNCHRONOUS OPERATION

The MC68030 bus may be used in an asynchronous manner. In that case, the external devices connected to the bus can operate at clock frequencies different from the clock for the MC68030. Asynchronous operation requires using only the handshake lines (AS*, DS*, DSACK1*, DSACK0*, BERR* and HALT*) to control data transfers. Using this method, AS* signals the start of a bus cycle, and DS* is used as a condition for valid data on a write cycle. Decoding the size outputs and lower address lines A0 and A1 provides strobes that select the active portion of the data bus. The slave device (memory or peripheral) then responds by placing the requested data on the correct portion of the data bus for a read cycle or latching the data on a write cycle, and asserting the DSACK1*/DSACK0* combination that corresponds to the port size to terminate the cycle. If no slave responds or the access is invalid, external control logic asserts the BERR* or BERR* and HALT* signal(s) to abort or retry the bus cycle, respectively.

The DSACKx* signals can be asserted before the data from a slave device is valid on a read cycle. An asynchronous read cycle is shown in Fig. 5.18. The length of time the DSACKx* may precede data is given by parameter #31 and both the data and DSACKx* must be valid until after AS* is negated. The hold times for DSACKx* and the data are parameters #28 and #29 respectively. These three parameters must be met in any asynchronous system to ensure that valid data is latched into the processor. Notice that no maximum time is specified from the assertion of AS* to the assertion of DSACKx*. Although the processor can transfer data in a minimum of three clock cycles when the cycle is terminated with DSACKx*, the processor inserts wait cycles in clock period increments until DSACKx* is recognised.

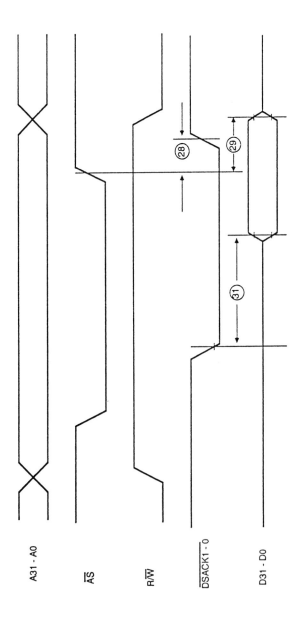

Fig. 5.18   Asynchronous read cycle timings.

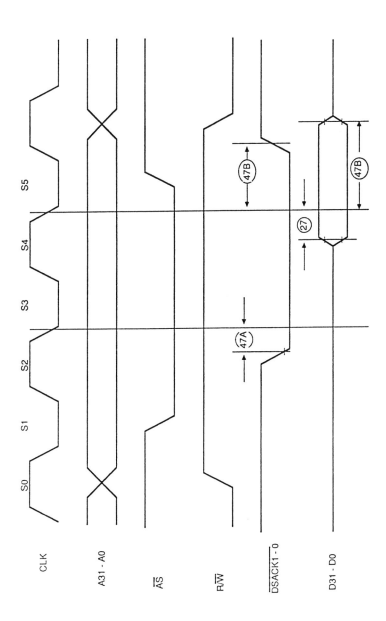

Fig. 5.19 Synchronous read cycle using DSACKx*.

5.19.3   SYNCHRONOUS OPERATION WITH DSACKx*

Although cycles terminated with the DSACKx* signals are classified as 'asynchronous' and cycles terminated with STERM* are classified as 'synchronous', cycles terminated with DSACKx* can also operate synchronously in that signals are interpreted relative to clock edges.

The devices that use these cycles must synchronise the responses to the MC68030 clock in order to be synchronous. Since they terminate bus cycles with the data transfer and size acknowledge signals (DSACKx*), the dynamic bus sizing capabilities of the MC68030 are available. In addition, the minimum cycle time for these cycles is also three clocks. A read cycle using this feature is shown in Fig. 5.19.

To support those systems that use the system clock to generate DSACKx* and other asynchronous inputs, the asynchronous input set up time (parameter #47A), and the asynchronous input hold time (parameter #47B) are given. If the set up and hold times are met for the assertion or negation of a signal, such as DSACKx*, the processor can be guaranteed to recognise that signal level on that specific falling edge of the clock, and valid data is latched into the data set-up time (parameter #27). In this case, parameter #31 for asynchronous operation can be ignored. Note that if a system asserts DSACKx* for the required window around the falling edge of S2 and obeys the proper bus protocol by maintaining DSACKx* (and/or BERR*/ HALT*) until and throughout the clock edge that negates AS* (with the appropriate asynchronous input hold time specified by parameter #47B), no wait states are inserted. The bus cycle runs at its maximum speed for bus cycles terminated with DSACKx* of three clocks per cycle.

When operating synchronously, the data-in set up and hold times for synchronous cycles may be used instead of the timing requirements for data relative to the DS* signal.

5.19.4   SYNCHRONOUS OPERATION WITH STERM*

The MC68030 supports synchronous bus cycles terminated with the synchronous termination signal (STERM*). These cycles, for 32-bit ports only, are similar to cycles terminated with DSACKx*. The main difference is that STERM* can be asserted (and data can be transferred) earlier than for a cycle terminated with DSACKx* causing the processor to perform a minimum access time transfer in two clock periods. However, wait cycles can be inserted by delaying the assertion of STERM* appropriately. A synchronous read cycle is shown in Fig. 5.20.

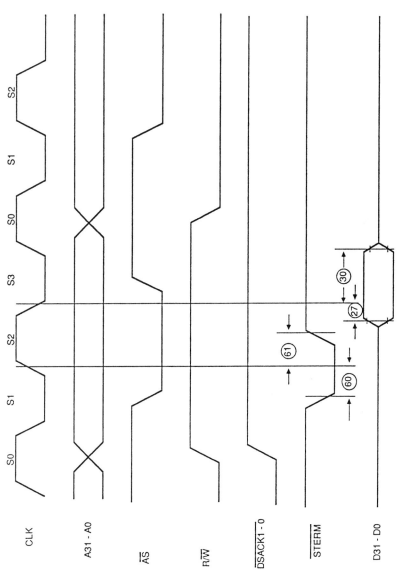

Fig. 5.20   Synchronous read cycle using STERM*

Using the synchronous termination signal STERM* instead of the data transfer and size acknowledge signals DSACKx* in any bus cycle makes the cycle synchronous. Any bus cycle is synchronous if:

- Neither DSACKx* nor the autovector signal AVEC* is asserted during the cycle
- The port size is 32 bits
- Synchronous input set up and hold time requirements (specifications #60 and #61) for STERM* are met
- The data also meets the set up and hold times for a read (parameters #27 and #30).

5.19.4.1 *Burst mode.* Burst mode operation requires the use of STERM* to terminate each of its cycles. The first cycle of any burst transfer must be a synchronous cycle as described in Section 5.19.4. The exact timing of this cycle is controlled by the assertion of STERM*, and wait cycles can be inserted as necessary. However, the minimum cycle time is two clocks. If a burst operation is initiative and allowed to terminate normally, the second, third, and fourth cycles latch data on successive falling edges of the clock at a minimum. Again, the exact cycles, and wait cycles can be inserted as necessary. A read BURST cycle is shown in Fig. 5.21. The first address presented by the MC68030 in the burst cycle will be the address of the data required at that time for the execution unit or the data unit. Hence A2 and A3 initial values will not always be 00, and the system hardware will be required to generate all the values of A2 and A3 during the burst cycle. Note the modulo addressing system used is identical to nibble mode drams. This does not mean that memory designs are limited to using nibble mode drams; both page mode and static column drams can be used with the addition of a modulo two counter.

Although the synchronous input signals (STERM*, CIIN*, and CBACK*) must be stable for the appropriate set up and hold times relative to every rising edge of the clock during which AS* is asserted, the assertion or negation of CBACK* and CIIN* is internally latched on the rising edge of the clock for which STERM* is asserted in a synchronous cycle.

The STERM* signal can be generated from the address bus and function code value, and does not need to be qualified with the AS* signal. If STERM* is asserted and no cycle is in progress (even if the cycle has begun) ECS* is asserted and then the cycle is aborted.

Similarly, CBACK* can be asserted independently of the assertion of CBREQ*. If a cache burst is not requested, the assertion of CBACK* is ignored.

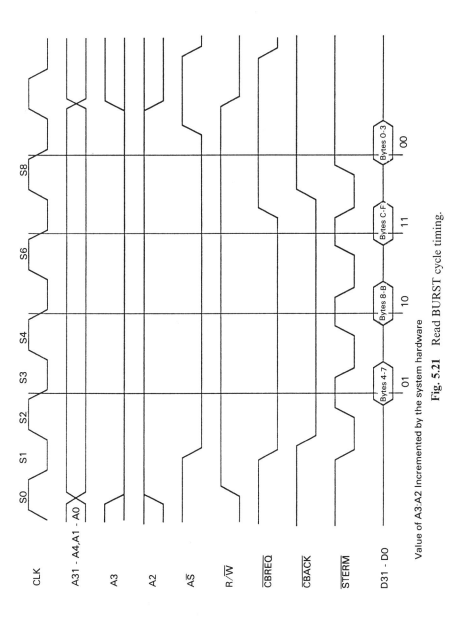

Value of A3:A2 incremented by the system hardware

Fig. 5.21 Read BURST cycle timing.

The assertion of CIIN* is ignored when the appropriate cache is not enabled or when CIOUT* is asserted. It is also ignored during write cycles or translation table searches.

5.20   On-chip cache memories

The MC68030 microprocessor includes a 256-byte on-chip instruction cache and a 156-byte on-chip data cache that are accessed by logical (virtual) addresses. These caches improve performance by reducing external bus activity and increasing instruction throughout.

Reduced external bus activity increases overall performance by increasing availability of the bus for use by external devices (in systems with more than one bus master, such as a processor and a DMA device) without degrading the performance of the MC68030. An increase in instruction throughput results when instruction words and data required by a program are available in the on-chip caches, and the time required to access them on the external bus is eliminated. Additionally, instruction throughput increases when instruction words and data can be accessed simultaneously.

As shown in Fig. 5.15, the instruction cache and the data cache are connected to separate on-chip address and data buses. The address buses are combined to provide the logical address to the MMU. The MC68030 initiates an access to the appropriate cache for the requested instruction or data operand at the same time that it initiates an access for the translation of the logical address in the address translation cache of the MMU. When a hit occurs in the instruction or data cache and the MMU validates the access on a write, the information is transferred from the cache (on a read) or to the cache and the bus controller (on a write) appropriately. When a hit does not occur, the MMU translation of the address is used for an external bus cycle to obtain the instruction or operand. Regardless of whether or not the required operand is located in one of the on-chip caches, the address translation cache of the MMU performs logical-to-physical address translation in parallel with the cache look-up in case an external cycle is required.

5.20.1   ON-CHIP ORGANISATION AND OPERATION

Both on-chip caches are 256-byte direct-mapped caches, each organised as 16 lines. Each line consists of four entries, and each entry contains four bytes. The tag field for each line contains a valid bit for each entry in the line; each entry is independently replaceable. When appropriate, the bus controller requests a burst mode operation to replace an entire cache line. The CACR is accessible by supervisor programs to control the operation of both caches.

System hardware can assert the cache disable (CDIS*) signal in order to disable both caches. The assertion of CDIS* disables the caches (regardless of the state of the enable bits in CACR, CDIS* is primarily intended for use by in-circuit emulators).

Another input signal, cache in inhibit (CIIN*), inhibits caching of data reads or instruction prefetches on a bus cycle by bus cycle basis. Examples of data that should not be cached are data for I/O devices and data from memory devices that cannot supply a full port width of data regardless of the size of the required operand.

The following paragraphs describe how CIIN* is used during the filling of the caches.

An output signal, cache inhibit out (CIOUT*), reflects the state of the cache inhibit (CI*) bit from the MMU of either the ATC entry that corresponds to a specified logical address or the transparent translation register that corresponds to that address. Whenever the appropriate CI bit is set for either a read or a write address and an external bus cycle is required, CIOUT* is asserted and the instruction and data caches are ignored for the access. This signal can also be used by external hardware to inhibit caching in external caches.

Whenever a read access occurs and the required instruction word or data operand is resident in the appropriate on-chip cache (no external bus cycle is required), the MMU is completely ignored, unless an invalid translation resides in the MMU at that time (see next two paragraphs). Therefore, the state of the corresponding CI bits in the MMU are also ignored. The MMU is used to validate all accesses that require external bus cycles; an address translation must be available and valid, protections are checked, and the CIOUT* signal is asserted appropriately.

An external access is defined as 'cachable' for either the instruction or data cache when all the following conditions apply:

- The cache is enabled with the appropriate bit in the CACR set
- The CDIS* signal is negated
- The CIIN* signal is negated for the access
- The CIOUT* signal is negated for the access
- The MMU validates the access.

As both the data and instruction caches are referenced by local addresses, they should be flushed during a task switch or at any time the logical to physical address mapping changes, including when the

MMU is first enabled. In addition, if a page descriptor is currently marked as valid, and is later changed to the invalid type (due to a context switch or a page replacement operation) *entries in the on-chip instruction or data cache corresponding to the physical page must be first cleared (invalidated)*. Otherwise (if on-chip cache entries are valid for pages with descriptor in memory marked invalid), processor operation is unpredictable.

Data read and write accesses to the same address should also have consistent cachability status to ensure that the data in the cache remains consistent with external memory. For example, if CIOUT* is negated for read accesses within a page and the MMU configuration is changed so that CIOUT* is subsequently asserted for write accesses within the same page, those write accesses do not update data in the cache and stale data may result. Similarly, when the MMU maps multiple logical addresses to the same physical address, all accesses to those logical addresses should have the same cachability status.

5.20.1.1 *Instruction cache.* The instruction cache is organised with a line size of four long words, as shown in Fig. 5.22. Each of these long words is considered a separate cache entry as each has a separate valid bit. All four entries in a line have the same tag address. Burst filling all four long words can be advantageous when the time spent in filling the line is not long relative to the equivalent bus cycle time for four non-burst long word accesses, because of the probability that the contents of memory adjacent to or close to a referenced operand or instruction is also required by subsequent accesses. Dynamic RAMs supporting fast access modes (page, nibble or static column) are easily employed to support the MC68030 burst mode.

When enabled, the instruction cache is used to store instruction prefetches (instruction words and extension words) as they are requested by the CPU. Instruction prefetches are normally requested from sequential memory addresses except when a change of program flow occurs (e.g. a branch taken) or when an instruction is executed that can modify the status register, in which cases the instruction pipe is automatically flushed and refilled.

In the instruction cache, each of the 16 lines has a tag consisting of the 24 most significant logical address bits, the FC2 function code bit (used to distinguish between user and supervisor accesses), and the four valid bits (one corresponding to each long word). See Fig. 5.22 for the instruction cache organisation. Address bits A4–A7 select one of 16 lines and its associated tag. The comparator compares the address and function code bits in the selected tag with address bits A8–A31 from

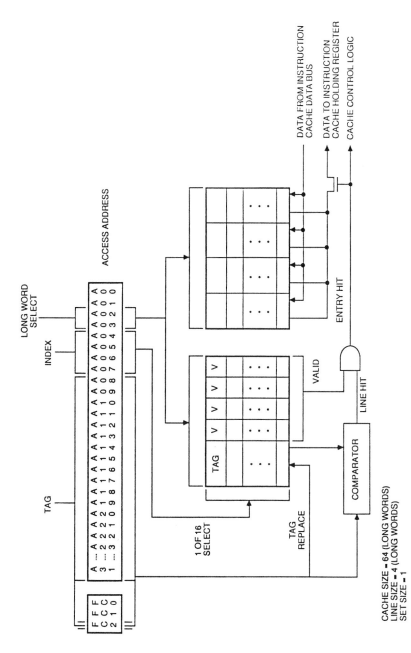

Fig. 5.22　On-chip instruction cache organisation.

the internal prefetch request address to determine if the requested word and the corresponding valid bit (selected by A2–A3) is set. On a cache hit the word selected by address bit A1 is supplied to the instruction pipe.

When the address and function code bits do not match or the requested entry is not valid, a miss occurs. The bus controller initiates a long word prefetch operation for the required instruction word and loads the cache entry, provided the entry is cachable. A burst mode operation may be requested to fill an entire cache line. In the function code and address bits match and the corresponding long word is not valid (but one or more of the other three valid bits for that line are set), a single entry fill operation replaces the required long word only, using a normal prefetch busy cycle or cycles (no burst).

5.20.1.2 *Data cache.* The data cache stores data references to any address space except CPU space (FC = $7), including those references made with PC relative addressing modes and accesses made with the MOVES instruction. Operation of the data cache is similar to that of the instruction cache, except for the address comparison and cache filling operations. The tag of each line in the data cache contains function code bits FC0, FC1, and FC2 in addition to address bits A8–A31. The cache control circuitry selects the tag using bits A4–A7 and compares it to the corresponding bits of the access address to determine if a tag match has occurred. Address bits A2–A3 select the valid bit for the appropriate long word in the cache to determine if an entry hit has occurred. Misaligned data transfers may span two data cache entries. In this case, the processor checks for a hit one entry at a time. Therefore, it is possible that a portion of the address results in a hit, and a portion results in a miss. The hit and miss are treated independently. Figure 5.23 illustrates the organisation of the data cache.

The operation of the data cache differs for read and write cycles. A data read cycle operates exactly like an instruction cache read cycle; when a miss occurs, an external cycle is initiated to obtain the operand from memory, and the data is loaded into the cache if the access is cachable. In the case of a misaligned operand that spans two cache entries, two long words are required from memory. Burst mode operation may also be initiated to fill an entire line of the data cache. Read accesses from the CPU address space and address translation table search accesses are not stored in the data cache.

The data cache on the MC68030 is a write-through cache. When a hit occurs on a write cycle, the data is written both to the cache and to

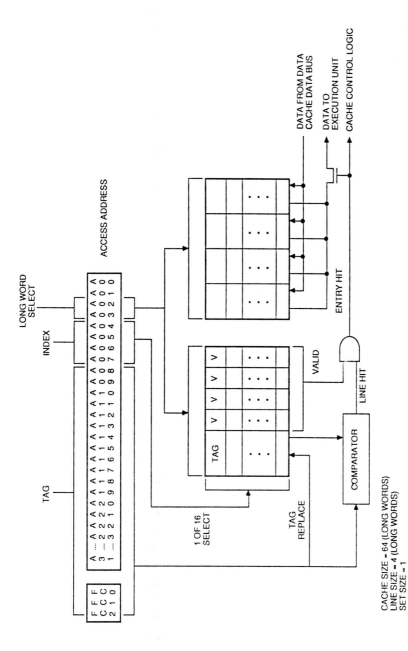

Fig. 5.23   On-chip data cache organisation.

external memory (provided the MMU validates the access), regardless of the operand size, and even if the cache is frozen. If the MMU determines that the access is invalid, the write is aborted, the corresponding entry is invalidated, and a bus error exception is taken. Since the write to the cache completes before the write to external memory, the cache contains the new value even if the external write terminates in a busy error. The value in the data cache might be used by another instruction before the external write cycle has completed, although this should not have any adverse consequences.

(1) Write allocation. The supervisor program can configure the data cache for either of two types of allocation for data cache entries that miss on write cycles. The state of the Write Allocation (WA) bit in the cache control register specifies either 'not write allocation' or 'write allocation' with partial validation of the data entries in the cache on writes.

When 'not write allocation' is selected (WA = 0), write cycles that miss do not alter the data cache contents. In this mode, the processor does not replace entries in the cache during write operations. The cache is updated only during a write hit.

When 'write allocation' is selected (WA = 1), the processor always updates the data cache on cachable write cycles, but only validates an updated entry that hits, or an entry that is updated with long word data that is long word aligned. When a tag miss occurs on a write of long word data that is long word aligned, the corresponding tag is replaced, and only the long word being written is marked as valid. The other three entries in the cache line are invalidated when a tag miss occurs on a misaligned long word write or on a byte or word write, the data is not written in the cache, the tag is unaltered, and the valid bit(s) are cleared. Thus an aligned long word data write may replace a previously valid entry whereas a misaligned data write or a write of data that is not long word aligned may invalidate a previously valid entry or entries.

Write allocation eliminates stale data that may reside in the cache because of either of two unique situations: multiple mapping of two or more logical addresses to one physical address within the same task, or allowing the same physical location to be accessed by both supervisor and user mode cycles. Stale data conditions can arise when operating in the 'no write allocate' mode, and all the following conditions are satisfied:

● Multiple mapping (object aliasing) is allowed by the operating system

- A read cycle loads a value for an 'aliased' physical address into the data cache
- A write cycle occurs, referencing the same aliased physical object as above but using a different logical address causing a cache miss and no update to the cache (has the same page offset)
- The physical object is then read using the first alias which provides stale data from the cache.

In this case, the data in the cache no longer matches that in physical memory and is stale. Since the write allocation mode updates the cache during write cycles, the data in the cache remains consistent with physical memory. Note that when CIOUT* is asserted, the data cache is completely ignored, even on write cycles operating in the write allocation mode. Also note that since the CIIN* signal is ignored on write cycles, cache entries may be created for non-cachable data (when CIIN* is asserted on a write) when operating in the write allocate mode.

(2) Read-modify-write accesses. The read portion of a read–modify–write cycle is always forced to miss in the data cache. However, if the system allows internal caching of read–modify–write cycle operands (CIOUT* and CIIN* both negated), the processor either uses the data read from memory to update a matching entry in the data cache or creates a new entry with the read data in the case of no matching entry. The write portion of a read–modify–write operation also updates a matching entry in the data cache. In the case of a cache miss on the write, the allocation of a new cache entry for the data being written is controlled by the WA bit. Table search accesses, however, are completely ignored by the data cache; it is never updated for a table search access.

5.20.1.3 *Cache filling.* The bus controller can load either cache in two ways:

(1) Single entry mode. This is when a single long word entry of a cache line is requested of the external hardware. Note this could be a single 32-bit transfer, either synchronous or asynchronous, or if the port size is not supported by the external hardware then the MC68030 executes all the asynchronous bus cycles necessary to make up a long word for the cache.

(2) Burst fill mode. In this mode, an entire cache line (four long words) is requested of the external hardware. See Section 5.19.4.1 for a description of a burst transfer. This mode is selected by software via the respective cache control register.

5.21   Memory management unit

The MC68030 includes an MMU that supports a demand paged virtual memory environment. The memory management is 'demand' in that programs do not specify required memory areas in advance but request them by accessing logical addresses. The physical memory is paged, meaning that it is divided into blocks of equal size, called page frames. The logical address space is divded into pages of the same size. The operating system assigns pages to page frames as they are required to meet the needs of programs.

The principal function of the MMU is the translation of logical addresses to physical addresses using translation tables stored in memory. The MMU contains an Address Translation Cache (ATC) in which recently used logical-to-physical address translations are stored. As the MMU receives each logical address from the CPU core, it searches the ATC for the corresponding physical address. When the translation is not in the ATC, the processor searches the translation tables in memory for the translation information. The address calculations and bus cycles required for this search are performed by microcode and dedicated logic in the MC68030. In addition, the MMU contains two transparent translation registers (TT0 and TT1) that identify blocks of memory that can be accessed without translation. The features of the MMU are:

- 32-bit logical address translated to 32-bit physical address with 3-bit function code
- Supports two-clock cycle processor accesses to physical address spaces
- Addresses translated in parallel with accesses to data and instruction caches
- On-chip fully associative 22 entry ATC
- Translation table search controlled by microcode
- Eight page sizes, 256, 512, 1K, 2K, 4K, 8K and 32K
- Separate user and supervisor translation table trees are supported
- Two independent blocks can be defined as transparent (untranslated)
- Multiple levels of translation tables
- 0–15 upper logical address bits can be ignored (using initial shift)
- Portions of tables can be undefined (using limits)
- Write protection and supervisor protection
- History bits automatically maintained in page descriptors
- Cache inhibit output CIOUT* signal asserted on page basis
- External translation disable input signal (MMUDIS*)

● Subset of instruction set defined by MC68851.

The MMU completely overlaps address translation time with other processing activity when the translation is resident in the ATC. ATC accesses operate in parallel with the on-chip instruction and data caches.

Figure 5.15 is a block diagram of the MC68030 showing the relationship of the MMU to the execution unit and the bus controller. For an instruction or operand access, the MC68030 simultaneously searches for a physical address in the ATC. If the translation is available, the MMU provides the physical address to the bus controller and allows the bus cycle to continue. When the instruction or operand is in either of the on-chip caches on a read cycle, the bus controller aborts the bus cycle before address strobe is asserted. Similarly, the MMU causes a bus cycle to abort before the assertion of address strobe when a valid translation is not available in the ATC or when an invalid access is attempted.

An MMU disable input signal (MMUDIS*) is provided that dynamically disables address translation for emulation, diagnostic, or other purposes.

The programming model of the MMU (Fig. 5.17) consists of two root pointer registers, a control register, two transparent translation registers, and a status register. These registers can only be accessed by supervisory programs. The CPU root pointer register points to an address translation tree structure in memory that describes the logical-to-physical mapping for user accesses, or for both user and supervisor accesses. The supervisor root pointer register optionally points to an address translation tree structure for supervisor mappings. The translation control register comprises fields that control the translation operation. Each transparent translation register can define a block of logical addresses that are used as physical addresses (without translation). The MMU status register contains accumulated status information from a translation performed as part of a PTEST instruction.

The ATC in the MMU is a fully associative cache that stores 22 logical-to-physical address translations and associated page information. It compares the logical address and function code internally supplied by the processor with all tag entries in the ATC. When the access address and function code matches a tag in the ATC (a hit occurs) and no access violation is detected, the ATC outputs the corresponding physical address to the bus controller which continues the external bus cycle. Function codes are routed to the bus controller unmodified.

Each ATC entry contains a logical address, a physical address, and status bits. Among the status bits are the write–protect and cache inhibit bits.

When the ATC does not contain the translation for a logical address (a miss occurs) and an external bus cycle is required, the MMU aborts the access and causes the processor to initiate bus cycles that search the translation tables in memory for the correct translation. If the table search completes without any errors, the MMU stores the translation in the ATC and provides the physical address for the access, allowing the bus controller to retry the original bus cycle.

An MMU translation table has a tree structure with the base of the first table defined by a root pointer descriptor. The root pointer descriptor of the current translation table is resident in one of two root pointer registers. The general tree structure is shown in Fig. 5.24. Table entries at the upper levels of a tree point to other tables. The table leaf entries are page frame addresses. All addresses stored in the translation tables are physical addresses; the translation tables reside in the physical address space.

System software selects the parameters for the translation tables by configuring the Translation Control (TC) register appropriately. The function codes or a portion of the logical address can be defined as the index into the first level of look-up in the table. The TC register specifies how many bits of the logical address are used as the index for each level of the look-up (as many as 15 bits can be used at a given level).

5.22 Development system support

Motorola's total development system solutions include the following:

(1) *In-circuit emulators* for all the M68000 family of microprocessors: MC68000, MC68008, MC68010, MC68020 and MC68030.
(2) *Hardware control station*, a controller that services each emulator and establishes the linkage to the host computer and user terminal. This is the Motorola HDS-200™.
(3) *System performance analyser or bus state monitor*, which monitors all the microprocessor activity and traces each selected bus cycle of the target microprocessor.
(4) *Source level debut*, used with a host computer system to provide full debugging capability at the source code level.
(5) *Cross support software*, consisting of assemblers, disassemblers, linkers, 'C' compilers, and debuggers used for software development on different host computers.

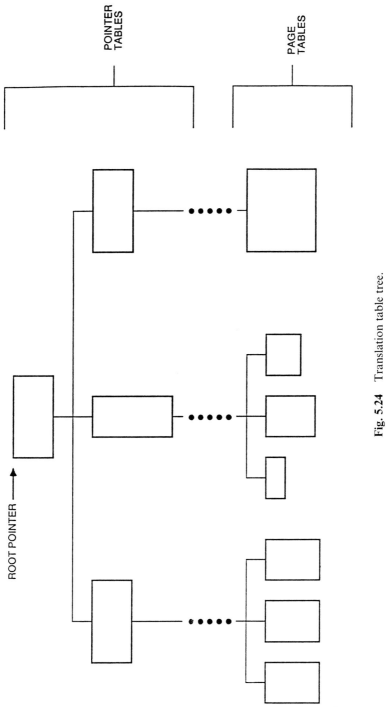

Fig. 5.24 Translation table tree.

(6) *Development system host computer*, a multi-user, multi-tasking computer running Unix™ System V, that hosts the hardware control station and cross support software.

5.22.1 HOST SYSTEMS

Motorola's cross development software has been ported to several host computer systems. The current hosts supported are the Motorola's M68DVLP, a VAX™ system, a Macintosh™ computer, or a SUN-3™ workstation.

5.22.2 HDS-300

An HDS-300 consists of the control station and control station software, which connects to an emulator via an interface cable set and to the host computer using an asynchronous serial interface. The HDS-300 and emulator look like an ASCII asynchronous terminal to the host computer. For stand-alone operation, an ASCII asynchronous terminal can be connected to the HDS-300 in place of the host computer. The HDS-300, in conjunction with the emulator, replicates all the functions of the target system microprocessor in its application environment, and can operate in a non-invasive mode supporting the traditional mechanisms for hardware and software debugging. The mode includes the fundamental capabilities of starting and stopping code, examining and altering processor registers and system memory, and of stepping through code by executing one instruction at a time.

5.22.3 REAL TIME BUS ANALYSIS

In-circuit emulation is supported by the Bus State Monitor (BSM) for the MC68000, MC68008 and MC68010, and by the System Performance Analyser (SPA) for the MC68020 and MC68030. The BSM and SPA work much like a stand-alone logic analyser, but are integrated with the emulators and capture bus cycles via the emulator's in-circuit probe. Both the BSM and SPA can capture all bus cycles in a trace buffer or selectively capture bus cycles as specified by the user.

5.23 Software support

There is currently a wide range of software support available for the M68000 family. This consists of the following software supplied by Motorola:

- Unix™ operating system, System V (the current AT&T release)
- Debug monitors for all the Motorola Computer System VME cards covering all the M68000 family of microprocessors
- High performance C compilers
- Real time operating system.

In addition to Motorola-supplied software, there is a wealth of third party software for the M68000 family. This consists of compilers, real time operating systems, multi-user/multi-tasking operating systems and application software.

References

1. *MC68020 32-bit Microprocessor User's Manual*, Prentice-Hall Inc., Englewood Cliffs, NJ.
2. *MC68881/MC68882 Floating Point Co-processor User's Manual*, Prentice-Hall Inc., Englewood Cliffs, NJ.
3. *MC68851 Paged Memory Management Unit User's Manual*, Prentice-Hall Inc., Englewood Cliffs, NJ.

Further reading

MC68000 Family Reference, Prentice-Hall Inc., Englewood Cliffs, NJ.
MC68030 32-bit Microprocessor User's Manual, Prentice-Hall Inc., Englewood Cliffs, NJ.

CHAPTER 6
The National Semiconductor Series 32000 Microprocessor Family

DAVID J. BRAMWELL MBCS

National Semiconductor GmbH, Furstenfeldbruck, Germany

6.1 Introduction

The Series 32000 family was designed as a chip-size main frame computer. Built from the start as a 32-bit processor, the designers did not have to try to adapt the new design to an existing 4- or 8-bit processor. In contrast to many competitive processors, Series 32000 has an orthogonal, symmetrical instruction set, i.e. everywhere it makes sense, an instruction can be used with any basic data object and any chosen address modes. Exceptions to the rule have been kept to a minimum.

At the time that the Series 32000 was designed, the VAX family was considered as a model of a good processor, and many features of VAX architecture are to be found in the Series 32000.

D. E. Knuth showed in a study[1] of 250 000 lines of FORTRAN code that 80 per cent of all assignments were of the form:

A op B

or:

A = B

This prompted the designers to make the Series 32000 a two-address machine, i.e. the general form of an instruction is:

operation_code   source operand, destination operand

which is interpreted as:

destination $<--$ $<$destination$>$ operation $<$source$>$

Memory is byte addressed, with the low order address of a multi-byte value corresponding to the least significant byte of the value. All addressing is linear; the Series 32000 has no segment or base registers.

All members of the family have a 32-bit internal structure; the external data bus may be 8, 16 or 32 bits wide as designated by the last two digits of the part number. The original processors have only 24 of the 32 potential address lines, giving a 16 Mbyte address space. In the later processors, the full 32-bit addressing is possible, giving a 4 Gbyte address space.

Floating point and memory management operations are handled by dedicated slave processors, considered as an integral part of the CPU; their instruction codes are part of the standard instruction set, and are enabled by setting an appropriate bit in the configuration register. To permit the user to attach a special purpose slave processor to the Series 32000, a set of custom slave instructions are also included in the instruction set, again enabled by a bit in the configuration register. The exact function of the custom slave instructions is, of course, dependent on the design of the slave processor. As technology matures, it is intended to integrate slave processor functions into the CPU chip, as has been done with the Timing Control Unit (TCU) in the 32CG16 and the 32GX32, and with the TCU and MMU in the 32532.

The Series 32000 was originally designed as a Unix™ machine, with instructions included to support high level languages. With the emphasis on structured and modular programming, the Series 32000 designers have included hardware support for program modules. Every program is considered to consist of one or more independent modules, each of which is represented by a module descriptor in the module table. The hardware mod register points to the descriptor of the currently active module. To allow for inter-module accesses, an external addressing mode is included; and call and return instructions (which save and restore the current module context) for external procedures are part of the instruction set.

The Series 32000 CPUs use two dedicated tables; the module table and the interrupt dispatch table. The module table contains a four-doubleword entry 'descriptor' for each software module in the program, the descriptor for the currently active module being pointed to by the mod register. The interrupt dispatch table contains an external procedure descriptor for the handler of each interrupt, trap and abort recognised by the system; the start of the table is pointed to by the interrupt base register. The 32532 and 32GX32 allow a direct exception mode, which uses the absolute address of the handler instead of the external procedure descriptor.

The Series 32000 processors have been employed in numerically controlled machine tools, Unix-based PC designs, instrumentation systems and are currently finding a major application as embedded controllers. The special instructions included in the 32CG16 have adapted it to the printer market. Coupled with the high speed FPUs and the other families of special-purpose chips from National Semiconductor, the 32CG16 and the 32GX32 provide a complete range of solutions to the page printer designer. When used with National's Advanced Graphic Chip Set, the Series 32000 provides a complete solution to the graphic terminal designer.

6.2   Chip family

6.2.1   THE CENTRAL PROCESSORS

The first processors of the range to be introduced were the 32016 and 32032, followed by the 32008 and the 32332. The 32532 was the natural extension of the family towards higher performance. The 32CG16 (see Fig. 6.1) is a variant of the 32016, adapted for the embedded printer market. The latest member of the family is the 32GX32 (see Fig. 6.2), introduced in 1989 as a high-speed embedded control processor.

The CPUs of the 32000 family are designed to be upward and downward compatible, i.e. a user program written for 32008 will run without change on 32532; and a user program written for 32532 will run on 32008, *without change*. The register set of all the processors, the instruction set of all the mainstream processors and the addressing

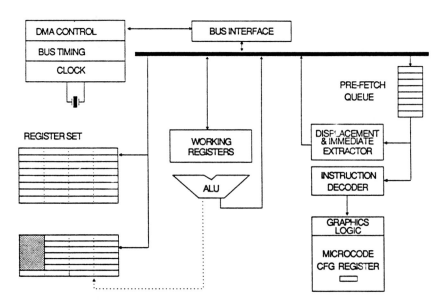

Fig. 6.1   32CG16 block diagram.

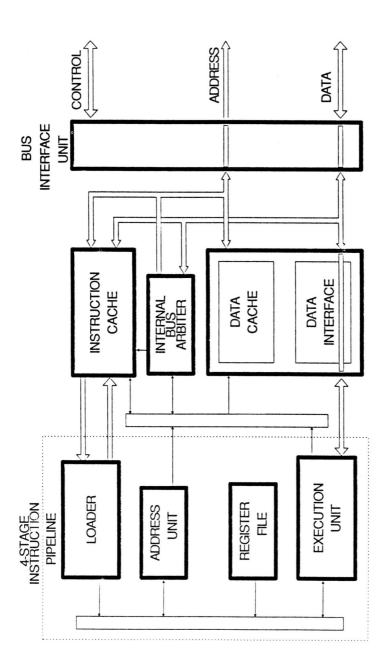

Fig. 6.2 32GX32 block diagram.

modes are the same. For the user this means that once the 32000 instruction set has been mastered, it does not matter which actual processor is used. For the system programmer, the 32532 and the 32GX32 have extra instructions for cache control.

The 32CG16 breaks away from the full compatibility in that the instructions for MMU and custom slave processors have been replaced by special graphic instructions, in order to satisfy the requirement from the printer market for a dedicated processor.

The 32CG16, 32332, 32532 and 32GX32 possess additional instructions to work with the 32381 FPU: the 32532 also includes the instructions necessary for the 32580 floating point controller with the Weitek WTL3164 floating point data path unit.

6.2.1.1 *Software compatibility.* With few exceptions, all the processors have the same instruction set:

- All slave processor commands are included in the CPU instruction set, and are enabled by bits in the configuration register
- The 32CG16 has the MMU and custom slave codes replaced by graphic codes
- The 32GX32 has no MMU instructions
- The 32532 and 32GX32 have additional supervisor mode instructions for cache management
- The 32332, 32532, 32CG16 and 32GX32 include the instructions for the additional operations of the 32381 FPU
- The 32532 includes the instructions for the 32580/Weitek 3164 FPU.

6.2.1.2 *CPU power and clock speeds.* The 32008, 32016 and 32032 run at 10 MHz, the 32332 and 32CG16 at 15 MHz and the 32532 and 32GX32 at 30 MHz.

The original processors required a TCU (32201 or 32C201) to generate the clock pulses, memory strobes and to manage the wait states. The 32GX32, 32532 and 32CG16 incorporate the TCU into the CPU chip.

The two-clock bus cycle of the 32GX32 allows it a peak performance of 15 VAX MIPS, and a sustained rate of 8 to 10 VAX MIPS. It will service an interrupt in 1.3 ms and can execute a context switch in 3.6 ms. The internal design of the chip gives a maximum internal memory bandwidth of 240 Mbytes, and an external bandwidth of 96 Mbytes/s.

Table 6.1 illustrates the performances on standard benchmarks by the processors.

Table 6.1   Processor performance on standard benchmarks

Clock frequency	CPU	TCU	FPU	Drystones/s	K Whetstones/s
10 MHz	32008	32C201	32081	870	320
	32016	32C201	32081	1190	385
	32CG16		32081	1300	385
	32032	32C201	32081	1400	425
15 MHz	32CG16		32381	1950	800
	32332	32C201	32381	3200	1100
30 MHz	32532		32381	16600	2400
	32GX32		32381	16600	2400
	32532		32580		
			+WTL3164	16600	8000

6.2.2   SLAVE PROCESSORS

Slave processors are considered to be an extension of the CPU. All the necessary instructions for operating the slaves are included as part of the CPU instruction set, and are enabled by setting the respective bits in the CPU configuration register. The communication protocol between the CPU and a slave processor is controlled by the four bus status bits, while any data which is to be transferred is passed on the normal data bus. Address decoding and memory access is made by the central processor; the slave processor has no access to memory.

6.2.2.1   *FPUs 32081, 32381 and 32580.*   The FPUs use IEEE formats for floating point representation, and provide move, compare, add, subtract, multiply and divide instructions. Normalisation is automatically carried out when an integer is moved to a floating representation. Three rounding instructions convert from floating point to integer representation.

The 32081 uses a 16-bit communication protocol, the 32381 a 32-bit protocol to suit the 32332, 32532 and 32GX32 processors.

The 32381 FPU includes the additional functions dot, poly, scale, and log.

For high-speed floating point operations, the 32532 can also use the 32580 floating point controller in conjunction with the Weitek 3164 floating point data path unit.

6.2.2.2   *MMUs 32082 and 32382.*   The MMUs handle address translation and demand paged memory management. The 32008,

32CG16 and 32GX32 processors are not able to use an MMU, and the 32532 has an MMU which is software-equivalent to the 32382 incorporated in the chip.

The MMU contains registers for hardware breakpointing, in addition to the registers needed for memory management. A translate look-aside buffer holds the logical-to-physical address conversion of the last 32 pages accessed. This enables address conversion to take place in one clock time in more than 95 per cent of all accesses.

6.2.3 PERIPHERAL PROCESSORS

In contrast to the slave processors, the peripheral processor is configured as a part of memory and accessed accordingly.

6.2.3.1 *ICU 32202.* No special instructions are needed for the ICU, since it is addressed as memory. The ICU allows for 8 or 16 external interrupts, depending on whether a 16- or 8-bit data bus is used for communication. In the latter configuration, a further ICU can be connected to any of the interrupt inputs, giving a theoretical maximum of 256 external interrupts. In the 8-bit bus mode, the additional input lines can be configured as general purpose I/O ports or additional interrupt pins. The ICU appears to the programmer as 32 byte addresses or registers, and includes internal programmable timer/counter possibilities.

6.3 Architecture

All processors use the same programmer's model, consisting of eight general purpose, eight floating point, eight dedicated registers, plus the registers of the MMU. This is illustrated in Fig. 6.3.

6.3.1 GENERAL PURPOSE REGISTERS

The eight 32-bit general purpose registers can be used to hold integer data values, index values or addresses. There are no specific accumulator or index registers. They may be accessed as a byte, word, doubleword and, in special cases, as a quadword register pair. When an operation affects a byte or word of a general purpose register, only the low-order byte or word is used, and any carry generated will appear in the C bit of the PSR, and not run over into the higher order part of the register.

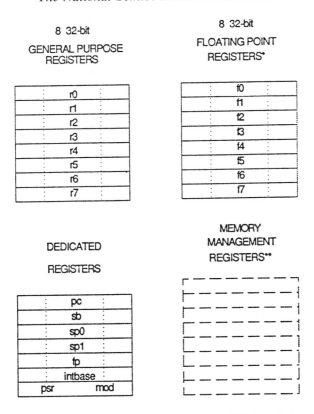

Fig. 6.3   The 32000 programmer's model. * With FPU installed and enabled
** Privileged access

6.3.2   FLOATING POINT REGISTERS

When an FPU is installed, eight 32-bit floating point registers are available. These may only be used for floating point operations, and may not contain addresses. They may be addressed as a single-length 32-bit floating point value or as a double-length, 64-bit long floating register pair. The 32381 and 32580 units have a set of eight 64-bit registers, of which the low-order 32-bits correspond with the normal floating point registers.

6.3.3   DEDICATED REGISTERS

The Series 32000 has a set of six 32-bit dedicated registers and two 16-bit dedicated registers, plus the configuration register. The names and functions are:

- PC *Program Counter*, holds the address of the next instruction to be executed

- SB *Static Base*, points to the global data area of the currently selected module
- FP *Frame Pointer*, points to the entry frame of the current procedure on the stack
- SP0, SP1 *User and Interrupt Stack Pointers*, point to the least significant byte of the last value stored on the respective stack
- Intbase *Interrupt Despatch Table Base Address*, points to the interrupt despatch table, entry vector zero
- PSR *Processor Status Register*, the low byte contains user accessible bits, the high byte is supervisor accessible, and indicates the current CPU state.

The bits of the PSR are as follows:

x x x x I P S U N Z F x x L T C

I	Enable interrupts
P	Trace pending
S	Stack pointer selector
U	User mode
N	Second operand more negative than first operand in a signed comparison
Z	Operands equal in a comparison
F	General fault flat, indicates overflow in integer arithmetic, until/while termination of string instructions, etc.
L	Second operand lower than first operand in an unsigned comparison
T	Trace bit
C	Carry bit, set by integer add and subtract operations.

- MOD *Module Register*, points to the module descriptor of the currently selected module. Since the MOD register is 16 bits long, the module table must be located within the first 64K addresses. This is illustrated in Fig. 6.4.
- CFG *Configuration register*, indicates which slave processors are installed. In the first series of processors, the configuration register is four bits, in the 332 and CG16 it is eight bits long, while in the 32532 and 32GX32, it is a 32-bit register, of which nine bits are currently used. The additional bits are used to indicate if the 32-bit slave protocol is to be used (32332), to select the CPU clock speed in the 32CG16, and to enable various CPU features in the 32532 and 32GX32. The various formats of the configuration register follow. In the 32CG16 the CFG is four bits:

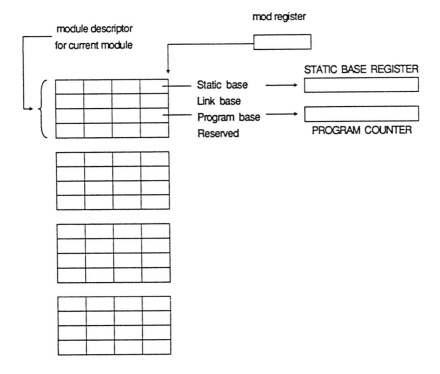

Fig. 6.4 Module table (in first 64K of memory).

C M F I

I	Indicates that interrupts are vectored
F	Indicates the presence of a 32081 or 32381 FPU
M	In conjunction with the C bit, provides clock scaling.
C	

In the 32532 and 32GX32, the CFG is a 32-bit register, of which nine are used:

LIC IC LDC DC DE 1 1 1 1 C M F I

I	Indicates that interrupts are vectored
F	Indicates the presence of an FPU
M	In the 32532, enables execution of memory management instructions by the on-chip MMU; in the 32GX32, this bit is reserved
C	Indicates the presence of a custom slave processor

The four one bits replace the protocol selection bits of the 32332, since these processors only accept the fast protocol.

DE   Enables Direct Exception mode
DC   Enables Data Cache
LDC   Locked Data Cache
IC   Enables Instruction Cache
LIC   Locked Instruction Cache.

In the 32008, 32016, 32032 the CFG contains four bits:

C M F I
I   Indicates that interrupts are vectored, typically because of the installation of a 32201 ICU
F   Indicates the presence of a 32081 FPU
M   Indicates the presence of a 32082 MMU
C   Indicates the presence of a custom slave processor.

In the 32332, the CFG contains eight bits, the four low order bits are as in the 32032, the upper four as follows:

P FC FM FF
FF, FM, FC   Indicate the use of the 32-bit 'fast' protocol for the custom slave processor, MMU and FPU, respectively.
P   Indicates that virtual memory pages of 4K are in use.

6.4   Instruction set

The instruction set of the entire family is essentially identical. As mentioned in Section 6.1, the only exceptions are the absence of MMU (32CG16 and 32GX32) and custom slave instructions (32CG16), the additional 32381 floating point instructions in the 32CG16, 32GX32, 32332 and 32532 processors, the cache control instructions in the 32GX32 and 32532, and the graphic instructions of the 32CG16.

6.4.1   CODE DENSITY

Every instruction has a fixed portion of one to three bytes long, which specifies the action and the address modes of both operands. This is followed by a variable length extension depending on the encoding of address modes.

One of the aims of the 32000 design team was to produce a system with a dense code; consequently, there are no restrictions about

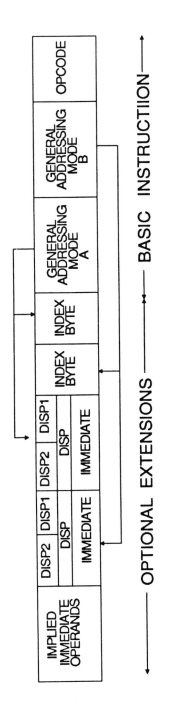

Fig. 6.5   General instruction format.

aligning code and data with address boundaries. Given the starting address of a multi-byte operand, the CPU will generate all the necessary addresses and memory enable signals. Naturally, non-aligned data will require more bus accesses than if it was aligned, and the assembler provides directives to align code or data as needed. In connection with these aims, it was decided to give the most commonly used instructions the shortest, and the less commonly used (but possibly more powerful), instructions the longer formats.

The general format of an instruction is given in Fig. 6.5.

The two general fields indicate which addressing modes are to be used. The displacement/immediate fields can each contain one immediate or one or two displacement fields, depending on the chosen addressing mode. If the general field indicates a scaled index, the index byte will show the general purpose register and the scale factor to be used.

Allowing for all possible addressing modes and addressing extensions, an instruction can be from 1 to around 30 bytes long.

It should be noted that all the fields beyond the fixed portion of the instruction are potential, i.e. if they are not needed, they do not exist. A field only appears in the code when it is needed. Such a variable system means that the code area of memory will not have 'holes' in it.

Statistics suggest that a Series 32000 program will be up to 30 per cent shorter than a comparable program using fixed length, aligned instructions.

6.4.2   DATA TYPES

The Series 32000 allows operations to specify the type of hardware data access required. All CPU operations specify whether the operand is to affect a byte (8 bits), a word (16 bits), or a doubleword (32 bits). Floating point operations can specify a floating point number (32 bits), or a long floating point number (64 bits). A single letter (b, w, d, f, l) is added to the operation code to indicate the operand length. A representation of hardware data is given in Fig. 6.6.

For example:

    addb r1,r0

will add the contents of the low order byte of general purpose register r1 to the contents of the low order byte of general purpose register r0, storing the result in the low order byte of r0. All values are considered as signed integers, and any carry or overflow goes to the C and F bits respectively in the PSR. Further:

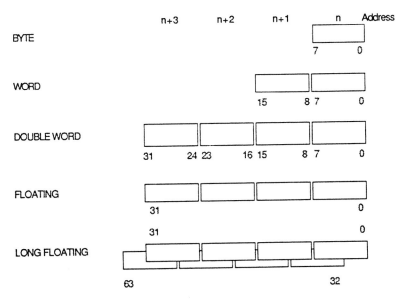

Fig. 6.6 Hardware data representation.

    addw r1,r0

will do the same job on the low order word (16 bits) whilst:

    addd r1,r0

will make the add using the complete contents of the two registers.

As the numbers are treated as signed integers, the above examples will use respectively bit 7, bit 15 and bit 31 as the sign bit.
Also:

    addf f1,f0

will carry out a floating point addition of the 32-bit values in floating registers f1 and f0 and:

    addl f2,f0

will make a double precision floating point addition. Where a register pair (64 bits) is addressed, the even numbered register must be specified.

Exactly the same instruction codes would be used if either, or both, operand was in memory; the appropriate addressing mode would replace the register name(s) in the preceding examples (see below):

    add r1,h'1000   # result in byte at hex address
                           1000

addw r1,h'1000	# result in bytes at hex address 1000,1001
addd r1,h'1000	# result in 4 bytes starting at hex address 1000

Instructions are provided in the Series 32000 to manipulate integers, BCD, bit fields, bits, strings and arrays. Operations on records and stacks are covered by appropriate addressing modes.

6.4.3   ADDRESSING MODES

The Series 32000 provides eight addressing modes, similar to many large computers, plus a scaled index modifier which can be appended to the others (except immediate or another scaled index).

In the following explanations, each example uses the same instruction code and operand length for clarity. The addressing mode under discussion is used as the source (left-most) address in each case, the same absolute addressing mode being used for the destination (right-most) address in all cases.

In the Series 32000 assembly code, an immediate value is indicated by a leading $; all other numeric values are treated as absolute addresses. For the examples, the absolute address has been specified in hexadecimal format, shown by a leading h'.

The standard addressing modes are:

(1) *Absolute*, where the actual memory address is specified in the instruction code, i.e.

   movd h'1010, h'1000

(2) *Immediate*, where the data value is encoded in the instruction, i.e.

   movd $25, h'1000

(3) *Register*, where the data is in one of the eight general purpose registers (or one of the eight floating point registers when appropriate), i.e.

   movd r0 h'1000

   See also Fig. 6.7.

(4) *Register relative*, where the data is in memory, the basic address is given in a general purpose register; a signed displacement (number of bytes) is added to this value to produce the effective address, i.e.

   movd 5(r0), h'1000

   See also Fig. 6.8.

REGISTER

movd   r0 , h'1000

DATA VALUE IS IN THE REGISTER

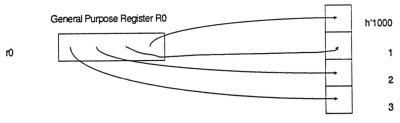

Fig. 6.7   Register.

REGISTER RELATIVE

movd 5(r0), h'1000

REGISTER POINTS TO DATA VALUE

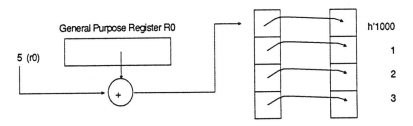

Fig. 6.8   Register relative.

To support high-level languages, the following addressing modes are available:

(5) *Top of Stack*, where the data is in memory and the address is in the Stack Pointer (SP) registers. Any modification of the SP is handled automatically by the processor. On write operations, the SP is decremented, then the value is transferred; in read operations, the value is transferred and the SP subsequently incremented. The address is:

movd tos, h'1000

See also Fig. 6.9.

Note that the Series 32000 does not have a push or pop instruction; all operations can access stack variables by means of the top of stack addressing mode.

TOP OF STACK

movd   tos , h'1000

REGISTER POINTS TO DATA VALUE

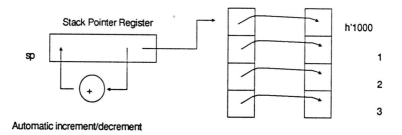

Fig. 6.9   Top of stack.

MEMORY SPACE

movd   5(sb)   , h'1000

REGISTER POINTS TO DATA VALUE

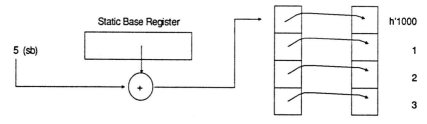

Fig. 6.10   Memory space.

MEMORY RELATIVE

movd 4(5(sb)) , h'1000

REGISTER POINTS TO ADDRESS

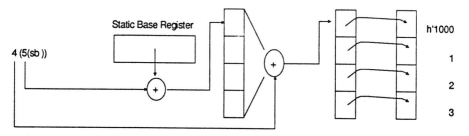

Fig. 6.11   Memory relative.

(6) *Memory space*, as in register relative mode, but using one of the dedicated registers instead of a general purpose register, i.e.

> movd 5(sb), h'1000

See also Fig. 6.10.

(7) *Memory relative*, as in memory space, but with a second displacement. The address calcualted with the first displacement is read, and the contents treated as a 32-bit address. The second displacement is added to this value to provide the effective address, i.e.

> movd 4(5(sb)), h'1000

See also Fig. 6.11.

(8) *External*, where the data is in memory, the address is given in the specified entry in the link table of the currently active module. A signed displacement may be added to this pointer value to produce the effective address, i.e.

> movd ext(1), h'1000

To each of these addressing modes, except immediate or another scaled index, a *scaled index modifier* can be added:

[rn:1], where rn represents one of the eight general purpose registers, and 1 represents the length of the index units, either b, w, d, or q (1, 2, 4, or 8 bytes).

See also Fig. 6.12.

SCALED INDEX

movd 4(fp) [r0:d] , h'1000

REGISTER CONTAINS INDEX COUNT

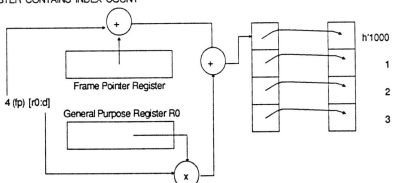

Fig. 6.12 Scaled index.

The specified general purpose register is read, the contents multiplied by the number of bytes represented by 1, and the result added to the effective address:

movd 4(fp)[r0:d], h'1000

Where a displacement is specified, a signed integer is stored in the instruction code. Displacement fields may be 1, 2 or 4 bytes long, with the first 1 or 2 bits being used as length indicator. Thus a displacement may be at a maximum of a 30-bit signed value.

In each of the preceding examples, the addressing modes used for the source could just as easily be used for the destination operand, with the exception of immediate.

6.4.4   INSTRUCTION TYPES

As the Series 32000 is designed to be an orthogonal machine, a full set of instructions is provided to process each type of supported data. As shown elsewhere, the instruction format of the Series 32000 is:

operation_code length, source address, destination address

A single instruction code covers all possibilities; the detail of the operation is given by the length character. For example, a move instruction has the mnemonic:

mov.

Moving integers is accomplished by adding the length codes:

b,
w,
d;

To move a floating point number, the codes:

f,
l,

are used.

Conversion of short integers to long is carried out with the special move instructions:

movx (sign extension)
movz (zero extension)

with two code letters indicating length of the source and destination operands.

Conversion of integer to floating point is made with the

mov

instruction and the letters of the integer source and floating point destination length.

6.4.4.1 *Arithmetic instructions.*   A full range of arithmetic instructions is provided, including add, subtract, multiply, divide, extended integer multiply and divide, packed decimal add and subtract, add and subtract with carry.

Carry and overflow conditions are indicated by the *C* and *F* bits of the PSR respectively. Whilst three bits are set automatically, they do not automatically generate a trap; the programmer must write his own handler.

Integer division is covered by two similar pairs of instructions, differing only in the way rounding is carried out. Each pair has an instruction for calculating the quotient, and one for calculating the remainder, using the same division algorithm. The pair *quo* and *rem* round towards zero, the pair *div* and *mod* round towards negative infinity.

6.4.4.2 *Logic and Boolean instructions.*   This group includes logical *and, or, exclusive or* and *complement* instructions. The arithmetic compare instructions will set the

Zero,
Negative and
Lower bits in the PSR

according to whether the two operands are the same, the second operand is more negative than the first, or the second operand is lower than the first, respectively. The comparison instructions treat the two operands as both signed and unsigned integers, and generate the N bit for signed and the L bit for unsigned values.

The *save condition* instruction will set the least significant bit of its destination operand if the stated condition is true, while the *not* instruction will invert the least significant bit of its destination operand.

In all instructions which affect bits of the PSR, the bit(s) are cleared at the beginning of the instruction, set as appropriate during the instruction, and left in that state until the next instruction which affects them. Instructions such as conditional branch and save condition refer to these bits but do not clear them.

6.4.4.3 *Bit instructions.* Instructions are provided to operate on any bit within an integer space. The bit instructions differ from the general pattern in that only one address is needed, but this is given as a base address and a bit offset. The base address may be specified using any of the standard address modes (except immediate), and the offset is expressed as a displacement within the integer length given in the instruction. There are instructions to test, set or clear a bit, find first bit set and invert a bit. Versions of the *set* and *clear* bit instructions exist which activate the processor interlock signal, making them ideal for semaphores in a multiprocessor system.

6.4.4.4 *Bit field instructions.* Bit field instructions are used to manipulate non-aligned bit fields, or fields within packed arrays. They enable the programmer to extract a group of bits from any position within an integer, and to copy the bit group to a byte boundary, or to insert a bit pattern from a byte boundary to a desired location within the integer, e.g.

extw r0, h'1000, r1, 11

will extract an 11 bit field from address hex 1000 and copy it into the least significant 16 bits of r1 (right justified, high order bits, zero filled). r0 specifies the starting point offset of the field in the base address.

6.4.4.5 *String instructions.* In order to suport string operations, which are so common in high level languages, the Series 32000 possesses a set of string manipulation instructions. A string of variable length can be moved to a new address with *movs*; the string can be skipped over with *skps*; two strings may be compared with *cmps*. The operations indicate either the integer length of the string elements or whether the operation is to pass via a translate table (in which case the operation is forced to byte length). An option field following the instruction code specifies if the operation should be carried out *until* or *while* specific patterns appear in the string.

String operations require their parameters to be set in the general purpose registers r0 through r4. Since all the parameters of the string operations are held in general purpose registers, and updated at each cycle, the strings may be of any length, and the operation may be interrupted after each cycle. The registers contain the following:

- r0 contains the number of string elements to move
- r1 contains the address of the source string
- r2 contains the address of the destination string

- r3 contains the address of the translate table
- r4 contains the search pattern to be used with the until or while option.

The string instructions look somewhat unusual in that they have no operand addresses, e.g.

movst u

Thus, if the value in r0 is greater than zero the CPU will move the byte from the address given in r1 via the translate table to the address given in r2 (provided that the translated pattern does not match the pattern in r4), the value in r0 is then decremented and the values in r1 and r2 incremented. The instruction can now be interrupted, and then the operation repeats.

If the until condition is met, the *F* bit of the PSR will be set, and the operation terminated.

For short strings, a move multiple and compare multiple instruction is available. Here, the source and destination addresses are given as normal, along with a displacement indicating how many of the specified integers are to be affected. Since the parameters of the operation are not held in a programmer accessible area, these operations are non-interruptible and are limited to a range of maximum 16 bytes.

6.4.4.6 *Arrays.* Further support for high level languages is given in the Series 32000 with instructions for checking the bounds of arrays and calculating the correct offset for accessing any element. The offset thus calculated is stored in a general purpose register and is designed to be used as the index in a scaled index address. If the subscript lies outside the bounds, the *F* bit will be set in the PSR.

When the array is established, a two-element variable must be specified for each dimension of the array. In the lower address must be the high limit of the subscript, and in the higher address the low limit.

Assume a two-dimensional array called table, the subscript ranges for the rows and columns in row_bound and col_bound respectively, and the number of columns per row in col_per_row (column high bound – column low bound). For this example, the table elements are assumed to be doublewords; all the other variables are assumed to be word length. In reality, any integer can be used.

To carry out the high level statement:

table [row, col] := val;

the following sequence of instructions would be needed:

```
checkw  r0,row_bound,row  #check 'row' is in range, store the
                          corrected value in r0
bfs     error            #else go to an error routine
checkw  r1,col_bound,col  #check 'col' is in range, result in r1
bfs     error            #else go to an error routine
indexw  r0,col_per_row,r1 #accumulate total offset. (r0 *
                          (col_per_row + 1) + r1) into r0
movd    val,table[r0:d]  #move source to array, using scaled
                          indexed addressing
```

6.4.4.7 *Procedures.* In order to effectively manage procedures:

enter and *exit*

instructions are provided which automatically:

- Create a reference frame on the stack
- Reserve space for local variables
- Save any chosen general purpose registers on the stack.

Parameters to be passed to a procedure by a calling routine are placed on the stack, from where they can be accessed by the procedure using frame pointer relative addressing (one of the forms of memory space addressing). Local variables are similarly accessed; the difference being that, from the frame pointer, local variables require a negative displacement, parameters a positive displacement.

As the Series 32000 was designed to support modular programming, procedures may be conceived as either internal or external. A call to an external procedure will push the current MOD register onto the stack, in addition to the return address, so requiring other displacements for accessing parameters; an external procedure must end with a return from external procedure, rxp instruction, instead of a normal return.

When a call external procedure, cxp, instruction is executed, the processor will:

- Save the MOD register as a double word on the stack
- Save the return address on the stack
- Copy the module field of the descriptor to the MOD register
- Copy the static base from the module descriptor currently indicated to sb register
- Add the program base from the module descriptor to the offset field of the procedure descriptor and move the result to the PC.

6.4.4.8 *The graphic instructions of the 32CG16.* The graphic instructions of the 32CG16 replace the MMU and custom slave instructions of its predecessors. These new instructions are grouped into BIT aligned Block Transfer (BITBLT), pattern fill and data compression, expansion and magnify. In all of the new instructions, the pattern area or frame buffer to be affected is defined by the contents of general purpose registers.

6.4.4.9 *Cache control instructions of the 32532 and 32GX32.* In any system using cache memory, it is essential for the processor to be able to maintain coherency of its data between cache and main memory. This is allowed for in these processors with the Cache Invalidate (CINV) instruction. The CINV instruction can invalidate either the entire cache or a 16-byte block within the specified cache.

6.5   Exception handling

Exception processing in the Series 32000 is based around a dedicated interrupt despatch table which is pointed to by the intbase register.

The interrupt despatch table is made up of a fixed portion, containing 16 entries (of which some are reserved for future use), followed by a region for vectored or ICU interrupts. In the case that cascaded ICUs are used, a third portion of the table, the cascade table, precedes the fixed entries.

The structure of the interrupt despatch table is given in Fig. 6.13.

The following additional interrupt entries follow the 'und' entry in the table in the 32332, 32532 and 32GX32 processors:

	[restartable bus error]
(Bus error trap)	[non-restartable bus error]
	[integer overflow]
	[debug]

Note: ()only in 32332, [] in 32532 and 32GX32.

Each entry in the positive portion of the table consists of an *external procedure descriptor* made up of a 16-bit module address and a 16-bit offset. (The entries in the negative portion of the table contain the absolute address of their corresponding ICU.)

The module address will replace the current content of the MOD register, and the offset will be added to the program base entry of the new module descriptor, to give the start address of the necessary handler routine. The change of context for handling an exception is accomplished by an effective CXPD (call external procedure with descriptor) instruction.

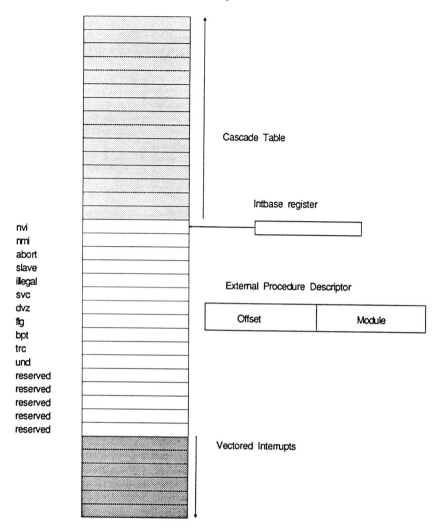

nvi
nmi
abort
slave
illegal
svc
dvz
flg
bpt
trc
und
reserved
reserved
reserved
reserved
reserved

Cascade Table

Intbase register

External Procedure Descriptor

| Offset | Module |

Vectored Interrupts

Fig. 6.13   32CG16 interrupt despatch table.

The concept of the direct exceptions is included in the 32532 and 32GX32 processors to speed up the context switch. When the direct exception mode is enabled by setting the DE bit in the CFG register, the entry in the interrupt despatch table is interpreted as an absolute address, instead of as an external procedure descriptor. The absolute address is loaded directly into the PC.

Exceptions in the Series 32000 are divided into hardware interrupts, software traps and memory access aborts. Hardware interrupts may be vectored, i.e. from an ICU, either single or cascaded; or non-vectored, i.e. no ICU present, as indicated by the I bit in the CFG register. In a vectored system, the ICU will return a vector indicating which input line has generated the interrupt. A position vector indicates that the interrupt is from the master ICU, a negative value shows that the interrupt has come from a cascaded ICU.

All exceptions will generate a vector value which indicates the offset of the corresponding entry in the interrupt despatch table. The offset is multiplied by four and added to the contents of the INTBASE register to access the table.

In the case of cascaded ICU interrupts, the master ICU will generate a negative vector which, when multiplied by four and added to the INTBASE, will cause one of the 16 negatively located entries to be read. This entry will contain the address of the cascaded ICU. When the CPU reads the address of a cascaded ICU, it will receive the vector of the actual interrupt, which is then added to the content of the INTBASE to give an access into the positive part of the table.

In the 32332, an additional entry in the fixed part of the table is used for a new bus error trap. In the 32532 and 32GX32, there are two bus error traps, for restartable and non-restartable bus errors, and in addition, an integer overflow and a debug trap. These bring the number of entries in the fixed part of the table to 15.

6.6 Hardware and software support

6.6.1 EVALUATION HARDWARE

6.6.1.1 *Development systems.* The Series 32000 development software is hosted on a number of machines. Currently, these are VAX and microVAX, SYS32-30, SUNIII and HP9000.

When run on a VAX host system, running either the VMS or ULTRIX operating system, the cross-compiler options are used, and the object code is produced to be down-loaded to a Series 32000 target.

An alternative is the SYS32 add-in co-processor board for PCs. Based around a 32332 CPU, the SYS32-30 is supplied with a full port of Unix System V.3, the GNX assembler, loader and debugger; the GNX compilers are available as options. Using the SYS32 development host, the object code can be produced in a native mode, and run on the development system itself, or can be cross-compiled, linked with the correct library versions and down-loaded to a Series 32000 target.

6.6.1.2 *Development boards.* Two development/evaluation boards are available to enable the software developers to carry out first trials on a known operational target before attempting integration with newly developed target systems. These are the GX32EB for users of the 32GX32 and 32532 processors, and the CG16EB to support the 32CG16 processor.

6.6.1.3 *Emulators.*

An In System Emulator (ISE), running under DOS, is available to support the 32CG16 processor. Hewlett-Packard have produced an ISE to run the 32532 and 32GX32 processors.

The CG16 ISE operates on a PC compatible in conjunction with the SYS32-30. Development is done on the SYS32 under Unix, the object code is copied into the DOS area with the Unix to DOS Copy (UDCP) command of SYS32 Unix. The ISE allows for zero wait state emulation at 15 MHz when running in the 512K emulation memory.

Address, data and status traces may be displayed in mnemonic or machine formats. Two hardware breakpoints are available, based on 16 predefined events, and there are 36 software breakpoints.

The HP64772A emulator can operate in a stand-alone mode, controlled by a terminal, or can be operated from a HP9000 processor or an IBM pc compatible. The emulator/analyser has a 512K emulation memory, runs at 25 MHz with zero wait states or 30 MHz with one wait state.

Operating in a window environment, the HP64772A can, for example, display source code listing, a symbol listing and a memory display in different windows, thus eliminating the need to continually change context during a debugging session.

6.6.2 DEVELOPMENT SOFTWARE

6.6.2.1 *GNX.*

The Series 32000 development software is known as GNX (GENIX native and cross software), and runs on the OPUS co-processor (SYS32-xx) under Unix System V.3 or on a VAX (or MicroVAX) under VMS or VAX/ULTRIX, under SUNIII OS or on an HP9000 under the HP-UX™. The components of the system are the 32000 assembler and debuggers, and optional C, FORTRAN-77 and Pascal compilers. To improve portability of the object code, the object files are produced in AT&T's Common Object File Format (COFF).

An advantage for the developer is the introduction of Compiler Technology Project (CTP) compilers. In the CTP software, a front-end processor is provided for the specific language and reduces the source to a Series 32000 intermediate language. An extremely effective optimiser can be used to perform selected or default optimisations on the intermediate code, and a Series 32000 processor-specific code generator then produces the executable code, carrying out 'peep-hole' optimisations for the selected target processor.

6.6.2.2. *Debuggers.* The GNX debugger is a symbolic debugger, allowing the user to debug high level language programs source line by source line. If needed, the generated machine code can be stepped through. Variables can be inspected and altered either by using their symbolic name or their machine address. It is recommended to carry out all symbolic debugging before any optimising is done as the resultant code is often not comparable with the source file.

The debugger is designed to work in native mode on the SYS32-xx, or in a down-load mode in conjunction with a Series 32000 target board using a monitor equivalent to one of the GNX monitors.

6.7   Demand paged memory management

The MMUs of the Series 32000 family operate a demand paged scheme. In the 32082, 512K pages are used, in the 32382 pages are 4K long. The 32532 with its built-in MMU follows the 32382 design. A two-tier page table scheme is used, with the first level table being resident and the second level tables being paged. A page table base register points to the start of the level one table. This is illustrated in Fig. 6.14.

The MMUs have two page table base (PTB) registers, PTB0 and PTB1. Each PTB points to a level 1 page table. Each entry in the level 1 page table points to a level 2 page table. The entries in the level 2 tables point to the physical memory page. In the 32082, the level 1 page table is 256 entries, each of 4 bytes; in the 32382, it contains 1024 entries. The level 2 tables are respectively 128 and 1024 entries; i.e. they are each one page long. The level 1 tables are memory resident; the level 2 tables are paged.

The dual space (DS) bit in the MMU status register determines whether user and supervisor addresses will be translated using the same or different mappings. If the DS bit is set, PTB0 will be used for user mode translations, and PTB1 will be used for supervisor mode address translations. When the DS bit is reset (no dual space enabled), all translations will use PTB0.

A virtual address is considered to consist of three parts. The most significant field is added to the PTB value to access the required page of the level 1 table. The second field is added to the value read from the level 1 table to give an entry into the level 2 table. The contents of the address read in the level 2 table is the page number of the physical page

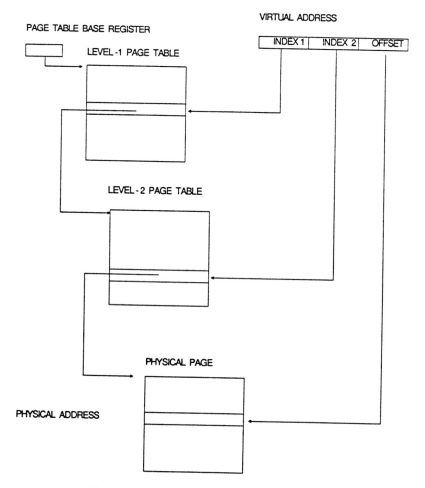

Fig. 6.14   Virtual to physical address translation.

in which the data is located. The third field of the virtual address is appended to the page number to give the physical address.

In order to speed up virtual to physical address translations, a translate look-aside buffer contains the last 32 physical addresses and their physical equivalent (in the 32532, the translate look-aside buffer of the on-chip MMU is expanded to 64 entries). Statistics suggest that a hit rate of about 97 per cent is achieved. In the event that the required address is found in the look-aside buffer, translation takes place in one clock cycle; otherwise, translation takes about 20 clock cycles.

Each page table entry contains status bits to provide the operating system with the information needed to decide which page(s) should be swapped out of memory to make space for loading a new page. These are the referenced bit, the modified bit, the valid bit and the protection level bits.

The referenced bit is set whenever the contents of a page are read or written; the modified bit is set only if the contents of a page are written, while the page is resident in memory. A page swapping algorithm can then find pages which have not been referenced within a given time-frame, or can determine whether a page to be swapped out must be copied back to disk. In the case that the modified bit is not set, there will be no need to write the page out, since the copy in memory is identical to the copy on disk.

The referenced bit is set by the MMU and cleared by the operating system; the modified bit is reset by the operating system when the page is loaded into memory, and set by the MMU whenever a successful write to the page occurs. The modified bit is only fully implemented in level 2 tables. The referenced bit in a level 1 table entry indicates that the level 2 page mapped by the entry has been accessed for translation, whether successful or not. In a level 2 table entry, the referenced bit indicates a successful access to the physical page which it maps.

The valid bit indicates that the mapped page is present in memory. If, in the course of translation a page entry is read with the valid bit reset, the MMU will generate an abort trap to the CPU.

The CPU must then call the correct operating system routine to load the required page into memory. Part of the trap reaction hardware in the CPU will ensure that the processor is returned to the correct state so that the instruction can be restarted after the return from trap has been executed. In most cases, this means that the instruction will be restarted, but in case of a string instruction, operation will continue from the current situation stored in the general purpose registers.

The last usage indicator in the page table entry is the protection level, 2 bits, which indicate how the page may be accessed in user and supervisor modes.

6.8 Bus timing

The Series 32000 has been designed to be able to support any variety of peripheral and memory devices. A complex logic in the TCU, or its on-chip equivalent in the 32CG16, 32532 and 32GX32, allows the normal bus cycle to be cleanly extended by the insertion of wait states.

The 32201 TCU requires, as input, a clock signal at twice the system frequency. From this it will produce two non-overlapping PH1 and PH2 signals for the CPU (and MMU if installed). The TCU generates ready and reset signals for the CPU cluster, and produces the correct read/write strobes for memory or memory-mapped peripherals.

A standard bus cycle consists of four states, indicated by the rising edge of PH1, named t1, t2, t3 and t4. When a MMU is added to a 32016 or 32032 CPU, an additional pulse, TMMU, is added after t1 to allow for address translation via the translate look-aside buffer. In the 32332, TMMU and t2 overlap.

In the 32532 and 32GX32, a bus cycle consists of two pulses.

A slave processor cycle, for communication between the CPU and a slave processor takes two clock pulses, and is the only bus cycle which cannot be extended.

The 32CG16 has an improved timing structure relative to the 32016, in that the address valid pulse occurs 5 ns earlier and wait states are sampled half a clock pulse later.

Wait states are inserted into the bus cycle by the TCU in accordance with wait request inputs. The TCU will indicate wait states to the CPU by holding the RDY line inactive.

The wait request inputs of the 32CG16 are cwait, wait-1 and wait-2. All three inputs are sampled at the end of t2. Up to three wait states are inserted for wait-1 and wait-2, then 1 wait for cwait. Cwiat is then sampled again, one wait state being inserted each time it is found active.

The 32532 and 32GX32 sample the ready input at the end of t2 in a normal cycle or t2b in a burst cycle; if the ready is inactive, the t state is repeated for another clock cycle, if the ready is active, the cycle is terminated normally.

6.9 Using the ICU as a timer

As has been briefly mentioned, the 32202 ICU contains two counters which can be programmed to generate interrupts. Figure 6.15 illustrates the ICU internal registers.

The two 16-bit counters, h-counter and l-counter can be used separately or as a single 32-bit register, according to the counter concatenate bit in the counter control register. They are both down counters, and will generate their respective signals when the count goes to zero.

The length of the count is programmable, the set-up routine must put the correct starting values into the h- and l-counter starting value registers. When the run bits in the counter control register are set, the starting values are copied to their respective counter, and the countdown then runs until the bits are reset.

Each time the counter goes through zero, the following clock pulse will reload the starting value to its register.

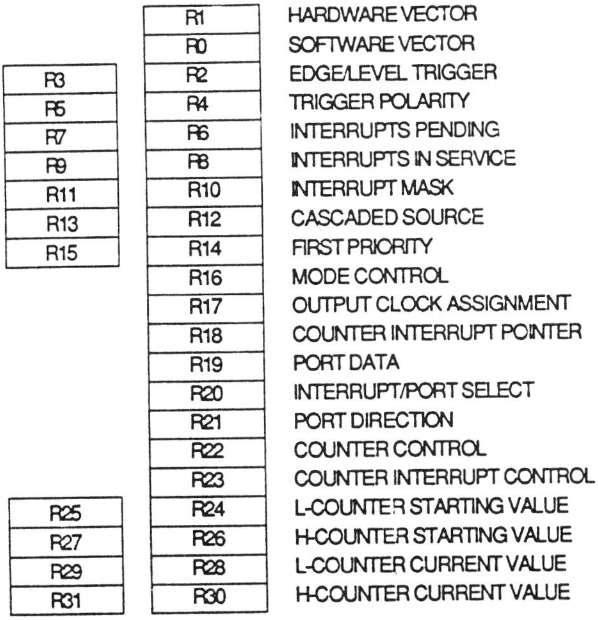

	R1	HARDWARE VECTOR
	R0	SOFTWARE VECTOR
R3	R2	EDGE/LEVEL TRIGGER
R5	R4	TRIGGER POLARITY
R7	R6	INTERRUPTS PENDING
R9	R8	INTERRUPTS IN SERVICE
R11	R10	INTERRUPT MASK
R13	R12	CASCADED SOURCE
R15	R14	FIRST PRIORITY
	R16	MODE CONTROL
	R17	OUTPUT CLOCK ASSIGNMENT
	R18	COUNTER INTERRUPT POINTER
	R19	PORT DATA
	R20	INTERRUPT/PORT SELECT
	R21	PORT DIRECTION
	R22	COUNTER CONTROL
	R23	COUNTER INTERRUPT CONTROL
R25	R24	L-COUNTER STARTING VALUE
R27	R26	H-COUNTER STARTING VALUE
R29	R28	L-COUNTER CURRENT VALUE
R31	R30	H-COUNTER CURRENT VALUE

Fig. **6.15**   ICU internal registers.

Each pulse to the counter will copy the new value of the counter to the respective counter current value register. If the program needs to read the counter value, the counter freeze bit in the mode control register is set. This prevents the counter value being copied to the current value register, and the program can read the current value register without risk. While the counter freeze bit is active, the countdown continues.

The clock input to the counters comes from an external source of maximum 2.5 MHz. A divide-by-four prescaler is provided (enabled by a bit in the counter control register) which allows a clock frequency of 10 MHz to be used.

In the 8-bit bus mode, setting the output clock assignment register will connect the output signal from the h– or h+l counter to one of the G0/IR0 . . . G3/IR6 lines. The state of the clock mode bit in the mode register will determine whether the output is to be a square wave or pulse.

The counter interrupt position register is used to indicate which interrupt positions are to be connected to the h and l counters.

In the 8-bit bus mode, the interrupt/port select register bits must be set to indicate which of the G0/IR0 . . . G7/IR14 pins are to be considered as general purpose I/O ports, and which as interrupt inputs. A pin defined in the output clock assignment register as carrying a clock signal cannot be redefined in the interrupt/port select register.

The ICU can be used to produce a clock output or to generate timed hardware interrupts. The same timing registers can be set up in cascaded as well as master ICUs.

6.10 Summary

The Series 32000 is a complete chip set solution applicable to many problem areas. Used in conjunction with other, compatible chip sets from National Semiconductor, the prospective user has a single supplier for his requirements.

In the necessarily brief descriptions of the Series 32000 features, I hope that the reader will have an insight into the power of the microprocessor family, as well as an impression of the simplicity of its symmetrical instruction set, and the ease of migration from one processor to another, thanks to the insistence on upward and downward compatibility.

The Series 32000 was the world's first commercially available 32-bit microprocessor with the introduction of the 32016. The power available to the user has been dramatically increased by the 32532. The 32CG16 has focused on the printer/terminal market.

Development does not stand still, and we may expect further advances in the family as technology progresses.

Acknowledgement

I would like to thank my many colleagues at National Semiconductor for the help they have given me in preparing this chapter.

References

1. *An Empirical Study of FORTRAN Programs, Software Practice and Experience*, pp 105–133 (Quoted in Series 32000 Databook), Knuth, D. E., 1986.

Further reading

National Semiconductor Microprocessor Databook.
National Semiconductor Embedded System Processor, Databook.
Series 32000 Programmers Reference Manual, Colin Hunter, Prentice-Hall Inc.
NS32CG16 Printer/Display Processor Programmers Reference Manual.

Index